NO EASY ANSWERS

The Trial and Conviction of Bruce Curtis

David Hayes

VIKING

VIKING

Penguin Books Canada Limited, 2801 John Street, Markham, Ontario, Canada
L3R 1B4
Penguin Books, Harmondsworth, Middlesex, England
Viking Penguin Inc., 40 West 23rd Street, New York, New York 10010 U.S.A.
Penguin Books Australia Ltd., Ringwood, Victoria, Australia
Penguin Books (N.Z.) Ltd., Private Bag, Takapuna, Auckland 9, New Zealand

First published by Penguin Books Canada Limited, 1986

Printed and bound in Canada by John Deyell Company

Canadian Cataloguing in Publication Data

Hayes, David
   No easy answers: the trial and conviction of Bruce Curtis
ISBN 0-670-81056-8

1. Curtis, Bruce. 2. Franz, Scott. 3. Murder —
New Jersey. 4. Trials (Murder) — New Jersey.
I. Title.

HV6533.N3H39 1986   364.1'523'0924   C86-093710-0

DEDICATION

To my parents, Margaret and Ralph Hayes,
who have always believed,

and, of course, to Maya for wit, wisdom
and support

ACKNOWLEDGEMENTS

An account of a true story can never be more accurate than the collective memories of its many characters and their willingness to participate. While court transcripts, police and media reports and other documentation help an author establish a chronology and connect the bones, flesh and blood emerges only when individuals give of themselves.

Bruce Curtis spoke to me agreeably and at length; my meetings with him were invaluable. It is also safe to say that I could not have written this book without the co-operation of Jim and Alice Curtis and Jim's sister, Lorraine Peever. They are ordinary people who found themselves in an extraordinary situation. Although their sole experience with the media prior to the summer of 1983 had been their reading of local newspapers, they chose to take their private sorrow to a public forum on the strength of a shared sense of outrage over perceived injustice to a member of their family. They gave unstintingly of their time and energy, sharing with me their joys and sadnesses, triumphs and defeats. They made no effort to hide from view even the most disturbing or humiliating aspects of this story. I owe them a tremendous debt of gratitude; they already have my deepest respect.

I am also grateful to Bruce Curtis's first lawyer, Michael Schottland, both for helping this layman understand New Jersey law and for reliving, to the best of his abilities, his ruminations and judgements about the case. And in the opposite corner, my thanks to first assistant prosecutor Paul Chaiet, who willingly shared his thoughts and presented the state's point of view.

For their specific contributions to the research of this book, I also wish to thank: Anne and Carol Curtis; Terry Rawlinson and Ted Podgis; Mike Shaw, Dan Casagrande and Joanne Legano; Professor Gerald Morris and Jennie Hatfield Lyon; Lieutenant William Lucia; Jennifer Wade; and Jim Stabile of the New Jersey Department of Corrections, who saved me a lot of legwork. Also, thanks to William Duerr, Frank Tenbroeck and John Stillwell; the teachers and former students at King's-Edgehill School who contributed their memories of 1981 and 1982; and Donya Peroff and Sue McKay, who helped transcribe countless tapes of interviews.

Many thanks to the Lucinda Vardey Agency — Lucinda, Lee Davis, Linda Turchin and, in England, Carolyn Brunton — for their efforts on my behalf.

A special acknowledgement to my friend and colleague Gary Ross, who encouraged me throughout this project and has had a great deal to do with shaping this writer into a writer.

This was my first experience with a book publisher, and Penguin Books Canada Limited fulfilled all my expectations. In particular, many hosannas to my editor, David Kilgour, whose judgement was always astute and whose handling of this project and its author was always sensitive, even at the most frantic times.

D.H.

A NOTE TO THE READER

I have tried to corroborate every significant event with as many accounts as possible. Sometimes different accounts of the same event conflicted. When a conflict couldn't be resolved, I chose the version that my knowledge of the case led me to believe was the closest to the truth. If I had serious doubts, I didn't include the event or the account.

Although there is no invented dialogue in this book, I occasionally took liberties with the order of words or sentences, dispensed with an ellipsis or combined several sentences dealing with a single thought in the interests of both clarity and brevity. I did so with the utmost respect for the people I spoke to, and never with the intention of altering the meaning of their thoughts.

INTRODUCTION

Prisoner number 93852 in the Bordentown Youth Correctional Institution in New Jersey is a soft-spoken, twenty-two-year-old Canadian. Shortly after a guard unlocks the E-1 tier door at 6:45 A.M., the prisoner rises, showers and returns to his cell for a breakfast of powdered milk and granola — supplied by his mother, who makes it herself in her farm kitchen in rural Nova Scotia. He has learned to avoid the overcrowded, potentially dangerous prison cafeteria. At 8:00 A.M. he walks down "the turnpike," a long, wide corridor from which all areas of the fifty-year-old prison branch out. He ignores the occasional taunts.

Once he passes the guard at the steel gate leading into the prison's school, he is among civilians: teachers hired by the New Jersey Department of Corrections but sharing none of the characteristics of most corrections officers. He spends as much time as possible here. He works with a young woman who handles the school's Continuing Assessment Program, a system of evaluating the educational abilities of inmates and placing them in appropriate programs. Since her office is isolated at the rear of the school, she has to be "very particular" about whom she takes on as her aide. She describes prisoner number 93852, Bruce Curtis, as "a quiet, sincere individual who is very conscientious and never complains." She agrees with her colleagues that Curtis seems "totally out of place" amongst the rest of the prison population. When he is not entering students' files into the computer, Curtis teaches illiterate inmates remedial reading and the basics of addition and subtraction. Although he has been taking correspondence courses from a Canadian university in philosophy, psychology and English literature, he also earns "brownie points" — a factor in the parole hearing he will face in 1992 — by attending courses provided by a local community college. In one, Business Mathematics, he was taught elementary fractions.

Twenty-five miles away, in Riverfront State Prison, a former high-school classmate of Curtis's, Scott Franz, follows a similar daily schedule. His quarters in this medium security institution, New Jersey's newest, are in B-1 South, where many of the windows face the Delaware River. He works as a clerk for the food services supervisor, seven days a week, 8:00 A.M. to 4:00 P.M. He has taken a graphic arts course and is a member of the Junior Chamber of Commerce.

Until February 1986, Franz was an inmate at the Youth Reception and Correction Center at Yardville, a progressive facility adjacent to Bordentown. At Yardville, he lived in a housing unit not unlike that of a college dormitory and enjoyed a relatively informal environment in what is sometimes described as the "country club" of New Jersey's prison system. On February 24, 1986, however, the Institutional Classification Committee reviewed several reports of alleged behavioural infractions and decided Franz was "too sophisticated" for the youth complex. He was transferred to Riverfront two days later.

In June 1982, both Curtis and Franz graduated from King's-Edgehill, an exclusive prep school in Windsor, Nova Scotia. Curtis, an honours student, had been a member of the debating team, a competitor on "Reach For the Top," CBC-TV's national quiz show for students, and the school's resident authority on J.R.R. Tolkien. He was to enter Dalhousie University in the fall, where he planned to study astrophysics. Franz, whose grades were average, was planning to attend Mount Allison, a small university in the neighbouring province of New Brunswick. But a summer holiday at Franz's home on the Jersey Shore ended in the shooting deaths of Franz's mother and stepfather and twenty-year prison terms for both boys.

Testimony at Curtis's trial suggested that Franz's stepfather, Alfred Podgis, was a brutal, domineering man and that the household Curtis entered in July 1982 became a domestic battleground. On the morning of the eighth day of the visit, Franz shot and killed his stepfather in an upstairs bedroom. A few moments later, Curtis shot Franz's mother, Rosemary Podgis, in a doorway between the kitchen and dining-room. (Later, Franz would maintain he had shot his stepfather in self-defence; Curtis would claim the rifle he was holding discharged accidentally.) After hiding the bodies, the boys fled. They were arrested five days later. Franz, who pleaded guilty to murder and testified against his friend, was sentenced to twenty years, the minimum for that crime in New Jersey. A jury acquitted Curtis of murder but found him guilty of aggravated manslaughter. He received the maximum twenty-year sentence for that offence, with ten years before parole eligibility.

Curtis's outraged family, convinced their son was a victim of circumstances beyond his control, launched a series of appeals that cost them in excess of $100,000. His aunt spearheads a grass-roots "Justice For Bruce Curtis" movement, made up of supporters from across Canada and the United States, that stages demonstrations and fund-raising drives, encourages media coverage of the case, and lobbies Canadian and U.S. officials. Bruce Curtis Defence Committees have been established in nearly every province. These efforts have kept the case alive but also served to mythologize it, a process already set in motion by the passage of time.

Questions remain: the only people alive who know what happened inside the Podgis house on the morning of July 5, 1982 are Scott Franz and Bruce Curtis. Their accounts of events leading up to and including the shootings of Franz's parents are similar but diverge at critical points. Were the shootings and their aftermath — described by Curtis's attorney as a teenager's understandable panic reaction to an extreme situation, and by the prosecutor of the case as "cold and calculated actions" —

reasonable under the circumstances? Did Curtis receive a fair trial and sentence?

Beside Curtis's desk in the prison school at Bordentown, a poster is taped to the wall. It is a photograph of the earth taken from space, accompanied by a line from the Danish philosopher Søren Kierkegaard: "Life can only be understood backwards; but it must be lived forwards."

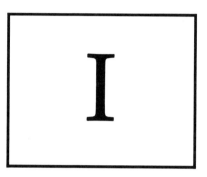

Now I don't know what it always was with us
   We chose the words, and yeah, we chose the lines
There was just no way this house could hold the
   two of us
   I guess we were just too much of the same kind
Well, say goodbye it's Independence Day
   It's Independence Day all boys must run away
So say goodbye it's Independence Day
   All men must make their way come
   Independence Day

Bruce Springsteen
"Independence Day"

Tuesday, July 6, 1982

As a commuter train pulled out of the Allenhurst, New Jersey station bound for Manhattan, sixty miles north-west, a blue-and-white cruiser nosed lazily onto Main Street. John Stillwell had been a patrolman in the Allenhurst police department for less than a year but was already familiar with this community of about a thousand, covering only three-tenths of a square mile. Allenhurst was founded at the turn of the century and developed into a summer retreat that was frequented by prominent members of society such as George Pullman, the railway car magnate, the tenor Enrico Caruso, and the Wupperman family of Cuba, distillers of Angostura Bitters. It was still a leafy refuge for those who could afford summer homes and those who sought to escape the cities and their equally crowded suburbs, providing the benefits of small-town life only an hour from New York. (An eighty-one-year-old ordinance prohibiting persons in bathing costumes on the streets of the town was still in effect, although no one could remember when it had last been enforced.) The town sat like a buffer between Deal, an exclusive summer community favoured by wealthy Syrian Jews from New York, and tough, tacky Asbury Park. Together, Deal and Allenhurst linked the larger centres of Long Branch and Asbury Park, which were in turn part of a larger chain of seaside resorts, stretching from Sandy Hook to Cape May, that made up the fabled Jersey Shore.

Stillwell drove past Jersey Central Power and Light, the town's only real industry, turned onto Edgemont Avenue and followed its winding route along the shore of Deal Lake. Edgemont Avenue was actually part of the Village of Loch Arbour, a few residential blocks and a beach club that was, for all intents and purposes and despite protestations from its four hundred or so residents, a southernmost neighbourhood in the town of Allenhurst. But Loch Arbour was self-governed, a decision taken in 1957 to retain its civic character and bring local government closer to the people. It proved to be an expensive autonomy: despite having one of the highest tax rates in the country, Loch Arbour contracted out to Allenhurst services such as police, ambulance, fire protection and garbage pick-up.

The early morning sun rising above the Atlantic Ocean promised a scorching July day. Even with his sunglasses, Stillwell shielded his eyes with the back of his hand. A week of rain had ended on Sunday, Independence Day, 1982, although in Allenhurst and Loch Arbour there were few signs that it was the day after the Fourth of July holiday weekend. The Stars and Stripes hung from poles at a number of homes, but Stillwell could not be sure how many of them had been put up for the occasion; many people who owned flags unfurled them at the beginning of the summer and kept them flying until the season's end. Stillwell glanced across the lake towards Asbury Park. The Fourth of July weekend always attracted a particularly large and high-spirited crowd of holidayers there, and during the afternoons the beach became so crowded it was impossible to find a space in the sand. Even the city's most rundown motels could boast of having no vacancies. As usual, there had been the occasional loud report, like gunfire, signalling an exuberant defiance of public ordinances restricting the sale and use of fireworks. On Sunday evening, thousands had convened along Asbury Park's boardwalk to watch the city's annual display paint the night with explosions of red, blue, green and white light. Although many local residents made the short drive over to enjoy the festivities, most left shortly thereafter, returning to the peaceful neighbourhoods they favoured over Asbury Park's hard-edged glitter and high crime rate.

As he drove along another tree-lined street, the radio in Stillwell's patrol car crackled. Later, Stillwell began his report this way: "At 7:57 this date this officer was detailed to 401 Euclid Ave., Loch Arbour, to check on the well-being of Mr and Mrs Alfred Podgis after their daughter Barbara called headquarters stating that they did not show up for work. Upon my arrival I observed a black ford [sic] and orange color jeep in the yard. After knocking on both the front and back door I received no answer."

Although Stillwell had observed two vehicles in the yard, he also knew that the family owned a van, and a German shepherd was generally chained outside. After walking around the house and detecting no signs of a break-in or other trouble, Stillwell decided the family had taken their dog and gone away for the long weekend. They had probably elected to stay an extra night and forgotten to phone their daughter. But when he notified Barbara Czacherski, she was still anxious. She authorized Stillwell to enter the house.

On the steps outside police headquarters, Stillwell met Chief James Newman as he was arriving for work. Newman, fifty-three years old, son of a Loch Arbour milkman, knew the pattern of life in his community intimately. It included break-ins, especially off-season when summer residents closed up and returned to the city, and plenty of municipal infractions, everything from barking dogs to traffic infractions. In the thirty-one years he had spent on the force — thirteen as chief — he had conducted only two homicide investigations in the area. Nonetheless, Newman did not dismiss the possibility that something was wrong at 401 Euclid.

"That's a fuckin' detective," gasped Scott Franz as the two-tone maroon Chevrolet van he was driving approached 401 Euclid Avenue. A green 1975 Oldsmobile with a CB antenna — Chief Newman's personal car — was parked in front of the house. Although Sam, the good-natured German shepherd sitting beside Franz, sensed the familiar neighbourhood and was panting eagerly at the prospect of freedom, Franz swung the van around the first corner and sped away in the direction of Asbury Park. He drove quickly and erratically, motion alone providing his actions with purpose.

In the passenger seat, Bruce Curtis stared straight ahead. He was a tall, gangly youth with a narrow face, pale, lightly blemished complexion and full lips. He sat hunched, as though his existence on earth at this time could be minimized by posture. There was a stretch of rocky coastline two miles from his home in Nova Scotia, on the shore of the Bay of Fundy. Children were warned never to swim there because a powerful undertow would drag them helplessly out to sea. A similar force seemed to be propelling him past a New Jersey landscape of malls, fast-food outlets and more malls. They had driven a long way and slept in the van. Now, at 8:40 in the morning, the events of the last twenty-four hours seemed like a hallucination. Sometime in the night he had awakened and seen the moon, bloated and scarlet-rimmed, disappearing into the black sky.

The two eighteen-year-olds had dissimilar personalities. Franz, a slight, curly-haired boy with a heart-shaped face, adopted a cocky, streetwise persona that usually served him well when he was engaged in his favourite pastimes — developing elaborate scams to earn money and, in his words, "hell-raisin'." He liked to believe he lived on a razor's edge by his wits alone, although this had been, until now, an adolescent conceit.

Curtis was a quiet boy, an honours student at King's-Edgehill, the exclusive private boarding school in Nova Scotia that he and Franz had attended. He planned to enter the science program at Dalhousie University in Halifax that fall. Like Franz, he adopted a persona — that of an aloof intellectual, a scientist equipped with a disciplined logical mind — that helped him cope with an inability to socialize easily. As Franz described him, "he was pretty intelligent. If you had a question, he could answer it and if he couldn't, he could find it pretty quick." But Franz also thought of him as "a deadbeat."

The home of Alfred and Rosemary Podgis was not unfamiliar to the Allenhurst police: 145 calls had been recorded over fourteen years, although Chief Newman later stressed that "calls" included routine visits. "There were all kinds of things," he said. "That dog barking, first-aid calls. Once Rosemary broke her arm, and an old gent — I think it was her father — lived with them until he died, so there were first-aid calls for him. But there was never a report of a fired gun in that house." But Newman had himself stood in the Podgis living-room for other reasons: a son, Mark, had been in trouble as a juvenile — stealing cars, break-and-enter, finally armed robbery. The last Newman had heard, he was in prison in Texas. And a daughter, Dawn, had been a runaway, in and out of detention homes. Only the youngest child was still at home, although he had been sent away to a private school.

"Never know," Newman remarked to Stillwell as they walked to their cars. "Someone can have a heart attack at night, or take a fall."

At 8:20 A.M., the two men arrived at 401 Euclid and conducted a "walk-around," knocking on the front and side doors. It was a big, rundown three-storey structure with a white stucco finish and black trim. There was a detached, two-car garage and a gazebo at the back of a huge yard. A window on the east side of the house was ajar, and nearby lay a wooden pallet of the sort used in warehouses. Stillwell propped the pallet against the side of the house, clambered through the window and opened the front door. At about that time, a third officer arrived on the scene. Captain Frank Tenbroeck, two weeks shy of his forty-second birthday, was the criminal investigator for the Allenhurst police. He was also an Asbury Park native married to a Loch Arbour girl. Not only did his in-laws live across the street at 414 Euclid, but Tenbroeck and his wife had rented a bungalow just three doors west of the Podgis property from 1967 to 1973.

"Goddamn, this place is a mess," exclaimed Stillwell, who wondered if there had been a fight. "It always looks like this," replied Tenbroeck. "They're not the cleanest people."

The furniture in the living-room looked askew, and papers, magazines and assorted paraphernalia were strewn everywhere. A large, brown couch beside the fireplace was opened into a bed, as though guests had been staying. Inexplicably, there was an orange-and-black handtruck ("4 Wheel Wonder") standing in the archway separating the living-room from the dining-room. In the kitchen, dishes were unwashed and cupboards open. A whisk had been left standing in a mixing bowl containing a milky mixture. The effect of this still life and a faint smell of cooking ("Something like bacon," Stillwell would later recall) suggested that someone had been there within the past twenty-four hours. Upstairs, beds were unmade.

Apparently because both Newman and Tenbroeck believed disorder to be the normal state of the Podgis home, or because all three men failed to entertain the idea of foul play on a sleepy summer's day in Loch Arbour, neither Newman, his chief investigator, Tenbroeck, nor Stillwell bothered to turn down the linen in the master bedroom or glance under the bed. Years later Tenbroeck would reflect on their visit. "We did a 'surface,' or 'on-scene' search. We eyeballed the place but didn't go into drawers or anything because we didn't have a search warrant. There was a cat in the house. I've always thought if that cat could have talked, it would have saved everybody a lot of time and money."

Franz pulled into the Hilton Inn, near Eatontown. In a corner of the rear parking lot he backed the van into a space used for waste disposal that was shielded on two sides by a tall picket fence. Had inquisitive guests on the upper floor of the hotel's east side been armed with binoculars, they would have seen two rifles being lowered from the back of the van into a storm drain.

"Maybe we should call my sister Barbara," Franz said, as though talking aloud to himself.

"Yeah, that's a good idea," Curtis replied.

"But she might not help. She might not want anything to do with me. We don't get along; she might not understand."

Curtis was insistent. "She's the closest. Let's call her. What's her number? I'll call her."

Truth is an elusive element at the best of times. Franz's sister Barbara never received a call. If Curtis did enter the Hilton Inn and telephone her, as he maintains, Franz must have supplied him with her home number, even though he knew she would be at work at the Englishtown post office.

"By that time Scott had come up with the idea of visiting his other sister, Rosie, in Texas," Curtis recalled. "I thought it was stupid to go all the way down to Texas to see someone when Barbara was right here. I mean, he was worried about things he'd done to Barbara in the past, but what we'd done was much bigger than some stupid, petty thing in the past. So I was really trying to get him to talk to Barbara because it was really stupid. But I wasn't doing it in an abrupt manner, you know, because he might, you know, break down or something. I didn't know what he might do."

As the van left the Hilton Inn and turned west onto Route 36, small copper-coloured objects were flung with great force out of its open windows into fields of scrub grass. The next stop was nearby Monmouth Mall, where a pair of cloth gloves were deposited in a dumpster behind the Abraham and Straus department store. Shortly before 1:00 P.M., Franz drove to the main office of the Central Jersey Bank, on Route 9 near Freehold, and cashed two cheques: one, for the amount of $200, was made out to Franz three days earlier and signed by his stepfather. The second was a $389 United States Treasury cheque in Franz's name. After buying a road-map, dog-food and apples, the boys travelled south towards Atlantic City. It was mid-evening by the time they booked a room in Hurrah's at Trump Plaza, a sparkling casino complex at the corner of Mississippi Avenue and The Boardwalk, where the boys wandered around the acres of one-armed bandits and gaming tables. The following day, Wednesday, they drove to Washington, D.C. where, like most visitors to the nation's capital, they explored the Capitol Building while Sam, who had escaped her leash and romped happily through the parks system, barely managed to elude a municipal dog-catcher. In Virginia, en route to Knoxville, site of the 1982 World's Fair, they were stopped by a highway patrolman for speeding. The officer, glancing inside the van, asked why they carried no luggage. A convincing charmer, Franz explained that his parents were meeting them in Knoxville with their belongings. ("That's why we were going so fast, sir. Sorry," he said sheepishly.) Released with a warning, the two boys stopped at a mall and purchased two red-and-white tote bags and a few articles of clothing. Once they picked up two hitch-hikers, who proved to be itinerant hippies for whom home was a network of obliging acquaintances throughout North America. They arrived in Knoxville early Thursday morning, so early that the sky was still dusky above a brilliant sunrise and it took them some time to find an open restaurant. After Franz picked up a Knoxville World's Fair souvenir T-shirt, they resumed their trip south.

Curtis and Franz kept the windows in the van rolled down.

Aside from its cooling properties, the rush of air was so loud —
"like white noise," said Curtis — that it made conversation
almost impossible. To a casual observer, the two teenaged boys
in the maroon van would appear to be on a summer holiday
adventure, but for holidayers they talked little, and when they
did they avoided the events that had prompted this motor trip
down the eastern half of the United States.

When Barbara Czacherski was called back a second time by the
police, she was informed that nothing was found inside the
house. She tried to return to her work but was deeply troubled.
The most consistent element in the often turbulent world of her
mother and stepfather was their jobs. They rarely missed a day,
and always notified her if they were delayed. Barbara was in a
position to know these details: as supervisor of operations at
the post office in nearby Englishtown, she was their boss. There
had been a history of domestic problems in her family's recent
past, including separations and a recurring pattern of loud,
drawn-out arguments that blew over a short time later like
summer squalls.

Al Podgis had been a divorced man with four grown children
when he married Rosemary, a widow, in 1969 after a year-long
courtship. Although his personality could once have been
described as bluff and engaging, it had soured over time into
malevolence. A large-boned six-foot frame carried 225 pounds,
and his face, lean, almost ascetic in boyhood photographs, had
become square and jowly, emphasized by a flat-top crew cut and
small grey moustache. His most striking feature, blue eyes that
had the ability to sparkle rakishly, were more often a hard,
gun-metal grey. He was disliked by his six stepchildren and
given to holding irrationally long grudges over long-forgotten
slights, even against his own children. Familial politics aside,
Barbara had received complaints about her stepfather's mean-
spiritedness from members of the public he encountered on his
rounds as a rural mail carrier.

Rosemary Podgis was a short, stocky blue-eyed woman whose

round face was accentuated by a habit of wearing her brown hair
in a ponytail or pulled severely up into a bun. She had not had
an easy life: after her mother threw out her alcoholic father, she
and her sister were raised alone by their mother. (Rosemary's
sister later died in her early twenties.) Rosemary's first husband,
Norman Franz, had died of complications following surgery.
Her eldest son, Norman Jr., died in a car crash, and a fire once
gutted the family home. As a counter clerk at the Englishtown
post office, she was well-liked by customers and co-workers,
although her cheery, talkative disposition disguised what
Barbara believed to be a weak spirit. Despite serious conflicts,
she conspired with her second husband to maintain an appearance of harmony at work and office social functions. The fact
that Rosemary, boisterous yet long-suffering, was involved with
a man Barbara regarded as brutish and domineering was a situation for which the strong-willed Barbara could find little
sympathy. Now, as she phoned their house again that day — she
had lost count of the number of times she had already tried —
the doubt all people harbour when considering dark thoughts
was exacerbated by memories of family feuds, vicious fights between Al Podgis and his stepchildren, and dubious explanations her mother had provided for what Barbara thought were
suspicious injuries.

At 1:50 P.M. Barbara called the Allenhurst police and spoke to
Tenbroeck. She told him again that her parents' absence was
highly unusual, and that her youngest brother, Scott, and a
schoolfriend from Canada were also staying at the house. She
also told Tenbroeck she had called the auto shop where her
brother was working for the summer, but he had not shown up
for work either. Tenbroeck promised to conduct a more thor-
ough search and advised her to call relatives. One thing she said
stuck in his mind. "Did you check everywhere? Could you
please check all the closets and the basement and places like
that? I don't want to find anything when I come down there
after work."

Tenbroeck and Stillwell entered the house and began a
systematic search. They looked in closets, under tables and in

spaces between furniture and walls where a person might lie injured. Then they looked in the basement; a clutter of the sort of junk that accumulates in basements was all they could see, but both men remarked on the smell of dog excrement that lay in scattered piles. On the second floor, Stillwell entered the sun-room and, finding nothing suspicious, walked along the narrow hallway and into the master bedroom. He noted with distaste that the same poor housekeeping that characterized the rest of the house was evident here. A pair of fans spun quietly in two windows, generating a slight breeze.

"At that point there was nothing indicating anything," Stillwell later remembered. "I just expected they weren't home. I figured they hadn't called their daughter because they'd forgot or something like that. But because of the instructions I'd received from the chief I turned the mattress over. Well, I'd seen blood and stuff, but I never expected to come across this. I mean, I didn't yell like a little kid but I remember saying, 'Holy shit, Captain, come here and look.' I felt a little shook up, because of the small-knit type of town that it was, and a little nervous. And I felt a little excited because I knew something had happened here and whatever it was, I had found it."

A massive amount of blood had soaked through a green sheet, mattress cover and mattress. It had soaked through the box-spring and formed a dark stain on the hardwood floor. There was a .22 rifle beside a copy of *Playboy* under the bed, which, along with a single-barrel shotgun in the adjacent bathroom and a pellet pistol, made three weapons found thus far. There was also a live round of .22-calibre ammunition. Calls were made to local hospitals to determine whether any members of the Podgis family had been admitted, but it soon became apparent that neither accident nor illness would explain what had happened at 401 Euclid Avenue. By 3:00 P.M., the Monmouth County Pro-secutor's Office had been notified that four persons were miss-ing, and foul play was suspected.

What had begun as a routine call to a house in Loch Arbour early in the morning of July 6 had, by mid-afternoon and thanks mainly to Barbara Czacherski's persistence, turned into a full-scale criminal investigation that was beyond the resources of the Allenhurst police department. The investigation changed in rhythm and tempo at 3:20 P.M. when the first county investigator arrived at 401 Euclid. William Lucia shook hands with Chief Newman, Tenbroeck and William Duerr, a patrolman who had relieved Stillwell, and was briefed on the details of the case.

A second-generation Italian-American whose father was in the garment business, Lucia was a wiry thirty-eight-year-old with black hair that he kept oiled and neatly combed. Two prominent creases enclosed the lower part of his nose and his mouth in parentheses. He favoured sharply tailored suits, although on a county investigator's salary his working garments were restricted to poly-cotton blends rather than costly designer silks. Whenever he rose, Lucia habitually straightened the knot in his tie and gave his jacket a smart tug while squaring his shoulders. He generally wore Italian loafers, and he walked with a welterweight's light, athletic step. His bearing suggested confidence, leadership and a dash of the dandy.

Raised in a Catholic family that implicitly emphasized pride, honour and the difference between right and wrong, Lucia developed into a headstrong, independent teenager. While attending high school he began playing in local rock groups and later, as the singer and saxophonist in The Jaywalkers, he often performed at The Peppermint Lounge in New York City as well as school dances around New Jersey. (To friends Lucia would admit "there was a lot of drugs around but that wasn't my thing; I never even smoked a marijuana cigarette.") In 1968, Lucia left the music business because "I saw a lot of guys, forty, forty-five years old, still beating their brains out trying to make it, and that psychedelic rock was totally against my grain." The only other career Lucia had ever considered was law enforcement. He became a patrolman in the seashore community of Monmouth Beach, but there was little room on a small-town force for a cocky, ambitious young man with a taste for glamour. In 1973, he joined the larger Ocean Township police department, where after five years of part-time plainclothes assignments, he was promoted to Detective Sergeant. In early 1980, he accepted a position as an investigator on the major crime squad of the Monmouth County Prosecutor's Office. Now, without appearing to yank authority from the local officers, Lucia began to take control of the investigation.

There had been no indication that the Podgises were planning a trip, and a next-door neighbour, Maurice Orlando, reported seeing their maroon van backed up to the side of the house at noon the previous day, Monday, July 5. While walking around the perimeter of the yard, Lucia discovered a box containing a child's badminton set and a tan-coloured vinyl bag in the bushes. An identification tag read: Bruce Curtis, R.R. #1, Middleton, Mount Hanley, Nova Scotia.

When Bruce Newman, an investigator with the forensic and technical services unit, arrived with photographic and videotape equipment in hand, the men toured the house. In the master bedroom, the local officers stood aside while Lucia and Newman moved with seasoned assurance.

"Bill," Newman called. "Take a look."

"Blood splatters," agreed Lucia, squinting close to the wall behind the bed. It was clear that someone had tried to wipe them clean.

That evening, while a search warrant and missing-persons teletype was being prepared, Lucia sat down with Barbara Czacherski in a room at the Allenhurst police headquarters. She was a short, slim woman with a tanned oval face and curly brown hair. Her composure did not disguise the fact that she was upset and nervous. While her husband and Tenbroeck looked on, Lucia sipped his coffee and listened to her recount her calls to the police.

"The next thing I heard was when the officer called back and advised me that I should come directly to the station after work. The officer asked me if my mother and her husband were fighting."

Lucia nodded, carefully writing her comments on a pad of paper.

"Who lived at the residence of 401 Euclid Avenue?"

"My mother, Rosemary, my stepfather, Alfred, and my younger brother, Scott, while not away at boarding school."

"Do you know if anyone was currently staying at the house?"

"Yes," Barbara answered. "A schoolfriend of Scott's from Nova Scotia was visiting. He arrived sometime during the middle of last week." She paused, then added: "I don't know his name."

"When did you see your mother and stepfather last?"

"I saw my mother last on Saturday, at approximately 2:30 P.M. at work."

"That would be Saturday, July 3, 1982, wouldn't it?" interrupted Lucia, writing the complete date into his report.

"Yes." Barbara replied. "I saw my stepfather last on Friday, July 2, about 3:30 P.M."

"When did you last see your brother?"

"I saw my brother Scott on Thursday at 5:30 P.M., with his Canadian friend. They were picking my mother up from work. This was the only time I saw his Canadian friend."

At this point Lucia knew he had no leads; in fact, he had nothing at all except a lot of blood, a Canadian boy's vinyl bag, and the knowledge that a van, a dog, and four people were missing. A crime had been committed; of that he was convinced, but he had no idea who was involved. A mass murderer could be responsible, or kidnappers. One or more of the missing people could be involved.

"Barbara, do you know of any existing problems between your mother, stepfather and Scott?" Lucia asked carefully.

Barbara nodded and cleared her throat. "There has been an unending personality conflict going on for the past thirteen years, all their married life. He has left physically to a new residence several times, but returned on all occasions."

Lucia glanced up. "What caused it?"

"Many times the source of the conflict was a problem between my mother's children and the stepfather. Several of the kids have run away and lived with me for years at a time. Scott and the stepfather had major problems up until two and a half years ago, when Scott finally went away to high school. The distance between them seemed to mend most of the problems. He is the youngest and last child in the house."

Later, Lucia stared thoughtfully at his notes. Barbara was, at this early stage of the investigation, his only reliable source of information, although he could not afford to rule her out as a suspect. It was possible, he speculated, that Scott had contacted her; after all, they were brother and sister, and she had been very insistent that the police check the house thoroughly. And there was another oddity. The Canadian boy's vinyl bag had contained, in addition to books, a pair of binoculars and various personal items, a prescription bottle with traces of a white powder, and a needle and syringe. At 11:20 P.M. Lucia telephoned the Royal Canadian Mounted Police detachment in Bridgetown, Nova Scotia and requested that the family of Bruce Curtis be notified that their son was missing.

That Tuesday, July 6, had also been a glorious summer day on Mount Hanley, in the province of Nova Scotia. "The North Mountain", as it was known locally, and a sister ridge to the south, protected the fertile Annapolis Valley ("We grow the best apples in the world," visitors have long been told, "just ask anyone around.") from storms blowing in from the Bay of Fundy. Being the first week of July, cherry trees were beginning to bear fruit. A fine salt breeze rustling the leaves of the maple trees and the big poplar in the front yard was Alice Curtis's only company that afternoon as she worked in the garden. Her husband, Jim, had retired eight years earlier from the armed forces but had been called up again in 1977 to take an administrative job that kept him in Halifax, the provincial capital about a two-hour drive east, during the week. He wasn't due home until Friday evening.

That night, exhausted from her labours as well as from the lingering effects of a blocked bile duct a few weeks earlier, Alice slept soundly. So soundly she was unsure how many times the phone rang at about 2:30 A.M. before she was startled awake. The caller, from the RCMP detachment at nearby Bridgetown, told Alice that a patrol car was sitting outside her house and asked her to speak to the officer. After first peering out a window to confirm this strange news, she donned a dressing-gown and stepped onto the front porch.

Although the presence of a law enforcement officer on her property at 2:30 A.M. was extraordinary, it was a measure of the Curtis family's uneventful existence that it had not yet occurred to her to feel disturbed. There was no hint that this moment foreshadowed a cataclysmic change in the previously orderly and, for the most part, contented world of Jim and Alice Curtis. The previous evening, Alice had risen to view a lunar eclipse but was too early. Returning to bed, she had slept through the night. Now, awakened at what would have been prime viewing time, she addressed the officer:

"Why didn't you come last night? I wanted to get up and see the eclipse."

The next morning she described the visit to her husband. "They wanted to know if I'd heard anything from Bruce, where he was, when he was coming home. And then they told me they're all missing: the parents, Scott and Bruce."

At that time, Jim and Alice Curtis agreed there was no reason to be upset, and little point in Jim returning to the farm. "There has to be an explanation," Alice reasoned, as Jim concurred. "Bruce said they're a well-to-do family. They have a van, and a guest staying with them. Maybe they've gone away for the long weekend, gone camping or something."

From the beginning, William Lucia believed the Podgis case would prove to be a homicide. Although officers had been shooing the curious away from the property and the tiny shore community was buzzing with gossip, nothing had appeared in the local newspapers yet because Lucia had little informa-tion himself. After Maurice Orlando, the Podgises' next-door neighbour, said he had seen the family van backed up to the side of the house on the holiday Monday, Lucia had been eager to question him further. While taking a formal statement on Wednesday morning, one bit of information caught his attention.

"My two sons told me that on Sunday evening, approximately 5:30 P.M., they spoke to Scott and his friend who were hiding in the tall grass at the rear of the property," reported Orlando. "They told my sons they were hiding because they didn't want to go to church."

Other investigators, working around the clock, were also turning up evidence. Two rings belonging to Rosemary Podgis had been found on a hutch in the dining-room. ("It's true," Lucia noted, "that people don't usually go away on a trip without their rings.") Two Winchester model 94 .30-.30 rifles had been found packed in cases in the back of an orange International Harvester Scout van, bearing the insignia of the U.S. mail, parked on the property. Two empty rifle boxes and a partially empty box of Winchester .30-.30 ammunition had been found in the garage at the rear of 401 Euclid. But the most disturbing discovery was made near the furnace in the basement of the house: two brown plastic garbage bags stuffed with blood-soaked pillows.

"About this time I began to lean toward at least Scott being involved," Lucia said. "And maybe his friend. One or both of them."

At 12:45 P.M. Lucia received a telephone call that confirmed his suspicions. An officer at the state police station in Lock Haven, Pennsylvania informed him that the bodies of a man and woman fitting the description in the missing persons teletype had been discovered the night before in nearby Ravensburg State Park. The woman, wearing a white nightgown and a pink, flowered bedjacket, had been wrapped in a sleeping-bag; the cause of death was not yet known. The man, naked and wedged into a trunk, had a gunshot wound to the head. Lucia called Barbara Czacherski and advised her to notify the rest of her family.

That afternoon, Dr Halbert Fillinger, a forensic pathologist and assistant medical examiner for the city of Philadelphia, was requested to perform two autopsies at the Lock Haven,

Pennsylvania hospital morgue. Although Fillinger had, on occasion, been flown by state police to the town — a small airport was located there because one of Lock Haven's local industries was a factory that built small aircraft — this time he packed his tools in his converted camera case and drove. At 8:00 P.M., Fillinger began work on a "well-developed, well-nourished white male" that lay on the morgue's old porcelain autopsy table. Because Lock Haven, like most rural hospitals, had no device for weighing bodies, Fillinger recorded an estimate into his handheld tape recorder. This was not an uncommon occurrence, and Fillinger felt he had become quite skilled at it. ("Sometimes you feel like a carnival barker.")

The body, he noted, appeared to have been lying on the ground, because soil and bits of leaves were present. There were signs of decomposition and areas of skin in which fly or ant larvae were embedded. But of greater interest was a 3.5-by-1.3-centimetre entrance gunshot wound behind the right ear. As Fillinger ran his fingers gingerly inside the hole, he felt a large amount of shattered bone. A gaping, star-shaped laceration, known as a stellate, began beneath the right eye and spread upwards towards the left forehead. Staring inside this opening, Fillinger observed fragments of bone and brain matter. With the help of the local pathologist, the scalp was slit across the crown from ear to ear and the skin peeled back. Fillinger skilfully sawed the skull-cap and lifted it off like the lid of a sugar bowl. He then repositioned the fragments by sliding them together and sewing them into a reconstruction of the face as it had originally looked. Speaking into his tape recorder, he said: "A reconstructed exit gunshot wound identified by reapproximating the extensive stellate lacerations of the face discloses a stellate 3-by-3.5-centimetre exit defect in the left forehead..."

The rest of Fillinger's examination included removing and weighing internal organs (this was accomplished by using a vegetable scale in the hospital commissary), taking fluid samples, and recording any other relevant medical characteristics. Thus he included a diagnosis of obesity, an enlarged prostate and some chronic kidney disease, although none of these contributed to the man's death. That, he concluded, was caused by a high-velocity gunshot wound to the head.

Turning his attention to the "well-developed, well-nourished white female," Fillinger noted the same evidence of decomposition that had been present on the first victim. An entrance gunshot wound measuring 1-by-1.3-centimetres was found to the right and slightly above the navel. A .30-calibre bullet, with copper and lead core intact, was recovered in the area of the left hip, which Fillinger was later able to determine had entered at a downward angle, tearing multiple loops of the small and large bowel as it travelled across to the left side of the pelvis before ending up by the left hip. He also noted three distinct areas of bruising on the scalp, which could have been caused by blows from a blunt instrument. Although the woman was listed as moderately obese and suffering from slight arteriosclerotic heart disease and minor kidney ailment, none of these were related to the cause of her death: a high-velocity gunshot wound to the trunk.

Interstate 80 begins north of Newark and cuts straight across the top of New Jersey before crossing the Delaware River and bisecting the state of Pennsylvania. It is a drive that takes motorists through forests of oak, maple and pine, wide valleys alternating with narrow mountain ranges. It is excellent country for camping, hunting and fishing, and disposing of bodies. Investigator William Lucia and Bill Duerr, the Allenhurst police officer assigned full time to the case, arrived late Thursday morning at the state police station in the sleepy village of Lock Haven. The local county coroner and assistant district attorney were waiting for them. Since bodies had been found in Ravensburg State Park before, and homicide was suspected, local officials had ordered autopsies performed and were preparing to begin their own investigation by the time fingerprint comparisons confirmed it was a New Jersey concern. Lucia and Duerr visited the Helt Funeral Home on Church Street to view the bodies. Duerr, recognizing Al Podgis immediately, told Lucia: "Not many people wear that flat-top crew cut these days."

Lucia and Duerr left the funeral home and drove along Interstate 80 to the PA 880 exit. They clocked 5.7 miles to the spot where the bodies had been pushed into a ravine. A trooper then led them to an embankment forty feet from the road. Although the evidence had been taken and stored, he explained the crime scene. Rosemary Podgis had been found wrapped in a sleeping bag and lying face down about seven and a half feet below the lip of the embankment. Next to her lay a foam mattress covered in a yellow sheet, two towels and a blood-stained handkerchief. A blue trunk containing Al Podgis had crashed seventeen feet before coming to a stop against an outcropping of rock, just seven feet from a dirt pathway. It was along this pathway, on Tuesday evening, that two men in search of a quiet spot to drink beer had discovered a knee protruding from the trunk. Investigators also found brown plastic garbage bags, a brown quilt, a white T-shirt, and several lengths of white nylon cord, one of which had come to rest in the branches of a hemlock tree between the path and a creek that ran below it. Inside the trunk were a number of items — including towels, sheets and blankets — that would later be turned over to Lucia and Duerr. Along with the rest of the evidence was a wedding ring containing five tiny diamonds and the inscription: "RFF to AKKP, 5-2-69," taken from the hand of Al Podgis.

Although a number of people were interviewed in connection with the case — several local residents reported hearing screams on Tuesday, but it was traced to a mother playing with her children in a nearby ball park — only one provided useful information. Before returning to New Jersey on Friday, July 9, Lucia took a statement from George Calvin Overdorf, a local farmer.

"I was coming down the road below my place when I saw a van behind me. I slowed down but it failed to pass me so I pulled off the main part of the road as I was driving my tractor with a baler and wagon behind it. When I pulled off, the van pulled alongside me and stopped. The passenger asked if I knew where Rauchtown Park was, with a lake being there. I told him there was a park here but there was no lake, only a dam, and the name of it was Ravensburg Park. He asked me if I could tell him how to get to the park and I told him. Then he asked me how they would know they were at the park and I told him it was right next to the road and he would see it. The van they were operating was blue with a purple background and there were three people in it."

"What did these people look like?" Lucia asked.

"I talked to the passenger and he was light complected with light sandy brown hair, between twenty to thirty years of age. I can't remember what he was wearing. The driver wore glasses and was dark complected with dark black hair.* The glasses had black thin framing all around, plastic I believe. I can't remember what he was wearing as far as clothing is concerned. The third party was between the two seats, inside and to the rear, and moved around a lot. I couldn't say whether it was a boy or a girl. I assumed it was a girl although I didn't see the person."

"What time would this have been, Mr Overdorf?" Lucia asked.

"The time that I saw this van was about quarter to one on Tuesday afternoon. The passenger thanked me for the information I had given him on how to get to the park. I had your office contacted due to the fact of what happened up at the park. I felt this information might be of some help."

"Thank-you," Lucia told him. "I think it was."

Lucia and Duerr returned to New Jersey later that day and delivered the evidence to the Monmouth County Prosecutor's Office for processing. "We would have had a time explaining ourselves if a police officer had stopped us," Lucia joked as they unloaded from his new Chevrolet Celebrity boxes of bloody towels, quilts and blankets, the foam mattress and, strapped to a roof rack, the blue trunk that had served as a temporary casket for Al Podgis. The following morning, Saturday, July 10, both men met at the Allenhurst police

---

*Although this description fits Bruce Curtis, his parents point out that he did not have a driver's licence and there was never any evidence that he drove the van.

headquarters where Captain Frank Tenbroeck greeted them with his latest findings.

Barbara Czacherski had called to let Tenbroeck know that the funeral would be held the following Monday and members of both the Podgis and Franz families would be coming to Loch Arbour. She also told him that a co-worker at the Englishtown post office, John Foley, had seen Rosemary Podgis on the July fourth weekend. When Tenbroeck interviewed Foley he uncovered the first indication of trouble at the Podgis home over the Fourth of July weekend.

"I had invited both Rosemary and Alfred to a picnic which I was having on July fourth at my house," Foley told Tenbroeck. "I asked her if she could bring a crock-pot and two warmers and she said, sure, and offered to make some cheesecake. I asked Alfred if he could bring a case of beer and he said, okay. On Saturday, in the morning, I asked Rosie if she was coming and she said she would be there with bells on. The picnic started about 1:00 P.M., and I noticed about 2:00 that Rosie and Al still weren't here. Then, approximately half an hour later, my father-in-law brought to my attention that a car had pulled into the driveway, and I noticed it was Rosie. She was holding the cheesecake in her hand and while she was approaching she was telling me that she couldn't stay. I asked why. She seemed embarrassed. It sounded like she said there were problems, or trouble, at home."

After spending the night at The Trail Dust Inn, a Best Western motel in Sulphur Springs, Texas, the two teenaged travellers and their dog rose on the morning of Saturday, July 10 to begin the last leg of their journey. Despite a night's sleep and a shower, Bruce Curtis felt dazed and his companion, Scott Franz, looked grim behind the wheel of their van. The boys had an unspoken agreement not to talk about certain things, and the silence grew heavy in the Texas heat. To whatever degree Curtis felt like a participant in the trip over the past few days, the present drive to Dallas was in Scott's hands. He was grateful to know there was a plan — "to reach Rosie and explain everything to her" — because inaction bred panic. When he learned Franz had stolen a telephone directory from the motel because he didn't know Rosie's phone number or address, Curtis had become upset. But at times of conflict, when his older sisters would pressure him to take sides in sibling disputes, for example, Curtis's defence was withdrawal. Now he occupied himself staring at the stream of billboards along the roadside.

When they reached the outskirts of Dallas, Franz developed an irritation in his eye and stopped at a mall to purchase ointment. Here the boys tried unsuccessfully to contact a schoolmate, a boy who lived with his family in Dallas and was, like Franz, an American who had recently graduated from King's-Edgehill School in Nova Scotia. Late that afternoon they stopped at the Holiday Inn in Richardson, a suburb of Dallas. Franz checked into Room 217, using a Carte Blanche credit card issued to Alfred K. Podgis. Curtis sat with the dog, Sam — "we were always sneaking her into our hotel rooms" — while Franz called directory assistance in an effort to find Rosie's number. Then the boys left the confines of the room.

At 8:07 P.M. Franz inserted the key into the door of Room 217. At the sound of footsteps both boys turned to see two Richardson police officers advancing towards them with their guns drawn. "Get on the floor!" one commanded, and Curtis would later recount how he looked over his shoulder to see who they were addressing. Shaking with fright, their arms were pulled behind their backs and they were handcuffed.

"Is there anyone in there?" one of the officers demanded, indicating the door.

"There's a dog," Franz told him. "A German shepherd."

"Is it dangerous?"

"No. Sam wouldn't hurt anyone."

Indeed Sam was pleased at the company. She watched curiously, tail pounding the rug, while the officers advised Franz and Curtis of their rights. They searched the underside of drawers, under the bed and behind the curtains. Then the officers gathered the boys' belongings and placed them in their duffel bags. The handles of the bags were placed over the boys' heads and they were led, still handcuffed, out of the room. The members of a wedding party that had just arrived and were milling around the lobby gaped in astonishment, a moment that Curtis would later remember as "exceptionally embarrassing."

The first newspaper story on the case ran in the *Asbury Park Press* the previous week under the headline: TWO SOUGHT IN LOCH ARBOUR COUPLE'S MURDER and began: "Two 18-year-old graduates of an exclusive Nova Scotia preparatory school are wanted in connection with the murders of the mother and stepfather of one of the teenagers." The story went on to say that "neighbours described Mr and Mrs Podgis as a likeable couple who kept to themselves" and estimated the time of the murders at "sometime between Sunday and Tuesday." Two days later a story in the *Red Bank Daily Register* speculated that the two fugitives might be trying to flee to Canada.

On the morning of Thursday, July 8, Mary Elizabeth Finnerty, the sixty-three-year-old secretary of the Loch Arbour Planning Board, called Frank Tenbroeck. For the past four years Al and Rosemary Podgis had been trying to subdivide their property, which occupied three lots. Their proposal had met with considerable resistance from those in the community anxious to preserve the character of the village. Now, in the wake of the publicity surrounding the deaths, Mrs Finnerty realized she might be able to contribute to the investigation. On Saturday afternoon of the holiday weekend, Mrs Finnerty was watching the first hour of a television special, "1776," when a telephone call disturbed her viewing.

"Mr Podgis telephoned me to inquire about the subdivision of his property," she told Tenbroeck. "I was able to answer him right away because I had established the status of the subdivision with the board attorney in anticipation of an inquiry from the Podgises. I was able to tell Mr Podgis that the subdivision had expired. He then talked for some minutes about his plan to sell the lot from his property even if it meant applying for another subdivision."

"At any time during the conversation with Mr. Podgis did you feel that something may have been wrong?" asked Tenbroeck.

"No."

"Do you remember anything else?"

"Yes," Mrs Finnerty said. "During this long conversation Mr Podgis mentioned that a boy he mentioned in an earlier conversation who had gone to school in Nova Scotia had succeeded at the school. He was very satisfied with the way that had turned out. I got the impression that he was rather proud of the boy's success there."

Any investigation into the circumstances surrounding death necessarily reveals a great deal about how people live. In Al Podgis's study, a second-floor sunroom at the back of the house in which neighbours often observed lights burning late into the night, a baseball-card collection valued at twenty thousand dollars was found. There were also tins containing commemorative coins: Kennedy half-dollars, Bicentennial quarters, a gold Canadian Centennial coin, wheat pennies. On the third floor, a section of the house kept locked and used only for storage, boxes were found containing items that had been purchased and saved, perhaps for future use or for gift-giving. Barbara Czacherski explained to the investigators that her stepfather was a hoarder, forever collecting things that might one day be of value. Scattered around the rest of the house were envelopes containing various sums of cash or savings bonds. Only Rosemary Podgis's wallet was missing. Thus William Lucia had, with a reasonable degree of certainty, concluded that robbery had not been a primary motive.

A total of ten weapons had been found at 401 Euclid: in addition to the pellet pistol, shotgun and .22-calibre rifle in the master bedroom, and two Winchester .30-.30s in the Scout, investigators collected a pump pellet rifle (Benjamin Franklin model), a derringer (Philadelphia Black Powder model) and boxes of .12-gauge and .22-calibre ammunition from the study. On the third floor they found a Springfield .22-calibre rifle,

Crossman BB gun and a starter's pistol that was missing its hammer. A copper-jacketed .30-.30 bullet was dug out of a hole twenty-four inches from the floor in the trim around the door leading from the second floor hallway into the study, and several small holes, probably .22-calibre, were found in the back wall of a closet in the master bedroom. Then there was the question of the two empty rifle cases and loose ammunition found in the garage.

At noon on Saturday, July 10, Lucia and Frank Tenbroeck began interviewing members of Al and Rosemary Podgis's families. Dawn Franz, Rosemary's youngest daughter by her first marriage, who was living in Fort Worth, Texas, near Rosie, said that she had talked to her mother and stepfather the previous Sunday, Independence Day, and that there hadn't seemed to be any problems. She added that her brother Scott, whom she described as a sissy and a mama's boy, would probably go to visit their sister Noreen in Eugene, Oregon, if he was in trouble. Lucia, bearing in mind Chief Newman's remarks about Mark Franz — "I always predicted he'd kill someone or be killed; that's why I thought Mark might have done it first thing" — asked Dawn about her brother. She told him Mark had been in jail in Texas over that weekend until she bailed him out on Tuesday, July 6.

Timothy Lee Podgis, a son by Al Podgis's first marriage who lived in Sarasota, Florida, told Lucia that he hadn't talked to his father and stepmother for three years. "He didn't want much to do with his children," Podgis said. His older sister, Terry, who lived with her husband in Bradenton, Florida, had visited her parents the previous March and described things as "normal." She said her father and stepmother seemed proud of Scott's achievements at school, and suggested that Lucia speak to her husband, Danial Rawlinson, about a conversation he'd had with Scott on the subject of drugs. At 6:13 P.M., Lucia interviewed Rawlinson by phone from Florida. Rawlinson told him that Scott had stayed with them for a few weeks in 1978 after he had run away from home. In March, when he and Terry had visited New Jersey, Scott had been home on a school vacation and told him he was into a lot of drugs. "He mentioned cocaine, Quaaludes and heroin," Rawlinson recalled, but added that he suspected Scott had been stretching the truth.

It was early evening by the time Lucia prepared to leave. "I'm taking my wife and kids out tonight before they forget what I look like," he grinned. Tenbroeck and Newman relaxed in the chief's office and discussed the case. "He was never a problem," Newman said of Scott Franz. "I watched him grow up. He used to come by the firehall when I lived next door to it." Tenbroeck, a longtime volunteer fireman, nodded. "I sometimes chased him away so he wouldn't get hurt. Our son was about three when we lived down the street and Scott would come over and play baseball with him. He was just a kid, a regular ten-year-old who meandered through the yards. Well-clothed, well-fed, never looked abused."

The conversation turned to Mark and Dawn Franz, and how their teenage delinquency had upset Al Podgis. "It's always tough for a stepparent," Tenbroeck remarked. "Mark, Dawn and Scott probably had resentment toward Al. I know Al tried to straighten Mark out; he threw him out of the house a couple of times but always let him back in."

"Mark was bad, Frank," Newman said. "The old man may have been a disciplinarian, but he was never a criminal problem."

Then they both had a laugh over the old-timer whose property backed onto the Podgises' backyard. When asked if he had seen anything unusual, he had confirmed that the maroon van had been backed up to the side of the house on the holiday Monday. The old man, Tenbroeck knew, sat in his backyard with binoculars watching his neighbours for signs they were abusing their pets. "He was sure that dog of Al's was being mistreated," Tenbroeck said.

"We could have arrested him as a peeping Tom under state laws," joked Newman.

"Yeah," Tenbroeck responded, "but if anybody'd seen anything funny going on there, it would've been him."

At 8:30 P.M., Tenbroeck and Newman were biting into cheeseburgers when the telephone interrupted their dinner. It was the fraud investigations branch of the Carte Blanche credit card company reporting that Al Podgis's card had been presented at the Holiday Inn in Richardson, Texas. Tenbroeck alerted the Richardson police and in less than half an hour received word that both Franz and Curtis were in custody.

Shortly after midnight, William Lucia returned home to find messages taped to his front door and the telephone ringing. After cancelling family obligations throughout the week, he had taken his wife, Cookie, and their three children to the boardwalk at Point Pleasant and later out to dinner. "I'd had no sleep all week," Lucia sighed. "Then at 1:00 A.M. I'm packing for Texas."

For Captain James Curtis and his wife, Alice, the months of May and June 1982 had been the busiest and most exciting in memory. Their eldest daughter, twenty-three-year-old Anne, was married on May 22 to Donald Blake Woodside, son of the chairman of the orthodontics department at the University of Toronto's faculty of dentistry, and a recent graduate in medicine from Queen's University in Kingston, Ontario. At the wedding, held in the solemn elegance of Trinity College Chapel on the University of Toronto's downtown campus, the Curtises stood proudly as Anne wed "a wonderful young man" who could scarcely have been a finer prospective husband for their daughter. Carol, the middle child, served as one of the bride's attendants and their youngest, eighteen-year-old Bruce, was an usher. A tall, introspective boy, Bruce looked uncomfortable in so large a crowd and dressed in unfamiliar formal attire, but the family later agreed he looked "handsome." The reception was held at the Royal Canadian Military Institute and the event was even written up in the society column of *The Globe and Mail*, the national newspaper. (In jest, a close friend of Anne's had convinced the columnist of the significance of the ceremony.) In the manner of society columns everywhere, the Curtises were said to "have a large farm by the ocean," a statement that was indisputable, considering their 750 acres located a mile from the Bay of Fundy in Nova Scotia, but conveyed a sense of baronial majesty to what was in fact a modest, rustic, decidedly middle-class life.

Three weeks later, after a honeymoon in Florida and Blake's convocation ceremonies at Queen's University, the couple returned to Toronto for Anne's graduation. After a distinguished six years of university life that had included twenty scholarships, prizes and medals, Anne was named gold medalist for scoring the highest aggregate average in the University of Toronto's highly rated and fiercely competitive faculty of medicine. It was, for Jim and Alice Curtis, who placed great value on higher education and encouraged their children to strive for distinction, a moment of overwhelming satisfaction. Next came Bruce's graduation from King's-Edgehill, the same private school that had nurtured Anne's development as a scholar. The fact that Bruce received no awards or medals at the ceremonies, as he had the previous year, surprised his parents, but his marks were strong and he was to enter Dalhousie University in Halifax that September.

Anne began her internship at University Hospital in London, Ontario on June 15, but was reading in the doctor's lounge of a hospital in nearby Chatham, where she was taking her first rotation in obstetrics, when she was unexpectedly summoned to the telephone. Blake informed her that her mother had called and that he had been unable to obtain a coherent message. He recommended Anne call her immediately.

Since her mother was a composed and taciturn woman who preferred to let events run their natural course before providing the family with a comprehensive account, she had only recently written Anne a newsy letter informing her that she had spent a week in hospital with an abdominal ailment, and that Bruce was in New Jersey. ("Expect he'll be back about the end of the week," the letter concluded.) The memory of speaking to her mother still haunts Anne. "I recall it vividly because it was so bizarre. My mother had known about all this for several days, since the RCMP came to see her, but hadn't wanted to let me know until she knew something definite because at that point Bruce still hadn't been found. She tried to tell me briefly about it but it was so odd I insisted she start at the beginning and go through it step by step. She told me that Bruce had started getting calls from Scott urging him to visit. When Mother heard about it she thought it would be great, a good graduation present. Then she told me how she had been the one who forced the issue and sent him down, really, because it was a big deal, with a lot of complicated arrangements, and Bruce was the type to resist anything complicated. She told me how they had sent him off and got a phone call that he had arrived safely, and the next thing she knew Mr and Mrs Podgis had been found dead.

"I remember trying to puzzle out in my mind what sort of bizarre circumstances could account for this. What sort of armed assassin could have done this? Then I thought, to kidnap a man, woman and two teenaged boys would take a gang. Why would they kill two and keep the others? And I can remember my mother quietly saying a couple of times that I should realize that from the police point of view, the two boys were suspects. I just dismissed that notion out of hand. You know, so much for that, let's work on real theories that have some potential."

On the plane to Dallas, William Lucia and Bill Duerr kept busy piecing together the many loose ends of the case. Duerr, a stocky affable man, had worked with his father on charter fishing boats along the Jersey coast before marriage and plans for a family convinced him to pursue his other interest, law enforcement. A keen reader of true-life crime stories, Duerr aspired to detective work and was unabashedly thrilled to be part of this investigation. "Lucia had a top reputation," he would later confide. "He was a professional and I was an amateur; this was my first homicide. I didn't lead the show." But Duerr brought to the investigation a valuable personal perspective. As a cop, he favoured "the social work approach, being a nice guy. I pride myself on knowing my community well." Duerr's own father had been a disciplinarian, and although he'd never raised a hand to his only son, there had been verbal battles during what Duerr now refers to as "the rebellious times." He had met

Al Podgis and found him to be a decent sort, but couldn't help wondering whether the man could have been secretly brutalizing his children.

Duerr had seen Scott Franz on the Independence Day weekend. As he told Lucia: "It was sometime before nine in the morning, on the Saturday. I was parked downtown, across from The Coffee Mill, when Scott drove up to my cruiser on his moped. He wanted to know what time the bank opened, and I told him nine. I asked him, 'how ya doing?' He said okay, that he'd just graduated from high school and was working for the summer before going back to Canada for college. I asked him how the family was doing and he said, fine. I remember his friend stayed across the street, the same kid I'd seen driving around with Scott the past few days."

Lucia listened with interest. He already entertained a couple of theories, but until he talked to Scott Franz nothing was certain. Although robbery had not been ruled out, the case most resembled a domestic dispute. Despite the disorder of the house there was no indication of any life-or-death struggle, nor were valuables taken. The rifle blast to Al Podgis's head had blown skull fragments down into a pillow, suggesting that the victim had not been an active participant in any activity other than, perhaps, sleeping. There had been an attempt at a cover-up — how else to explain the bloody pillows stuffed into garbage bags in the basement, the wiping of bloodstains off the walls — yet it had been so sloppily executed that it suggested panic rather than ruthless professionalism. The report from Texas had mentioned only the two boys: if they had ever been hostages, which Lucia doubted, they were alone when they checked into the hotel in Richardson and apparently in no hurry to call police. That Rosemary Podgis had also been shot was a bigger mystery. There was nothing to indicate that she had been disliked by any of her children, so Lucia could think of no motive for deliberately shooting her unless she had threatened the killers in some way. The Canadian boy's role was also unclear. He might have been forced to accompany his friend, perhaps at gunpoint, although Lucia's instincts told him otherwise. Inside the bag belonging to Curtis that was found at the back of the Podgis property, in addition to the needle and syringe, empty pill bottle, and plastic bag containing an as yet unidentified substance, was a diary filled with half a dozen pages of morbid, vaguely pathological ramblings.

Lucia and Duerr were met in Dallas by Ken Roberts, an investigator with the Richardson police department. He informed them that Curtis had requested to see an attorney but that Franz seemed willing to answer questions. (In fact, Franz had also asked to see an attorney; he had been given a list of names and telephone numbers and had tried, unsuccessfully, to reach one.) Behind the Richardson police headquarters was a one-storey, red-brick structure that had once been a doctor's office but now housed Richardson's criminal investigations division. Roberts gave Lucia and Duerr his crammed office, formerly a doctor's examining room, that now contained two desks and two chairs and left room for little else apart from its occupants. At 6:45 P.M., after Roberts had led Franz into the room and closed the door behind him, Lucia said: "Hello Scott. I'm Detective Lucia, and of course you know Officer Duerr. We're here to investigate the deaths of your mother and stepfather."

The interrogation of Franz, Lucia knew, was critically important. "My humble feeling about police work," he often said, "is that despite all the forensic advancements and all the statistics, it still boils down to dealing with people face to face. More cases are solved by getting somebody to talk to you than by fingerprint analysis." Lucia was fond of describing himself as an "unlicenced psychiatrist" when he conducted interrogations. "My job is to put you in that chair and get you to tell me something that'll put you in jail for the rest of your life. You could sell a lot of vacuum cleaners with that talent."

After reading Scott Franz his constitutional rights and asking him to sign a waiver, Lucia began, slowly, with a rambling monologue that gave him time to size up his prey. The boy, dressed in a Knoxville World's Fair T-shirt and jeans, looked very young, and his fingers trembled when Lucia lit his cigarette. He denied any knowledge of his parents' deaths, stating that he and his friend Bruce had left the house last Monday on a trip that took them to Atlantic City, Knoxville and finally Texas where they had been inexplicably arrested. ("No, we were nowhere near Pennsylvania." "Nowhere near it, Scott?" Well, Franz conceded, they might have driven through the lower part of the state.) It was, Lucia noted, an unconvincing performance. There was too much self-righteous swagger and absolutely none of the remorse or even curiosity one would expect from a person who had just learned that his parents had been killed. After a period of deceptively casual probing punctuated by long and, for Franz, visibly unsettling silences, Lucia began to draw his circle of questioning tighter. ("I could get a better chronological statement out of a ten-year-old!") Gradually the boy's blustery efforts at denial weakened. Finally, Franz admitted that he had had problems with his stepfather prior to leaving the house, an admission upon which Lucia pounced.

"It's done, Scott. We have certain evidence that makes it pretty obvious there was some involvement on your part. Hey, you committed a crime, and even little lies you tell me now can look like big lies later. There's another person; you don't know what he's going to say, do you?"

Franz swallowed. He flicked the filter of his cigarette in a rat-a-tat rhythm.

"We know you know more than you're telling us," Duerr told him gently.

"It's to your advantage to tell us the truth," Lucia continued. "Look, everybody makes mistakes, so get it out on the table."

At 8:30 P.M., after nearly two hours of questioning, Franz said weakly, "Yeah."

"Yeah what?" asked Lucia.

"Yeah, I shot him."

At 9:45 P.M., after running through this new version of events in which Franz admitted he had shot his stepfather and said that Bruce Curtis had shot his mother, Lucia asked him to repeat the account while he typed it into a statement.

"My stepfather, Al, and I were having problems over some items missing out of the house that he was blaming me for taking, but I didn't. My friend, Bruce Curtis, flew down from Nova Scotia to visit me. Bruce got there on Tuesday, June 29. My stepfather and I went to pick him up at the airport. His plane was late and my stepfather was mad because he thought he had to pay for parking longer. During the rest of the week, my step-father kept picking on me. On Thursday, July first, I went to the post office and picked up the mail. I brought it home and put it on the table. My social security cheque was in the mail. He said he couldn't find it and accused me of taking it. I later found it and gave it to him and he was still mad." (Since the death of his father, Scott had received monthly cheques from the govern-ment — Al and Rosemary carefully monitored their arrival.)

"The next morning he asked me if I was going to take a shower. I said, no. He later told my mother that he had asked me if I was going to work and I had said no. I know he asked me if I was going to take a shower. He left for work without giving me a ride and got mad because I didn't go to work. On Friday night my mother came home and her and my stepfather got into a fight over me not going to work. She tried to keep me away from him and took Bruce and I out to dinner.

"Saturday, my mother went to work. I was out cutting the grass and I saw my stepfather bring six of his rifles and some towels and lock them up in the four-wheel-drive Scout.* I got afraid when I saw him put the rifles out there. I also forgot to mention that he had punched me twice on the right shoulder when I didn't go to work. After we saw him with the guns, Bruce and I took off to Burger King in Asbury Park. After we left Burger King we went to my house to see if my stepfather had gone to the baseball-card dealer like he said that he was. When we got there he was home so we left and went to Seaview Square Mall. I called my house but didn't say anything. My mother answered and said to come home, that he wouldn't hurt me, but I hung up.

"Bruce and I got back to my house about 10:00 P.M. We were

*In the end, only four rifles were found.

afraid to go in so we went into the garage and got into the camper. Around midnight I looked around the house. Most of the lights were on. I could see my stepfather through the window, still at his back desk. I went back to the trailer. A little while later my mother came out with my dog, Sam. She opened the garage door and said, 'Scott, if you're in here answer me, come into the house and we will straighten the whole thing out.' We didn't answer and she went back into the house.

"Bruce and I went across the street for a while to see if the lights went off. They didn't, so then we went under the porch to listen, to see whether or not we could get in. I couldn't get in if the door was locked because he had taken my moped keys and my house key was on the ring. While under the porch we heard my mother and stepfather arguing in the kitchen, and I heard him say, 'he's no better than Mark.' Then I heard my mother scream. He came out to bring the moped into the house. I heard him cursing and he said something about killing me. After a while, all the lights went out and my mother came out and we talked. After we talked she told me she would leave the door open and for us to come in and sleep on the couch, and we did.

"Sunday morning, Bruce and I woke up before them, about 6:15 A.M. I went upstairs and got our sneakers out of the white bathroom and brought them down. Bruce wanted his traveller's cheques and I went back upstairs. I got his bag and then I was looking for my cheque-book when I heard a noise. I thought it was my mother, but then I heard a gunshot. At that time I was standing in his office room. He couldn't see me where I was standing. Then I ran down the stairs. He was standing in the hallway with a rifle. We hid Bruce's bag outside by the bushes, then we went to the Asbury Park boardwalk. We ate at Perkin [Steak and Pancake House]. We went to Nick's Amusements and won a badminton set and a frisbee. Then we went to the free beach.

"When we got back to my house, at about 4:30 P.M., we got Bruce's bag from the side of the house. We hid the bag and the badminton set in the grass and waited for my mother to go to church. While we were out there the Orlando kids saw us and I told them we were hiding because we didn't want to go to church. My mother didn't come out so we went to the Tastee Sub Shop in Loch Arbour. We bought a couple of subs and Bruce paid for them with a ten-dollar traveller's cheque. Then we went to the Asbury Park boardwalk and waited for the fireworks. We watched the fireworks and then we went back home and went into the camper and waited around again.

"A short while later, I went to the Scout and opened the door with a piece of wire. I took out two rifles, I think they were .30-.30s. One of them was loaded. I think there were eight shells. I equally divided them and loaded both guns. Sometime after midnight, Bruce and I went into the house with the rifles and went to sleep on the downstairs couch. On Monday morning, I woke up around 7:00 A.M. and talked with my mother. I told her I wasn't going to stay around and wait for him to kill me. She said that he was only trying to scare me, that he had missed me. My mother went into the kitchen to make Bruce and I French toast. I told Bruce that I was going upstairs to take a shower and that if my stepfather tried anything I was going to shoot him. I also said something to Bruce to the effect that if he had to shoot to go ahead and shoot. I'm not sure exactly what I said to Bruce.

"I went upstairs and put the rifle I had in the pink bathroom and I went into the white bathroom to get something. My step-father was laying in bed. I saw his arm drop to the side of the bed. There was a .22 rifle by the side of the bed. I ran to the pink bathroom and got the rifle I had. He was getting out of bed with the rifle in his hand and I was going into his room. He started swearing and I said, 'don't even try it, because that will only give me a limp but this will finish you.' He started arguing with me about my brother, Mark, and me stealing and then he fired a shot in my direction. I freaked out and something fell on the mirror. He looked in that direction and as he looked I ran toward the door and fired. After I fired I went into the hallway and when I looked back I saw blood splattered on the wall.

"The next thing I heard was another shot. Then I heard my mother groaning or crying. I stayed upstairs for a couple of minutes and then I went downstairs and saw her lying between the dining-room and the bar-room in the doorway. Bruce was standing there screaming something to me like, 'what are we going to do?" At first I said I didn't know, and then I said we've got to get rid of the bodies. A little while later Bruce and I brought my dark blue trunk upstairs. I was starting to get sick.

"Bruce wiped down the walls in my stepfather's room. Bruce and I lifted the mattress and got my stepfather in the trunk. We also put the bedclothes, sheet, blanket and some towels in the trunk. Then Bruce and I went to Sears at Seaview Mall and bought some white nylon rope. I remember now that we went to Sears before we put him in the trunk because we used the rope to pull him off the bed into the trunk. We went downstairs and I told Bruce to take my mother's rings off. He did, and washed them off, and I put them on the buffet in the dining-room. I put them there so one of the family could have them. Then Bruce put my mother in a sleeping bag. He tied the sleeping bag with some of the rope that we had bought. We went upstairs and tied the trunk with some of the rope and brought the trunk to the entrance of the stairway with the handcart and took it downstairs. I backed the van up to the side door. We loaded the trunk into the van, and then the sleeping bag with my mother. We cleaned up a little more and put garbage bags in the cellar. We put the guns we used into the van. We took Sam and left.

"We took the parkway and headed toward Pennsylvania after some discussion. We took Interstate 80 west. We stopped at a rest area close to Ravensburg and looked at the map, got off at the next exit and went to a state park. We picked out a spot and backed the van up. It was about 9:00 P.M. There was a drop there and we dumped the bodies. We headed toward home. When I went by my house I saw the police car and I think a green detective car so Bruce and I kept on going. After that we drove to the Hilton Inn in Tinton Falls. We parked there and Bruce went in and called my house and there was no answer. We decided that we had to get rid of the rifles. I dumped the rifles in a sewer drain in the rear of the Hilton by a dumpster. We headed back toward the Eatontown Circle and started throwing the rifle shells out the window, one by one. We went to the Monmouth Mall and threw out the gloves we had used into a garbage can. We bought some clothes at the mall. We went to Atlantic City for a day, then headed for the World's Fair, and then we came to Texas and were picked up by the police."

"Did Bruce say anything to you about shooting your mother?" Lucia asked.

"Yes. I asked him how far away he was when he shot her and he said about this far, and showed me with his hands. He said something about the length of the muzzle."

"Did he say why he shot her?"

"He said something about being afraid."

Shortly after 2:00 A.M., Franz was taken to a holding cell in the basement of the Richardson police headquarters. (In order to separate the two boys, Curtis was being held by police in the nearby town of Plano.) Lucia then called Paul Chaiet, the county prosecutor responsible for the case, at his home in Oceanport, New Jersey. Chaiet agreed to send someone immediately to retrieve the weapons at the Hilton Inn. "Nice work, Bill," he added.

Neither Lucia nor Duerr had eaten since they had arrived in Texas, twelve hours earlier. At 5:00 A.M. they drove to the International House of Pancakes and ordered breakfast specials. Both men were struck by the lack of remorse Franz had shown. "Scott told us that in the same situation he would have done it again," recalled Duerr. Lucia was certain Franz was not telling them everything, but for now he had told them enough.

Something had gone terribly wrong in New Jersey. This much Alice Curtis had known as soon as the RCMP contacted her, on the night of Thursday, July 8, to inform her that the bodies of Al and Rosemary Podgis, her son's hosts, had been discovered in a ravine. A plump woman, her face fleshy but glowing with the ruddiness of farm living, Alice sat down heavily on the gold-patterned sofa in the living-room to sort things out. She was accustomed to life, with all its surprises, disappointments and emergencies, unfolding coherently; tragedy, in its most brutal dimensions, had not visited the Curtis family. When sharp pains in her stomach caused her to double over four days before Bruce left for New Jersey — a blocked bile duct had been the source of the complaint — she made arrangements to get herself to the hospital, since her husband was away on business and Bruce had never learned to drive, and instructed her son to finish preparing the homemade bread for baking. That was Alice, orderly even in times of crisis. Now Bruce, a boy whose intellect, Alice had feared, was developing at the expense of his instincts, had been pushed out of the nest and become entangled in violent circumstances beyond his control. Like a fly in a spider's web, she thought. Which reminded her that she had known nothing about Scott Franz or his family when she had agreed — no, she would never let herself forget it, she had advocated — that Bruce take this vacation.

The next morning, Friday, after speaking to his wife, Jim Curtis left his office immediately. As a radio specialist in the Royal Canadian Air Force, Jim had been involved in search-and-rescue operations, military exercises, and peace-keeping efforts abroad through the Cold War period of the 1950s and 1960s. He finished his active career in operational training before retiring in 1974, at the age of forty-five. Three years later, when the Canadian Armed Forces was experiencing a shortage of middle-management personnel and Jim was feeling the pinch as inflation eroded his pension, he gladly accepted administrative duties at Maritime Command Headquarters in Halifax. It was usually with great satisfaction that he departed the busy port city of 94,000 and returned to the salty, pine-scented air and rural pace of the Annapolis Valley, but today he felt a profound foreboding. A genial, controlled man not given to emotional outbursts, whose normal speaking voice was an uncommanding lilt, Jim Curtis could, by drawing his stocky, five-foot-nine-inch frame erect and emphatically snapping each word, project himself authoritatively. He adopted this manner when he walked into the RCMP detachment at Bridgetown and respectfully demanded to know "what the hell is going on."

Although the RCMP clearly told him less than they knew — no mention was made of certain allegations that his son and

Scott Franz had been involved in a poisoning incident at King's-
Edgehill, for example, although that information would become
known to those investigating and prosecuting the case in New
Jersey — they had probably received fewer details from New
Jersey authorities than the Curtises believed. When Jim asked
whether Bruce's luggage had been found at the Podgises' house,
he was told it had. That made the abduction theory more plausible, while providing little cause for optimism. Two people
were dead, and if the police were unable to find two teenagers
after four days, the likelihood of finding them alive seemed
remote. Jim had asked for the name of someone to contact in
New Jersey. An RCMP officer gave him Barbara Czacherski's
number.

The next morning, Jim Curtis called Barbara and asked
whether his son was still alive. He later described her as "very
pleasant, very agreeable, very concerned," although she asked
a few peculiar questions. "She wanted to know whether Bruce
was left-handed. The way Al Podgis was shot, they figured the
rifle was aimed from that shoulder. (Bruce was right-handed).
Then she wanted to know what kind of kid he was. She asked
whether we'd ever had any trouble with him. I said, no. It felt
kind of funny being asked by this stranger whether you'd ever
had any trouble with your child."

He also told Barbara that Bruce was very quiet, an honours
student who didn't drive, use drugs or even drink beer, as far as
he knew. When Barbara asked him about guns, Jim told her that
he had three in the house but that Bruce never touched them.
(All of this information appeared in Captain Tenbroeck's report
of Sunday, July 11, following a conversation with Barbara.)

For several days the Curtises had noticed their telephone
behaving strangely: a series of clicks, then the line would go
dead. Since Bruce was considered a suspect, they were convinced the RCMP had bugged their line in order to gather information about his whereabouts, an accusation the RCMP denied.
("The bastards have never admitted it yet," Jim Curtis complains
angrily to this day.) On the weekend, an anxious Lorraine
Peever, Jim's sister, called from her home in Brantford, Ontario.

"Alice, Anne told Mother and I that Bruce has disappeared, and that the people he was staying with are dead."

"Yes, that's right," Alice replied cautiously.

"Well, what's going on?"

"We don't know what the blazes is going on," Alice told her.

An amazed Peever listened as Alice confirmed that an impossibility was fact, and voiced her suspicions that the phone was wiretapped.

"Do you want Mother and I to come down and stay with you?" Peever asked. "We don't think you should be alone, with Jim away in Halifax."

"No, no. Not at the moment," Alice reassured her. "I'm fine."

At 10:00 A.M. on Tuesday, July 13, Barbara called Alice and informed her that Scott and Bruce had been arrested in Dallas. "Scott said that he shot our stepfather," Barbara told her. "And Bruce shot our mother. They're both being charged with murder."

Alice hung up the phone. Her first reaction was relief at the news that Bruce was alive, followed by a feeling of confusion. Everything about her surroundings seemed unfamiliar, like the geography of a nightmare. She would describe the moment bitterly: "We went right from the top, that great fancy wedding of Anne's and her graduation with a gold medal, followed by Bruce's graduation...and then the bottom fell out."

Alice, who had never been one to dispatch bulletins updating the family as news unfolded, first notified her husband, then Anne. Several hours later the phone rang.

"Has there been any news?" It was Lorraine Peever.

Alice cleared her throat self-consciously. Whenever she used the phone she imagined a tape recorder being activated.

"Well, yes. Have you spoken to Anne?"

"Not since yesterday," Peever answered.

"Bruce has been found."

Alice's voice dropped so low that Peever was convinced her nephew was dead. She asked uncertainly, "Is he alive?"

"Yes. He's been arrested."

"Arrested?"

"He's been charged with murder."

Peever was silent for a beat. "That's ridiculous, Alice. It's ridiculous. There has to be some kind of reasonable explanation."

Alice, who did not want to say more over the phone, replied worriedly, "Well, let's hope so."

The Curtises' neighbours expressed disbelief and shock, followed by a great outpouring of sympathy and support. Barry Dragan, a fellow air force officer, was haying some of his property outside Middleton when Jim Curtis dropped by. Curtis was "self-composed and self-contained, as usual" when he told Dragan about Bruce's misfortune. Since Dragan's wife, Hope, was a nurse and Alice was so recently out of the hospital, Curtis asked whether she would "visit Alice, to calm her down a little." Dragan told him: "It just doesn't fit the picture of the kid. He's polite, respectful, shy. It has to be a mistake."

Muriel Armstrong, who lived down the road from the Curtises' farm, was plunged into a tizzy. "I saw him the day before he left," she cried despairingly. "His ma took ill and he didn't have a driver's licence so he couldn't even take her to the hospital. Next day he was baking the bread his mother'd started. He'd kneaded it and let it rise but not enough before it went in the oven. He was upset 'cause it would be no good. There was this mad, cold-blooded killer baking his mother's bread?"

The Curtises, with Barbara Czacherski's assistance, began making arrangements to retain a lawyer in New Jersey. On Tuesday, July 13, Jim sent a telegram to Bruce in Dallas County Jail. With characteristic formality, he wrote: HEARD WHERE YOU ARE FROM SCOTT'S SISTER BARBARA. HAVE CONTACTED CANADIAN CONSUL IN DALLAS, A MRS BLACK. CONTACT US THROUGH HER IF YOU NEED ANYTHING. WILL BE TO SEE YOU IN NEW JERSEY. AM ARRANGING LEGAL COUNSEL THERE. JAMES CURTIS.

One of the many points of lasting bitterness that remain with the Curtises is their charge that no one from the Canadian consulate in Dallas, nor the consulate in New York, under whose jurisdiction New Jersey falls and where Dallas officials claim the information was relayed, ever visited Bruce or contacted Jim and

Alice at that time. The telegram was returned three days later. By the time it had reached Dallas County Jail, Bruce and Scott were already en route back to New Jersey.

At first glance, the inventory of items seized in Texas by a meticulous pair of New Jersey investigators revealed little of significance. But William Lucia was aware that successful prosecutions often depend not on the observation of suspects *flagrante delicto*, or on dramatic eleventh-hour confessions, but on the methodical accumulation of detail. Amongst Bruce Curtis's possessions found in the Holiday Inn room was a Timex wrist-watch, toothbrush, pocket-knife, used tissues, assorted articles of clothing, Sears hair dryer with attachments, cloth pouch and notepad from Hurrah's in Atlantic City, and currency totalling $20 in American money and $12.25 in Canadian. Scott Franz's possessions included a broken Criterion wrist-watch, Canadian cigarettes (du Maurier), clothing, a sealed envelope containing $299.76 (U.S.), an empty wallet, ointment for eye irritations, a King's-Edgehill school ring, ball-point pen and shoe horn from Hurrah's, Holiday Inn matches and soap, matches from the Best Western Trail Dust Inn in Sulphur Springs, Texas, and a paper bag bearing a Sears imprint containing shampoo, shaving cream, razor and two sixteen-ounce bottles of Coca-Cola. Among his identification cards and personal papers were the home and business numbers for his sister Noreen J. Franz, in Eugene, Oregon, a business card from A-1 Specialty Services and Supplies Inc., of Englishtown, New Jersey, and a handwritten note from a girl named Heather Cuthbert that read: "Scott, please write me over the summer. I will write if you give me your address. (Please?)"

On the afternoon of Monday, July 12, after Curtis had been brought to Richardson police headquarters and given an opportunity to talk with Franz alone, the boys agreed to waive extradition. "Look," Lucia told Curtis, "it's my understanding from the Texas authorities that you want to see an attorney. So I'm not going to ask you any questions. The only way I can start talking to you is if you initiate a conversation. Don't expect me to start talking to you. I'm not going to violate your rights."

Curtis nodded. He looked at Lucia curiously, like someone awakened from a dream. His first night in jail had not been easy. "They took away my shoe laces and my glasses, and there was a drunk across from me yelling all night so I didn't get any sleep. Then in the morning they gave me coffee and a hamburger. I don't drink coffee and I couldn't eat the hamburger so I hadn't eaten anything at all." Glancing quickly up at Lucia, a man he would describe as having "this slicked-back hair and was, like, gimme some of this, always looking in mirrors and wore golden bracelets," he said that he still wanted to speak to a lawyer but that he would let him know if he changed his mind.

Later Lucia turned to Duerr. "Is this one st-range, Billy, or what?"

"A strange one," Duerr concurred, although privately he was less certain. Curtis did give the impression of being strange, but he might have been confused, or paralyzed with nervousness.

Lucia shook his head, squared his shoulders and straightened his jacket. "The kid," he declared, "is weird."

When the van was searched by Duerr the next day, he discovered an envelope containing assorted toll and motel receipts, a Hurrah's bag filled with maps, tourist brochures, fireworks and other paraphernalia. But Duerr took particular note of two things: a green bed-sheet and a wallet belonging to Bruce Curtis that contained, among other cards and papers, a card dated 1977, indicating that Curtis had completed a hunter safety training program.

That evening, Lucia, with Duerr present, interviewed Franz again. Lucia asked him whether he could account for his whereabouts last August, when a body connected to an unsolved crime had been found near Ravensburg Park in Pennsylvania. Franz said he had been working at his summer job at A-1 Specialty Services and Supplies in Englishtown, and knew nothing about it. Lucia already suspected as much, but wanted to observe the boy's reaction to a question about which he knew nothing. Earlier in the day, Lucia had received a call from Chief

Newman in Allenhurst reporting that Lucia's request that the RCMP in Nova Scotia provide information on the boys had produced unexpected results: although no charges had been laid, Franz and Curtis were suspects in two separate poisoning incidents, involving a teacher and two students, at the private school they had attended.

"What about these attempts at poisoning two students, Scott?"

Franz could not disguise his surprise. According to observations that Duerr later typed into a report: "Scott Franz indicated that he knew who did it, but would not give the name of the person involved. Scott Franz further stated he knew the incident wouldn't have killed anyone. Investigator Lucia asked Scott Franz if Bruce Curtis did the poisoning. Scott Franz wouldn't say yes or no, just that he didn't want to give the name."

Late in the afternoon on Wednesday, July 14, two Richardson police officers drove Lucia, Duerr and their two handcuffed prisoners to the airport, taking a detour along the way to show the New Jersey investigators the spot where John F. Kennedy had been assassinated. At one point Lucia turned to Curtis, who had quietly ignored the occasional remark directed his way, and asked, "What's the matter, cat got your tongue?" At the airport, after a surprise meeting with two fellow Monmouth County investigators who were also escorting a prisoner, Lucia and Duerr removed the handcuffs before boarding American Airlines Flight 154 bound for Newark. Before parting, one of the Richardson police officers turned to Curtis and said, in a thick drawl, "you ain't got no jackrabbit in ya, do ya?"

"Excuse me?" mumbled Curtis blankly.

The Texan repeated himself.

Curtis stared at him. "I don't know what you're talking about."

"You're not gonna run off, are ya?"

Curtis flushed. "No," he answered thickly.

The party of four arrived in Lucia's car at Allenhurst police headquarters at 11:15 P.M. A pack of journalists was gathered around the entrance, along with a smattering of curious townsfolk who had kept abreast of the infamous local boy through daily media reports. The case contained all the necessary elements for high drama: a sleepy seaside community shocked by parricide; a local couple who were either so ordinary or so discreet that no reporter could find a source of ill-will to quote; a teenaged son, variously described as "quiet" and "a peaceful kid," and his accomplice, a mysterious Canadian visitor, both prep school graduates.

Cameras captured the moment when the car doors opened: first Curtis, a surprisingly tall, skinny boy with black hair and large glasses, stepped forward with Lucia at his side. As he walked he stared at the ground, manacled wrists held in front of him, hands clasped with both index fingers extended, touching at the tips and pointing towards the concrete as though divining a water source. Franz followed, still wearing his Knoxville World's Fair T-shirt, shielding his face from view. After being processed and fingerprinted, the two boys were taken to Monmouth County Correctional Institution in Freehold to await arraignment. The next day, Scott Franz and Bruce Curtis were jointly indicted on a total of six counts, including the first-degree murders of Al and Rosemary Podgis.

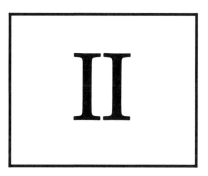

II

Canada and the United States enjoy a long-standing and remarkably co-operative relationship founded on similarities and proximity. But many Canadians regard their powerful southern neighbour, with its pervasive influence on Canadian social, economic and cultural life, with equal parts attraction and aversion, respect and disdain. In 1980, the Canadian government published a study that was in keeping with a tradition of defining the Canadian identity by pointing out the differences between the two countries. Canada, the study reported, had lower rates of divorce and infant mortality, cheaper health care and less poverty. Most significantly, Canada experienced less crime: Americans were three times as likely to be raped or murdered. This was confirmed by U.S. statistics: rates of violent crime rose 47 percent during the 1970s, and another 10 percent in 1980. Murders were committed every twenty-four minutes, more than half of them private affairs involving families or friends. The arrest of their son propelled Jim and Alice Curtis out of the peaceful Annapolis Valley and into precisely this dark corner of the American Dream.

On Saturday, July 17, the day before Jim and Alice were

scheduled to visit Bruce and meet with a lawyer in New Jersey, Bruce phoned home. Although the call lasted only a few minutes, in accordance with regulations at the Monmouth County jail, Alice was relieved to hear his voice. "Well, this is a great conclusion to your graduation present," she finally told him. "It's all so ridiculous," her son replied, buoying Alice's spirits. "I thought that was great," she says now. "It was going to be all sorted out. This was all a big mistake."

The next afternoon, Jim and Alice flew to Philadelphia, Pennsylvania, rented a car and drove east across the border into New Jersey. It was a blazing, humid day, the temperature close to 90 degrees — "hotter than Hades," complained Alice, who found the heat suffocating. To their surprise, the flat farmland, sprinkled with horses, dairy cattle and roadside vegetable stands, did not appear so different from parts of Nova Scotia. In appearance, central and southern New Jersey is unlike the crowded industrial north, with its petroleum refineries, chemical plants, smelters and urban decay associated with cities like Newark and Jersey City. With a population nine times that of Nova Scotia in an area one-third the size, New Jersey has been stereotyped as a bedroom community serving New York and Philadelphia, an image that was created at least as early as two hundred years ago when Benjamin Franklin referred to it contemptuously as "a barrel tapped at both ends." Its notoriety as a centre for organized crime began during Prohibition, and an incredible tradition of municipal- and state-level political corruption was, during the early 1980s, being upheld by a panoramic exposé of bribery known as the Abscam Scandal.

Public demand to reduce violent crime had resulted in a state law, the 1981 Graves Act, imposing a mandatory three-year prison term on anyone using a gun to commit a crime. And following years of criticism that the state's "revolving door" parole system was a disgrace — a person sentenced to ten years in prison in 1980 was eligible for parole as early as one year and nine months later — new legislation had been prepared that would ensure that those convicted of violent crimes served at least half of their sentence before coming before a parole board.

In conservative Monmouth County, in particular, the courts had a reputation for taking a hard line against crime, meting out the harshest sentences in the state.

The Monmouth County Correctional Institution, in Freehold, is a one-storey structure solidly constructed of brick, masonry and steel. It is entirely enclosed, except for the front entrance, by a fourteen-foot perimeter fence of heavy-gauge security mesh crowned by barbed wire. In the summer of 1982, conditions within the facility had so deteriorated as to assume crisis proportions. With state prisons overcrowded, inmates scheduled for transfer to a state institution often languished in county jails ill-equipped to handle the overload. Monmouth County jail was designed to accommodate 285 prisoners but routinely housed 400. The "A" and "B" tiers of the Grand Jury wing, where Curtis and Scott Franz were held, consisted of four sections, each containing eight single cells. But in addition to the eight prisoners the section was meant to hold, eight more slept on mattresses on the hallway floor, among them two terrified teenaged boys.

Curtis says he doesn't remember what they talked about, but the subject of the murders came up at least once, during a phone call between Scott and his sister Dawn that Dawn later related to William Lucia. According to Lucia's report, Scott told his sister that the shooting of their mother had been an accident. Then he passed the phone to Curtis, who told Dawn, "I'm really sorry. I didn't mean to do it." (Dawn answered, "If it was an accident, it can't be helped.")

When Jim and Alice saw their son they were shocked. He looked nervous and gaunt, and his eyes stared dully at them through a glass partition smudged with fingerprints and kisses. Since they had been warned not to discuss the case, Jim and Alice awkwardly recounted local gossip about people he knew on Mount Hanley and showed him snapshots of Anne's wedding. "He looked terrible," Alice reported to Lorraine Peever. "He was just kind of with-it and that's all. The prison psychologist said he'd examined him and decided he wasn't imminently suicidal. He said he'd told Bruce to try and act a little tough. I just looked at this guy, because I knew Bruce couldn't act tough. I don't know how he's going to survive in there."

Scott Franz was being represented by a local attorney named Tommy Smith. With Barbara Czacherski's help, the Curtises had been put in touch with Joe Dempsey, an experienced attorney who lived in Interlaken, just a few blocks from Loch Arbour. Although Dempsey was intrigued by the case — he had followed the media reports and had teenaged children of his own — he was also fighting a cancer that left him too debilitated to bear so demanding a responsibility. Instead, he contacted Michael Schottland, a stocky, aggressive criminal lawyer with whom Dempsey had collaborated in the past. Schottland agreed to act as chief counsel and had met Curtis for the first time at his arraignment the previous week.

Michael Schottland grew up on a chicken farm not far from Freehold. His paternal grandfather had been an assistant district attorney in Manhattan, and although Schottland's father never went beyond high school because of the Depression, his son describes him as "a frustrated lawyer who was very happy when I went to law school." As a college student in the early 1960s, Schottland worked part-time as a gardener for George Chamlin, an attorney ten years his senior with a practice in West Long Branch. When Schottland entered Rutgers Law School, he began clerking for Chamlin during summers. After he passed his bar examinations, Chamlin hired him in 1966. Asked to characterize his partner, Chamlin answered: "He had an awful lot of ambition. There was no mountain he wouldn't climb in his quest for justice; no cause he wouldn't take, often to our financial detriment. I'd say, you can't afford to take that case, and he'd say, look, these people require justice. Who's gonna give it to them?" Schottland waves his arm dismissively at the memory. "Yeah, when I started out I had a reputation as a big liberal, taking all kinds of crazy cases: the American Civil Liberties Union, criminal stuff. I just felt law was an instrument for social change, and that lawyers should use the system to right wrong. I guess I've become a little more realistic, but to a certain extent I still believe that."

The Curtis case came to Schottland at a time in his career when, at forty-one, his reputation established, he had decided to decline handling future murder trials. Aside from the fact that they were emotionally draining, usually thankless undertakings, Schottland was a family man—he had four children by his first marriage and an infant son by his second wife, Rosanne—and owned several horses. After two decades of hustling he was ready to ease up a little. Within the firm of Chamlin, Schottland, Rosen, Cavanagh and Uliano, he had become the masterful jack of all trades who specialized in cases of great complexity—everything from negligence and malpractice to his pet project, representing the top harness racers on the eastern seaboard. He had taken the Curtis case "because I like Joe [Dempsey] and he wanted me to do it," but associates knew it had more to do with Shottland's personality than his respect for Dempsey. When Chamlin learned some of the details of the Podgis murders, he asked his partner: "How the hell are you gonna win this one?" Schottland grinned. "George, the impossible is just a little more difficult to achieve."

On the evening of Tuesday, July 20, Schottland and Dempsey met with the Curtises at the American Hotel in Freehold, where they discussed the general contours of the case and finalized their relationship. "I see it as manslaughter," Schottland explained. The Curtises, despite their best efforts to hide their shock, winced. "I think you should be prepared to expect him to serve about three years in prison." Schottland was unwilling to create false hopes even though he had not entirely ruled out the prospects of an acquittal. That the boys had done the shooting was irrefutable: Curtis had already told Schottland that the gun had gone off accidentally in his hands, killing Rosemary Podgis, and Franz had given a statement to that effect. But there was evidence that the boys had been terrorized by Franz's father. The state would have to prove *mens rea*, literally "evil mind" but usually translated as "guilty intent." Did Curtis intend to murder his friend's mother, or was it an accident involving some element of negligence? The circumstances raised more questions than they answered, but the state held a

wild card: Franz was vulnerable to an overture from the prosecutor's office to testify against Curtis in return for a plea-
bargaining arrangement, although Schottland believed Franz's
case was defensible. He was glad Tommy Smith was handling
the case; he knew Smith to be a combative lawyer who, when he
was performing at the peak of his powers, was possibly the best
in the county. The fact that Curtis and Franz had dumped the
bodies and fled was an unfortunate, but not necessarily insur-
mountable, complication.

"They're very nice people," Schottland said to Dempsey after
the Curtises were gone.

Dempsey agreed. "People are often disordered when they talk
about their life at home, and what they consider important. The
feeling they gave me is that they're simple, lovely people, and I
mean simple in the most complimentary sense of the word. I'm
also concerned because this case contains legitimate ambigui-
ties, but there's an overwhelming conviction within the community that these boys murdered the mother and father as part
of a psychopathic lark."

Schottland made a mental note to find out more about the
family. If Curtis was the naive country kid described by his
parents, his background could prove an important element in
his defence.

"Yeah, they're nice people," Schottland repeated. "And
befuddled. They've come off their farm up in Canada and
walked into a maelstrom."

Jim Curtis, the eldest child of Harold and Jennie Curtis, was
born in 1929 and grew up in Canning, a farming community
near the towns of Brantford and Paris in southwestern Ontario.
A sister, Lorraine, and a brother, Don, followed in three-year
intervals. Brantford, well-placed on the banks of the Grand
River, was originally an Indian settlement. Later it was colon-
ized by immigrants from England, Ireland and Scotland, among
them the parents of Harold and Jennie Curtis. Seven miles
away, the beginnings of a second community had formed at the

confluence of the Nith and Grand Rivers, where large plaster-of-Paris beds were found. A mill producing plaster for sale to farmers as fertilizer was so successful that the community was named Paris. The prosperity of both towns was guaranteed in 1840 when a canal was built permitting access to Lake Erie and major shipping centres such as Buffalo and Cleveland.

Lorraine remembers her older brother as "a solitary boy" who loved to take long walks by the river flats across from the family house, and rise before dawn to check his muskrat lines. In a photograph that perfectly captures his rustic childhood, nine-year-old Jim, holding a white rabbit, is kneeling barefoot beside a woodpile. The war years dominated the childhoods of Jim and Lorraine. Their father was a sheet-metal worker employed by Brantford Coach and Body, a manufacturer of custom vehicles such as hearses and ambulances that began assembling military vehicles during the war effort. The children picked milkweed pods, used in the manufacture of life preservers, and left them in bags by the roadside for the Red Cross to pick up. Lorraine sold war savings bonds and joined a church group, Canadian Girls in Training, and Jim joined the Air Cadets as a teenager. Jim shared an aptitude for mathematics with his father who, although not formally educated, enjoyed working through algebra and trigonometry problems as a hobby. Harold Curtis also tinkered with radios. "We had the first non-battery radio in our parts," remembers Jim Curtis with pleasure. "My father built it himself."

On summer nights, the children sat outside their house under an immensely quiet and black country sky, listening for the drone of aircraft. Suddenly powerful searchlights would stab the sky, guiding the planes in for a landing at a nearby air base, where the Royal Canadian Air Force trained pilots in night flying. Once a plane crashed in a neighbour's farm field. Jim and Lorraine were astonished to see the pilot clamber from the cockpit, draw his service revolver and stand guard until air force officials arrived. "These things made an impression on the mind of a child," Lorraine explains. "I think this is where Jim picked up his interest in the air force."

In 1947, Harold Curtis finally satisfied a private dream to work for himself. With the help of two co-workers at Brantford Coach and Body, he started a business designing and manufacturing playground equipment. Materials were scarce so soon after the war, so Harold Curtis travelled the countryside looking for scrap metal — old windmills were one source — in order to build his teeter-totters and slides. His first "factory" was a rented garage on a lonely country road that a local ghost was said to haunt. None of the children know what inspired their father to launch the business. While they agree he may have guessed that service-men would be returning home and starting families, it is unlikely that he foresaw the prosperity and urbanization of the 1950s. It seemed no one was more amazed than Harold Curtis when his company, Paris Playground Equipment, slowly began to prosper.

By the time Jim finished high school, Paris Playground was still a struggling two-man operation that provided full-time jobs only for his father and a welder. Although Jim attended three semesters at the University of Western Ontario with the intention of studying business administration, he was not destined to go into the family business. (That opportunity would come to the youngest, Don, a gregarious and able manager who would eventually succeed his father.) So no one was surprised when, in 1953, the young man with the love of the outdoors, a fascination with aircraft and an aptitude for science and math, joined the air force.

Jim received his training as a flight cadet in London and Clinton, Ontario, and later graduated from the Air Navigation School in Winnipeg, Manitoba as a radio officer. He was stationed at Namao, part of a large air force base in northern Alberta, and began flying search-and-rescue missions, often in the far north. "We used to get some good fishing up there," Jim recalls fondly. "Lake trout. About the same size as salmon. You couldn't find one under five pounds. We'd land somewhere, like Great Bear Lake, and somebody would catch a twenty-five pounder. You could look down, maybe fifteen feet, into that crystal-clear water and see them."

In August 1957, a new housing officer arrived at Namao, a young woman who had driven alone from her last posting in Ontario, across the country to northern Alberta, in a sleek red Dodge with swept-back fins. She was thirty-one-year-old Alice Pilgrim, a farm girl and former teacher who, acting on the destiny suggested by her surname, had left behind her old life in favour of the air force and the excitement of travel in Canada and overseas. Alice, like Jim Curtis, was an eldest child. She was born "back in the hills" on a stony farm not far from Combermere, Ontario, at a spot where the Madawaska River was so wide it looked like a lake. Her mother, Bertha, died of infection following the birth of Alice's youngest brother, leaving her husband, James, with four young children to raise in the middle of the Depression. Following the defeat of the ruling political party in a provincial election, James Pilgrim lost his job as road governor for the township. When he learned of the promise of work in Timmins, about three hundred miles north-west, he left his children with relatives and moved to the rough-and-tumble gold mining town. When he remarried in 1936, the two eldest children — Alice was then ten — joined him.

When she finished high school, Alice, who wanted to become a librarian but knew she could not afford to attend university, became a teacher. But after five years of teaching in Timmins she became increasingly dissatisfied with her choice of career and, unlike many young women stuck in small towns, decided to make a radical change. In May 1951, during the first post-war expansion of Canada's armed forces, the Royal Canadian Air Force began actively recruiting women to its ranks. The following year Alice enlisted and was sent for basic training to a depot in Quebec. In the summer of 1953, she was stationed in Soellingen, near Baden-Baden in Germany. It was a time she still remembers with pleasure. "If nothing else, that first two years in the service was just marvellous because of Germany. My father was from England, so I visited the English relatives and took all kinds of trips, from Italy down to Greece and Egypt, then down the Nile to Aswan."

Upon her return to Canada, Alice was stationed in New

Brunswick. After receiving her commission from the ranks, she was appointed administrative officer at a base in Ontario and then sent to Namao. The arrival of this friendly new officer, with her round cheeks, wavy hair and beautifully arched eyebrows, was greeted with an interest to be expected at an air base. One of the enlisted men upon whom she made an impression was Jim Curtis. Nine months later they were married and Alice, in keeping with military policy at the time, was released from the ranks.

In September 1958, Jim Curtis was sent to Canada's east coast, to the Operational Training Unit at Base Summerside in the tiny province of Prince Edward Island. Their first child, Anne, was born on the first of December, less than two months before Jim was posted to Greenwood, a large base in Nova Scotia's Annapolis Valley. Greenwood was growing rapidly by the late 1950s, as Canada's role in post-war international affairs expanded. As a member of the United Nations, Canada was involved in the Korean War, the 1954 armistice in Indochina and an Emergency Force established during the Suez Canal crisis in 1956. Throughout the 1960s, Canada would contribute to UN peacekeeping activities in the Congo, Cyprus, Lebanon, Yemen and Kashmir. As a radio operator experienced in transport flying and search-and-rescue, Jim was often sent abroad. But in 1959 his main concern was to find a permanent home. As a young officer with a new wife and child, he found himself at the end of a long waiting list for Greenwood's limited on-base quarters. Many service families settled in Middleton, but houses proved to be scarce and prices high. Finally, Jim paid $9,000 for 750 acres on top of nearby Mount Hanley, not far from the Bay of Fundy. Early settlements were built along the bay, where sailing ships could unload coal and take on shipments of apples. Port George (formerly Gates' Breakwater), near the Curtises' farm, was a thriving centre when Middleton was little more than a hamlet, but settlers had left the mountain for the rich, protected soil in the lowlands by the time the railway opened up the valley. To want to live on the mountain in 1959 was simply considered odd. "There was a stigma about the mountain," explains Alice. "People were thought to be a bit backward here. If they could have accomplished anything they'd have moved to the valley. But we didn't care about that."

Their new home, a farmhouse built in the mid-nineteenth century, was in disrepair: the basement leaked, the insulation was poor, and the pipes in the kitchen and bathroom — really a partition across a corner of the woodshed — froze in the winter. But Jim and Alice loved it. It was the closest Jim had ever experienced to his childhood in Richwood. Renovations seemed a small price to pay when one considered the pleasures: digging the first garden, finding a spinning wheel in the remains of an original settler's homestead. That first spring, Jim returned from a walk with an armful of morels, a rare edible mushroom that he ruefully notes he's never seen on the property since. Of Nova Scotians, the novelist Margaret Atwood once wrote in an article in *The New York Times*: "Their social style today — deadpan, ironic, skeptical, laconic — can overlie a generosity and helpfulness that will be brought out for you as a visitor when it becomes clear that you are not malevolent or a total fool." Although Ontario-born, Jim and Alice Curtis never felt like visitors in Nova Scotia. They felt as though they had come home.

In the summer of 1962, the family returned to Prince Edward Island when Jim was sent to Summerside's Operational Training Unit as an instructor. Since damage during Anne's birth had made further attempts at child-bearing difficult for Alice, the Curtises adopted two more children, Carol and Bruce. "When we got Bruce home he cried for a week," recalls Alice. "He'd been farmed out to a family with a lot of kids who'd loved him to death. I really thought he wasn't going to adjust and we'd have to send him back. Then he just quit crying. His mother was a nurse or a nurse's aide. She wasn't married."

"About all we know about the father," adds Jim, "was that he was a sometimes carpenter, sometimes fisherman who was very tall. So we expected him to be tall."

"He had a lovable, docile nature and a little round baby-face that became quite lean as he got older," continues Alice. "He lived under the domination of two fairly bossy, aggressive sisters. Not that they were deliberately mean or anything, but there was a certain amount of push-pull all the time."

Jim Curtis chuckles. "As far as Bruce was concerned, it was all pull. The girls once dressed him up as a girl, like he was a doll. He was the baby and never very assertive."

"He just handed it to me, the gun, and I said, 'What am I supposed to do with this?' And he didn't say anything."

Michael Schottland stared at his client. Bruce Curtis sat in a chair opposite him, his long legs apart and his long fingers entwined. He slouched, like a rag doll losing its stuffing, wearing beige prison-issue shirt and trousers. Although Schottland knew Monmouth County jail rarely engendered good health, Curtis looked exceptionally thin and pale.

"We just lay down on the couch and put the guns between us. And we had a cover that we put over the guns and over ourselves. I would wake up, in a half-daze, and fall back asleep. It wasn't a restful sleep."

"What happened Monday morning?" Schottland asked.

"I was sort of in a daze, half in and half out of sleep, and I heard his mother talking and they were talking about going back to Nova Scotia. Scott said we were going back to Nova Scotia, and she said, 'At least have breakfast before you go.' Scott suggested French toast."

"Where was Mr Podgis?"

"Upstairs. Then Scott said he couldn't take it any more, that he had to have a shower because he felt really gross, grimy, y'know."

Curtis spoke slowly and often inaudibly. There were frequent pauses when Schottland would prompt him to continue. His speech was thick, as though his tongue was swollen, and when he wasn't talking in a monotone, he sang in graceful hills and valleys, like someone reading to a small child. Occasionally a sound would slip out that was halfway between a giggle and a moan.

"Scott took a gun with him?"

"Yes."

"Did he say anything to you about shooting his stepfather?"

"Well, maybe. I don't remember."

Schottland frowned. "What do you remember next?"

"I remember hearing a shot."

"How many shots?"

"I don't remember how many. I think there were four. I know I heard several."

Schottland leaned forward. "What did you do next?"

"I grabbed the gun and ran and she was coming around the corner and it went off."

"It went off?" Schottland interrupted. "You mean you pulled the trigger?"

"I dunno. I mean, I don't know if I pulled the trigger or if it went off by itself."

"Why did you pick up the gun?"

"I don't know. It was like my emotions were dictating me. It was like fear and not knowing what was going on."

"And you don't know whether you fired the gun?"

"I don't know whether when I jumped back my hand moved too and I pulled the trigger or if it just went off. It was just a blur."

There was a long silence. The fluorescent lights emitted a low whine and occasionally voices would rise and then recede outside the door. Schottland finally addressed his client. "Okay. What did you do then?"

"I just stood there."

Curtis stared down at the floor. His hands trembled. Outside the door, someone called something that echoed down the hallway. A steel door clanged shut. "All I remember is like my whole head is ringing. Like the blood in your ears is making them ring or whatever. I just stood there and it was like my whole mind was, like you become a big, black cloud, sort of like in trauma, twisting around."

"What do you remember next?"

"It was Scott coming down the stairs. He came over, and I don't know what the time period, he said something."

"Try to remember exactly what he said."

"I'm not sure. Something like 'What happened?' Then he went over to his mother."

"What did he do then?" Schottland asked.

"He's saying, 'She's dead, she's dead. What happened?' Then he said, 'I can't leave her like that, I can't leave her like that.' He kept repeating it."

"Why didn't you call the police?"

"It didn't occur to us," Curtis answered falteringly. "It just didn't seem like something they should be involved with right away. They were more like, they would be told exactly what had happened later on."

Schottland began to lose his patience. "Knock it off."

Curtis giggled nervously. "They had problems with other children. And they always handled it within the family, y'know. So that's how Scott wanted to do it, to work it out within the family, y'know, explain it to them, figure out exactly what to do."

"Why did you clean things up?"

It took a long time for Curtis to answer. "See, it wasn't a quick decision. Like, we were sort of standing around, doing nothing. Scott's big concern was that he couldn't leave his mother lying there like that. The initial thing was to take them out of the house and put them somewhere."

Schottland spoke so sharply that Curtis jumped. "Why did you pack up those bodies and drive them to Pennsylvania?"

Curtis stiffened and twisted slightly in his chair. "I don't, I can't analyze it. This feeling of total dread, about what you had done. You had to somehow alleviate the pain in your mind and anything you could do to do that, you did."

Schottland stared at him.

"We wanted to take them out of the house. For some reason that was a major point of Scott's. So we got them out of the house. And the other thing too was it was sort of like washing away sins to clean up. Because if you replace everything and make it as if nothing had ever happened, then you would return the house to its original state. And then if your mind went back to the house, it would appear to be not as it *had* been, but in its original state."

When Schottland was leaving, he repeated his warning not to

talk with Scott Franz. "It's the worst thing you can do, Bruce. You talk to Scott about anything and it may come back to haunt you."

Sitting in his office, Schottland leaned back in his chair and rolled a pen thoughtfully between his fingertips. He was pleased that the Curtises had agreed to his recommendation that the defence team include, in addition to one of his partners, Charles Uliano, and Joe Dempsey's limited participation, the services of a private investigator. Dennis Fahey, a former police officer who had set himself up as an "evidence consultant," sat across from him. He was a tall, solidly built Irishman with a boyish face and severely close-shorn hair. Coincidentally, Fahey had already assisted the prosecutor's office with part of its investigation. When Scott Franz revealed the place where the rifles had been hidden, he also said that he and Bruce had thrown shells out the window of their van. Fahey, who was teaching a course in crime scene investigation to Explorer Scouts at Fort Monmouth Academy, was asked to conduct a search using his class. One live round and two spent casings were eventually found in the fields along the south side of Route 36 near the Hilton Inn.

"What's Curtis like?" Fahey asked.

"It's hard to say," admitted Schottland. "He's not an open kid. If you want to know, he's a little strange. I don't know whether he was strange before this incident or whether we're seeing the after-effects of going through the trauma of what he went through. Can't tell you."

Schottland knew that the exhaustive gathering of information was critical to a successful defence. The state always has a jump on the defence attorney, since a full-scale investigation conducted by a well-funded county prosecutor's office gets underway as soon as a crime is reported. In recognition of that imbalance, the prosecutor in New Jersey must, by law, provide the defence with the results of its investigation, known as the Discovery. But some of the prosecutor's findings might not become available until shortly before the trial date, and Schottland knew he faced a capable and determined adversary.

First-assistant prosecutor Paul Chaiet specialized in murder cases and rarely failed to obtain a conviction. Schottland's instructions to Fahey were straightforward: gather information on witnesses and the Podgis family, talk to Bruce and visit the crime scene to test the fidelity of his story, and interview Scott Franz.

Schottland rose and shook Fahey's hand. "I'd kinda like to find out what the hell happened here."

Jim and Alice Curtis's world had always revolved slowly, timed to the seasons and the Fundy tides, except when the air force intruded. Jim was often away — in Puerto Rico, Bermuda, Scotland, Greenland, Nigeria, the Congo — and once, in 1966, he took the entire family with him to California while he attended a six-month training course at a U.S. air force base. But he was happiest on Mount Hanley, tending to a large vegetable garden and a succession of farm animals. The Curtises were neither "of Mount Hanley" nor "of the valley." Although their surname was not associated with the history of the region — a history that, in Nova Scotia, was thought to have begun ninety-nine years before the Pilgrim Fathers stepped onto Plymouth Rock — they sought out its backwoods charm and unabashedly embraced it. They abhorred pomposity and kept to themselves. If anything, they were "of the service," a phenomenon common to those parts of Canada and the United States where a large military population shares a region with residents whose ancestors cleared the forests. Although the two groups co-exist peacefully and often band together over matters of local concern, the distinction between them never vanishes. The Curtises' small circle of friends consisted of several military families — chiefly Barry and Hope Dragan, Grant and Barbara Mimms, and others who had at various times been stationed in the area — and their closest neighbours, the Barteaux and the Armstrongs. Social activities centred around barbecues and occasional visits to the Officer's Mess at Base Greenwood.

The Curtis children were farm children. Their backyard was

acres of meadow, field and forest. The tallest man-made structure in sight was a church spire. The children would pick cattails in the swamp at the back of the property and watch their mother tap off the bright yellow pollen to make pancakes. Each child had an apple tree, the largest Anne's, the smallest Bruce's, with gnarled branches perfect for climbing. A pony was named Francis, after a talking mule of the movies. Each child had a cat, and the family owned several dogs over the years: a collie that died when its leg was caught in some farm machinery; Freckles, the incorrigible Brittany spaniel; Tip, a sheep-dog whose instincts were so powerfully developed that even after Jim sold his sheep it raced around the farmhouse as if it could herd the four walls.

Saturday night was bath night. As the eldest, Anne took the first bath and had the privilege of the hottest, cleanest water. Carol came next, and Bruce last. Then Alice made popcorn and the family settled down to watch the Saturday night movie on one of only two television signals available on the mountain. The next morning the children went to Sunday school at the Baptist church down the road, where Anne and later Bruce played piano, and where Bruce and Carol staged puppet shows and amateur theatrical productions with the younger children.

Connections

Anne: "It was very quiet on the farm. I had a friend half a mile away, but Carol wasn't so lucky. There were kids roughly her age but she was always the odd one out. There really weren't any kids appropriate for Bruce, so there was nothing for him to do but read. The bookmobile came while we were in school and Mum would bring home several grocery bags full of books. She'd try and remember what we'd read, but sometimes she'd have to look inside the dust jacket to see if it had been signed out to Mount Hanley before. If it had, it was probably to us.

"We rarely went to the movies. In fact, we were rarely off the mountain except for trips to Ontario in the summer. We rarely went to Halifax. I remember the big production when we moved to California for six months. The first house we stayed in was like Disneyland. We were used to a simple farmhouse and this house had wall-to-wall carpeting, a stereo and a tape machine, and air-conditioning. There was a swimming pool right around the corner. I couldn't get over this plush, suburban subdivision with its manicured lawns and houses that went on forever."

Carol: "Our parents were pretty strict, y'know? Not too much so, but we did what we were told, type of thing. All the other local kids got in trouble but we were home by ten o'clock. I'm glad it was that way. You hate it when you're a little kid but now I'm really glad.

"We kind of lived a sheltered life. We were very sheltered kids, being on the mountain most of the time. If you wanted to go anywhere, Mum or Dad had to drive you. Even when I learned how to drive, my parents wouldn't let me drive their cars. That was the rule, and what Daddy says, goes.

"Dad wasn't around much when we were kids. He was in the air force so we'd hear that he was in Greenland. But where is he *this* week? Iceland? Oh, okay. I wouldn't say it's a super-close family. Like some kids can talk to their mother about everything, right, like a buddy. But my mother's quite a bit older than me, so there was a generation gap type of thing. When we were kids we used to kiss Mum goodnight when we went to bed, but we never kissed Daddy. I fooled around with my mother a lot. I used to grab her so she couldn't move and say, 'tell me you love me or I won't let you go.' You would never, ever do that with my father."

Bruce: "The first thing I remember was when I was four-and-a-half. My mother was doing the laundry and there were soap bubbles on the surface of the water. I've always been fascinated by water. I would go down to the bay and watch the waves crash for hours. To this day I'll take a cup of liquid and watch it swirl around.

"My parents were always reading. It's just their natural way. They were always encouraging us to learn and, y'know, find things out. I was eager to learn and they were always telling us stuff, y'know, like the history of an area as we were driving through it. So it was always a learning experience.

"I started reading when I was very young, but never fiction. I was only interested in facts. I wanted to learn about everything. I read books on animals; we had an encyclopaedia on animals so I read that. I was also interested in ancient Greece so I read about Archimedes and Socrates when I was very young. I was fascinated by maps. We had this big atlas and I would sit for hours going over countries, y'know, their capitals, major rivers. I remember being terribly worried about the end of the universe. I'd come out at night and just stare at the stars for hours, trying to come to terms with that concept.

"My father and I would go out into the woods and he'd teach me how to tell different types of trees, the difference between red spruce and white spruce and that sort of thing. We'd see tracks in the snow and he'd know what type of animal it was. He can whistle very well and knows all the bird calls. He goes out and imitates them, and the birds come up really close and follow him."

Anne, the first child, was serious and studious, a precocious girl. By the time she reached grade eight, Jim and Alice knew she needed a greater challenge than a rural school could provide. They considered sending her to live with Jim's sister, Lorraine, in Ontario while she finished high school, but Anne was not keen on moving so far away from the family. Finally, they enrolled her in Edgehill, an eighty-year-old private girls' school with an excellent reputation that was located in Windsor, just sixty-five miles away. While Anne blossomed in Edgehill, Jim and Alice found themselves forced to re-evaluate their own future. It was 1973, and Jim was less than a year away from the compulsory retirement age of forty-five. (It would forever irritate him that a short time later this ironclad regulation was loosened.) The farm did not bring in much income, and it would be difficult to finance their educational aspirations for their children on a captain's pension. Eventually, Jim and Alice elected to buy a house in Paris, Ontario, while keeping the farm. Jim held shares in Paris Playground Equipment along with Lorraine and his younger brother, Don, who was now its president. Perhaps it was time, Jim reasoned, to get involved in the family business. They would be close to his mother — his father had passed away a year earlier — and to Alice's family. Since Anne was unsure what field she wanted to enter, she would benefit from the career counselling available in the area's first-rate school system, and could choose from a number of top universities located in southern Ontario.

That fall the Curtises moved into a two-storey brick house on Banfield Street in Paris and the three children were enrolled in local schools. It was, for Anne, Carol and Bruce, a stimulating change from Nova Scotia. Accustomed to the isolation of Mount Hanley and the limitations of a local rural school, they were delighted to find dozens of children in their neighbourhood and extra-curricular school activities such as drama groups, photo clubs and chess tournaments. Anne and her cousin Corrine took part in theatrical presentations. Bruce played chess, worked in a library, and was taken to the Royal Ontario Museum in Toronto. Although he missed the open spaces and the ocean, there was a valley beyond the train tracks behind his house through which the Nith River wound past woodlots and corn fields. He also spent a great deal of time at his grandmother's house. Jennie Curtis lived only a few doors away, in what was once a cottage connected to a larger estate next door. In the spring, lilies of the valley were splashed across a lawn shaded by a walnut tree and a pair of butternuts. In the summer, the pink blooms of a hydrangea marked the entrance to her driveway. The flowerbed was planted with tulips, irises and poppies. In the autumn, when leaves and twigs from a neighbour's Carolina poplar littered Jennie's backyard, Bruce gathered them into piles and placed them carefully on the compost heap.

"When he was very young he was shy, shy to the point of being fearful of his environment," says Lorraine Peever. "I used to fear he was autistic, but then when he got a little older he grew out of his fearfulness, although he remained a shy boy."

On report cards during this period, teachers described him as polite, studious and withdrawn. "Bruce was not one to talk an awful lot," recalls Brian Merritt, his teacher for grades five and six. "He was introverted, really, but a very clever boy. Schoolwork came easily to him. Each year I would ask the children what they wanted to be when they grew up. The usual answers were things like secretary, racing car driver, stewardess, hockey player, magician. In grade five Bruce said he wanted to be a microbiologist, and in grade six he said biologist."

When Bruce called on his friend, Leslie Turner, he would knock on her back door and then hide behind the garage. If no one was at the door, Leslie's mother would tell her daughter that Bruce was outside waiting for her. "We were both shy," says Leslie. "That's why we became friends. He'd run around the side of the house when people were coming, even a pedestrian." She remembers "having intellectual discussions" sitting on the fence in his backyard or on a nearby bridge overlooking the Nith River valley. "I remember we were questioning the existence of God then. We even called ourselves atheists."

Another schoolmate, Craig Larlee, was Bruce's best friend in Paris. He echoes many of the observations of others, although he hastens to add that Bruce was not entirely meek and passive. "He was quiet, like everyone says," recalls Craig. "And he always had a fascination with science, and with the occult, magic and astrology. But when he knew people well he was likely to try and dominate them, usually intellectually. He was definitely not an average kid, and he took great pride in not being average."

Unlike their children, for whom Paris offered unimaginable bounty, Jim and Alice were not happy. Although Paris was considered a small town, urban development in southern Ontario intruded on rural areas, and it was more crowded than the Curtises were used to. The weekend and holiday traffic driving east towards Toronto was so heavy that Jim and Alice dreaded visiting Alice's family near Bancroft. Puttering around a tiny, fenced-in backyard made them yearn for the vastness of Mount

Hanley. Gradually it occurred to Jim that "what we had left behind in Nova Scotia was what everybody in Ontario was busting their necks to get." After a temporary falling-out developed between Jim and his brother, Don, it became clear that Jim's future did not lie in the family business. He worked as a salesman and took a television repair course; later he spent a summer in Alberta learning about Leaf Cutter bees in the hope of developing an income-producing apiary when the family made its inevitable return to Nova Scotia.

The Curtises, unwilling to interrupt Anne's progress in high school, waited until she graduated before selling their house and moving back to the farm in the summer of 1976. Anne did not object — she was entering the University of Toronto that fall — and they assumed it was a return to paradise for Bruce, who spent countless hours exploring the Bay of Fundy shoreline, bringing home jars filled with tiny fish, frog's eggs and thread-like eels that had migrated north from the Saragossa Sea. But Bruce soon discovered he had little in common with his childhood friends, now teenagers. Jim and Alice regarded the school in Lawrencetown as good enough for Carol — "she's at least as bright as Bruce but not a student; she's so hyper she can't sit still long enough to study" — but knew that it was as unchallenging for Bruce as it had been for Anne.

———————————Connections———————————

Anne: "I used to talk a lot to my mother. I'd come home from school and tell her in minute detail the goings-on of the day. My parents were very interested in education, and I probably told them how terrible the school in Lawrencetown was. They were particularly disturbed that girls my age, thirteen and fourteen, were getting pregnant and dropping out of school. My parents were afraid I'd get caught up in the Lawrencetown syndrome and develop the same ambitions as the other kids: none. We had a lot of discussions about whether I should move to Ontario, but I really didn't want to leave Nova Scotia and move in with my

Aunt Lorraine. It was around that time that mother saw an advertisement for Edgehill, an Anglican church school for girls. So I went there and it turned out to be very good. Then one year later we moved to Paris.

"Carol seemed to have different values than Mum and Dad. She liked clothes, lots of them. She liked TV and never liked to read. I remember Carol used to visit the Armstrongs down the road. Mrs Armstrong had always wanted a girl, and she was bouncy and talkative, more like Carol's temperament.

"Bruce was a very solitary boy. He didn't have much in common with the kids in the area so he'd go for long walks in the woods alone. He said very little, but when he did it was often the best crack of the evening. He was very witty. He was a bit inclined to avoid conflicts between Carol and I. Carol was always trying to draw him in on her side, and I would try to neutralize him. His usual defence was retreat. There were only two ways of getting Bruce to do anything. One was to draw him out slowly, coax him, and the other was to make a plan and present it as an absolute. Once things got rolling he was less likely to oppose it."

Carol: "Anne was the smart kid. She played piano, she sang, she was in the school plays. You get the idea. I don't think she did a lot of helping around the house. She was older, and she didn't really hang around with the local kids.

"I don't know if Bruce and I were buddies. He thought I was more of a pain than anything else, but that's pretty normal. When we were young we played swings, or we'd go swimming or play in the tree-house with the neighbourhood kids. We'd play tag, y'know, or back-in-the-woods. When we got older we'd play games once in a while, but by then Bruce would rather read his books or catch butterflies. I'm serious. These local kids would be out snaring rabbits or shooting at birds and Bruce would be [in a sing-song cadence] *running through the fields with his net.*

"He used to lock me out of his room. He was quiet, liked to be alone and liked his books. He'd say, 'Carol, leave me alone,' and he'd lock his door with one of those little hooks but I'd just pop it up. So then he got this great big magnet and put it over the hook so I couldn't lift it. Bruce was also the smart kid. He played chess and was into these strategy games. Like we had this game, RISK. It got to the point where I wouldn't play with him because he beat me so bad. That was Bruce. He'd read books while I watched TV. I don't read books. I don't like any serious type of thing.

"Bruce was so smart that he once corrected the geography teacher. Kids said to me, 'Your brother *corrected* Mr Murray.' I don't think there were many who didn't like Bruce. Maybe some of them were a little jealous 'cause he was so smart, y'know, 'cause I doubt he had any marks under 90. I'm not stupid, but I'm not up to this 95-average type of thing. About school and stuff he was real confident. He knows he's smart. He doesn't care what anybody thinks about him either. If somebody didn't like him that was too bad. Not super-social."

Bruce: "Carol was very active and spirited and all that, and I got along with her. I can be very active and spirited too, but only with people I know very well. Carol knows how rambunctious I can be but the rest of the people think of me only as sitting down and reading a book. Anne is very studious, everything that I'm supposed to be but really I'm not.

"There were three of us who were very good friends in Paris. One of them was Craig Larlee. We'd go down around the gravel pits and have very long talks. We built this raft and sailed down the river, making up stories about hidden treasure and caves. And we made up our own strategy and tactics games, y'know, based on ancient Greek mythology. We'd pick names from the *Iliad* or whatever. I went to the theatre and entered chess tournaments.

"When we came back to Nova Scotia I was really happy, because I saw all my friends and they were overjoyed because we'd all started out in kindergarten together. It was like one of the group had returned to the flock, y'know. But after a while it wore off because I realized that in Paris my perceptions and interests had changed. I just drifted away from my old friends because we didn't have any mutual interests anymore. I was interested in acquiring knowledge, and all they were interested in was cars, y'know, and who would get drunk first. In school there were about ten of us who were, like, the bright students. I used to talk to Patricia [Hirtle] and Valerie [Milo] and Don Llewellyn 'cause they were interested in stuff.

"We took these tests every year at Lawrencetown that rated you. I came out very high and I guess my parents realized that I was very bright and Lawrencetown was totally boring me. So they sent in an application to King's-Edgehill and got a brochure that told what kind of clothes you had to wear all the rules and regulations. I really wasn't too thrilled about going to a private school, y'know, but I wanted an education."

Bruce's closest friend at Lawrencetown was Valerie Milo, a lanky redhead whose family lived across from the school. Valerie was a keen student who shared Bruce's feelings of detachment from their peers. "Both Bruce and I found it difficult because we were considered outsiders. There was a group of us — Patricia Hirtle, Patty Daniels, Donny Llewellyn, Bruce and I — who were friends. We worked on projects together, and Bruce and Donny played chess. Bruce was a bit emotionally immature, I guess, and relatively sheltered, but his intellectual side was developed. Anytime he didn't get great marks, it was because he was bored. Instead of having to prove to the teachers he could get 100 percent every time, he just clicked off."

Milo remembers one occasion, in grade nine, when she and Curtis prepared an elaborate presentation on Greek mythology for a history class. Twelve poster-sized, full-colour illustrations were accompanied by a detailed fifty-page text. Their teacher, praising their efforts, turned to the back page and wrote: 105/100. Curtis was enraged that the teacher hadn't bothered to read it. For their second assignment, Milo suggested a short write-up. "Bruce said no. He put three pages of writing in front and three at the back with a stack of blank loose-leaf pages in between. The teacher never looked at it, just gave us 102/100. Bruce was quite irritated he wasn't caught."

Milo was impressed by her friend's resolve in such matters. "Bruce was very aloof and I always envied him. He was brought up to appreciate things above and beyond Lawrencetown, above and beyond the local community. He considered himself a scientist and an atheist. He wasn't accepted by the jocks in the class who all the girls worshipped. They had no time for him but it never seemed to bother him. He had no time for them."

In 1980, Jim and Alice enrolled their son in grade eleven at King's-Edgehill, the private school Anne had attended that had since merged with the neighbouring boys' school to form a co-educational academy. The Curtises hoped Bruce would benefit both from the high academic standards at King's-Edgehill — it offered the International Baccalaureate, a program of study for high achievers that was recognized world-wide — and from the social atmosphere of a boarding school. "We'd had such a favourable experience with Anne there," Alice says. "And Bruce wanted to go. He wanted to get away from Lawrencetown."

"But if we hadn't sent him there," Jim adds sadly, "he would never have met Scott — "

Alice interrupts him. "And none of this would have happened."

The Winchester model 94 .30-.30 rifle, bearing serial number IS29924, was manufactured at the Winchester Arms Factory in New Haven, Connecticut. It was a lever-action rifle — because of its short, twenty-inch barrel, it would more correctly be called a carbine — with an Illinois Sesquicentennial (1818–1968) medallion on the stock and the inscription, "Land of Lincoln," etched in wood below the chamber. On June 17, 1968, the weapon was shipped to Westside Hardware in Ashtabula, Ohio and was purchased five months later by Alfred K. Podgis of Lakewood, Ohio.

The Winchester model 94 .30-.30 rifle, bearing serial number NRA24538, was also manufactured at the Winchester Arms Factory. It was a level-action rifle with a twenty-four-inch barrel that had on its stock a medallion commemorating the centennial of the National Rifle Association (1871–1971). It arrived at Dayton Gun Headquarters in Dayton, Ohio, on April 22, 1971. Six months and two weeks later it was on the premises of the Cleveland Sports Headquarters. On December 23, two days before Christmas, the gun was purchased under the name Barbara J. Franz. (Barbara Franz, later Czacherski, told investigators she did not remember buying the gun. She suggested her mother may have purchased it in her name. In either case, the weapon ended up among the possessions of her stepfather, Alfred Podgis.)

Both Winchesters were commemorative weapons that could have been purchased as collector's items. It is generally advised not to fire collector's items in order to retain their value. But both weapons were capable of being fired, as was demonstrated on at least one occasion: Monday, July 5, 1982, the day after Independence Day, a national holiday once celebrated by the firing of guns in the streets before the practice was symbolically replaced by organized fireworks displays.

As far as county detective William Lucia was concerned, his investigation was unfolding like most: slowly, involving many steps in many directions in order to take a single stride forward. Scott Franz's admission that he had shot his stepfather was by far the most dramatic piece of evidence, and he had implicated his Canadian friend in the death of his mother. Efforts to trace the boys' movements, by interviewing the staff at the Hilton Inn, where the guns had been jettisoned, and local gas stations, had proven fruitless. But records kept by the sporting goods department of a Woolco store in Ocean Township — corresponding to a receipt found in Bruce Curtis's suitcase — indicated that Franz had purchased a box of .30-.30 ammunition on July 1, four days before the shootings. Franz had claimed that his mother had asked him to buy the ammunition for his stepfather, but Lucia doubted the story.

On August 17, more than a month after the boys were arrested, Lucia and Captain Frank Tenbroeck talked to Barbara Czacherski at Allenhurst police headquarters. When Lucia told her that she did not have to tell them about her conversations with her brother since his arrest, and that if she did it could be used in court, Barbara told him: "My family and I are interested in learning the truth, the same as you are." Most of what she recounted was familiar to Lucia: Scott had told her there had been arguments; he had been accused of stealing items from the house by his stepfather. During the Independence Day weekend, Scott maintained that his stepfather had taken a shot at him. He became convinced Al Podgis intended to kill him. On the morning of July 5, after his stepfather fired two shots at him, Scott closed his eyes and squeezed the trigger. Lucia noted that Scott had told Barbara his stepfather was "kind of in a half up and half down position with his head next to the wall." This did not correspond to information that had emerged from forensic analysis, but Lucia did not mention it.

After shooting her stepfather, Barbara continued, Scott said that he heard a shot downstairs and found her mother lying on the floor. "Scott told me that Bruce said he had shot her accidentally," Barbara said. "But he said Bruce did most of the cleaning because he was throwing up."

"Did he say anything about buying any ammunition?" Lucia inquired.

"He told me he bought ammunition before the weekend, that our mother sent him to buy it for Al."

"Was that the sort of thing your mother might have done?"

Barbara paused, then looked at Lucia. "I don't think there's any way that my mother would send Scott or any of the kids to buy ammunition for Al, knowing Al's temper."

"Can you think of any reason why Scott would want to shoot his mother?"

"There's no way," Barbara replied firmly, "that I can believe Scott would help kill our mother."

Two weeks later, Tenbroeck telephoned Scott's sisters, Rosemary Cox in Texas and Noreen Hovis in Oregon. Both women agreed that Scott did not get along with his stepfather, and that the family environment had been particularly harmful to the youngest Franz children: Mark, Dawn and the baby, Scott.

They also said Scott had told them that the shooting of their mother by Bruce Curtis had been an accident. Neither believed that their mother had instructed Scott to buy ammunition. "I think Scott needs psychiatric help," Noreen concluded.

Al and Rosemary Podgis were born in Cleveland, Ohio — Al in February 1924, Rosemary two years later — although they would not meet for another forty years. The Cleveland of their childhood, located where the Cuyahoga River meets Lake Erie, midway between the coal and oil fields of Pennsylvania and, by Great Lakes freighter, the iron mines of Minnesota, was the country's fifth largest city and a major industrial centre. It was the home of Republic Steel, American Steel and Wire, and the Aluminum Co. of America. The promise of jobs in "the Sheffield of America" had brought farmers, tradesmen and immigrants over the Allegheny Mountains to Ohio. By the turn of the century, more than half the populations of the United States and Canada lived within a five hundred-mile radius of Cleveland; it was a measure of the city's stature that Henry Luce, deciding Cleveland was closer to the heart of America than New York, relocated the offices of *Time* magazine there from 1925 to 1927. The city's most illustrious magnate was John D. Rockefeller. In 1870, Rockefeller created Standard Oil Co. of Ohio; by the time he retired twenty-five years later, the huge Standard Oil trust controlled 90 percent of oil manufacturing in the U.S. By 1911, the year the Supreme Court broke up the monopoly, gasoline had replaced kerosene as the chief product in Standard Oil's refineries and Cleveland was, until supplanted by Detroit, the nation's automotive capital. When Al and Rosemary were young, its streets were filled with made-in-Cleveland cars with names like Winton, Chandler, Baker-Raulang, Peerless and Hupmobile.

Al's parents were Lutherans who emigrated from Germany just after the turn of the century and settled on Cleveland's south side. Alfred Kenneth Karl was the eldest — two older half-sisters had died from scarlet fever when they were toddlers — followed by his brother and sister, Erwin and Arlene. Al's father was a mould-maker with the Otis Steel Company (later absorbed by the Jones and Laughlin Corp.) where he worked on, among other things, the first turbine used to generate hydro-electric power at Niagara Falls. But the Podgises, like many working-class families, suffered during the Depression. At one time Al's father lost his home, and there were gloomy Christmases that none of the children forgot.

Al graduated from Greater Cleveland High School just as World War II was ending. A photograph taken at the time showed a handsome, angular-faced young man with round, wire-framed glasses that lent a preppish quality to his features. It did not reveal, nor even suggest, two other appealing characteristics: he stood an athletic six feet, two inches and had a gift for easy chatter with strangers that made him a born salesman. He began working for Star Bakery, a local firm founded in 1893. He would hold his job as a deliveryman-salesman for twenty-five years and provide his children with an enduring memory of growing up: the cupcakes he brought home in the evenings. He married Twyla Kerr in 1947 and a year later their first child, Terry, a daughter, was born. Three sons, Ted, Tim and Tom, followed.

In 1952, Al was transferred to Star Bakery's new plant in Geneva, a town on Lake Erie fifty miles east of Cleveland. Twyla worked at the Geneva Rubber Company, first in the factory, later in its administrative offices, while Al brought in extra money from part-time jobs in the evenings. By then Al and Twyla were making payments on their first house in Cleveland and a second one in Geneva. After visiting Twyla's parents in Florida, Al purchased a duplex in Siesta Key, near Sarasota on Florida's west coast, where he taught the children to swim. When Star Bakery closed its plant in Geneva six years later, Al began working in the Cleveland area again. He and Twyla bought a fourth house in Mentor, a country town halfway between Geneva and Cleveland; it was a compromise that meant both of them had to drive twenty-five miles to work. The new house, a four-bedroom split-level with a family room, two fireplaces, a double-car

garage and a swimming pool, was located in a leafy neighbourhood near a sports and recreation complex. An enthusiastic
baseball fan, Al found time to umpire Little League games and
take the children to see the Indians play at Cleveland Stadium.
He was also active in the Boy Scouts at the local Methodist
church; he particularly enjoyed taking his troop on summer
camping trips around Lake Erie into Ontario, where he developed a life-long fondness for Canada.

It was around this time that Al began working as an insurance
salesman for the Peninsular Fire Insurance Company, a Newark,
New Jersey-based firm with offices in Cleveland. But the pres-
sures of supporting a family and four mortgages strained the
marriage. In 1966, the year Terry graduated from high school, Al
and Twyla were separated. After selling their four properties
and dividing the proceeds, Al was bitterly disappointed: they
had earned back their equity and little more, although he knew
the properties would have increased in value if they had held
onto them. (He was right: the lot in Siesta Key, for example, is
now part of an exclusive, multi-million dollar community.)
Twyla bought a house in Geneva and lived there with her three
sons. Eighteen-year-old Terry, disenchanted after watching her
parents' marriage disintegrate, went on a vacation to Florida
with two girlfriends and stayed there. Later Twyla also moved to
Florida to be closer to her parents, taking Ted and Tom with her;
Tim remained with his father. Al eventually bought a single-
family home and triplex in Lakewood, a suburb northwest of
Cleveland. It was while he was working evenings as a desk clerk
for a motel chain that he met Rosemary Franz, a gregarious
widow employed at one of the chain's other motels.

Rosemary Franz, née Farron, had always been told her pale
skin and hearty laugh came from her Irish ancestry. She had
been raised a devout Roman Catholic by her mother, Margaret.
When Rosemary was a child, her mother had thrown her
hard-drinking husband, Leo, out of the house and raised her
two daughters alone. Rosemary's sister later died when she
was in her early twenties. In November 1946, shortly after
graduating from high school, Rosemary married Norman Franz,

a soft-spoken man of German descent who worked at the Tin-nerware Products factory in Cleveland. They were living in near-by Parma when a son, Norman Jr., and two daughters, Barbara and Noreen, were born. Later they moved to Brunswick, a rural town south of Cleveland, where they lived on a dirt road and knew everyone in the community. Four more children followed: Rosemary, Mark, Dawn and, in 1964, Scott. Norman and Rosemary complemented each other: Norman was a good pro-vider and father who was happy to let Rosemary play the role of matriarch.

At the time that Rosemary met Al Podgis in 1968, she was recovering from two personal tragedies in as many years. In September 1967, Norman Franz unexpectedly died of a per-forated ulcer after undergoing surgery on his oesophagus. Four months later her eldest son, Norman Jr., perished in a car crash.

Rosemary and Al's courtship was brief. Al was forty-four, no longer the lean wolf of his youth, and he was nursing the pain of a broken marriage. Rosemary, at forty-two, knew that an eligible suitor who did not bolt at the sight of six children was a God-send. Never mind that he was a Lutheran who had married — and divorced — a Methodist. Rosemary didn't want to be alone for the rest of her life. Al's daughter, Terry, had returned from Florida and was living with her new husband, Dan Rawlinson, on the second floor of her father's triplex. She remembers spending Thanksgiving Day with Al and Rosemary in 1968. "He really liked her," she says. "They had a lot in common. My father loved families, so he was thrilled to be marrying somebody with six small children."

Al and Rosemary were married the following May, and dif-ficulties soon followed. Rosemary's children, especially the boys, were unused to discipline — their late father furnished them with little and their mother's loud voice failed to disguise her lack of resolve. Al, who had been the master of his first household, expected good behaviour from his stepchildren. They, in turn, resented the stocky stranger who suddenly tried to bring new order into their lives. When Al offered to adopt the youngest stepchildren, Dawn and Scott, the proposal met such violent opposition from the rest of the Franz children that it was abandoned. Barbara, the eldest, maintains that she left home following an argument with her stepfather during which he overturned the kitchen table in her direction.

It was also hard on Rosemary to face the possibility of excommunication because she had wed a non-Catholic divorcé, and some of her relatives who disapproved of the marriage ostracized her afterwards. It was not without some relief that Al and Rosemary greeted the news that Al's insurance company was transferring him to Newark. The couple, looking forward to a fresh start, began searching for a home in New Jersey. They eventually settled on a rambling, three-storey house at 401 Euclid Avenue, a few blocks from the ocean in the Village of Loch Arbour.

Connections

Ted Podgis: "My father's parents were real strict, and that caused him to be a bit stubborn all his life. He had principles. He believed his children should clean up, take out the garbage and that kind of thing. And he'd give you a good licking if you didn't do it.

"Thanksgivings we'd go down into rural Ohio to visit an aunt. She'd make candy and my brothers and I would go out in the woods and cut Christmas trees. Our father had an old dilapidated shotgun that he'd let us shoot every now and then. That was a big thrill as a boy. But he'd never go hunting or anything. He never had time."

Tom Podgis: "For the most part, we were happy living in Mentor, in the big house. We did stuff together with our dad even though he worked a lot. I remember he had this camera that had six big floodlights on it. I tell you, you'd be blinded for ten minutes after opening a present at Christmas if he got you in the eyes with that thing."

Terry (Podgis) Rawlinson: "My father usually had two jobs. They needed three different incomes to support all their properties. I feel they wanted to buy too many things instead of just enjoying their lives."

Twyla Parker (formerly Podgis): "He was a hard worker who worked long, long hours. Even though the kids only really saw him on weekends, he would take an evening off for a special function. He was always there for family parties, the Little League, Boy Scouts.

"His object in life was to own things so that in old age his kids would be taken care of. He had an obsession with property. He never forgot his mother and father once lost their house. The trouble was, he couldn't resist buying property no matter how far he was in debt."

Barbara (Franz) Czacherski: "Rosemary, my mother, was pretty, fun-loving, loud and outgoing. She didn't socialize a lot, but she was very popular at work. She had a real personality that helped her make friends. My grandmother, who's still alive, was very much like my mother: very fun-loving, all Irish. She threw my grandfather out, so Gramma had to work all the time. She raised her two daughters, then my mother's sister died. Gramma had a hard life.

"My father, Norman, was German. His parents were pretty laid-back, quiet type of people. He wasn't a big man, probably about five-feet-six or five-feet-eight, and gentle. Nothing like Al Podgis. He worked in a factory and my mother was usually a cashier in a store or a bookkeeper. They didn't have money for babysitters so my mother waited until Dad got home from work. Then she'd work till late at night."

Terry (Podgis) Rawlinson: "When my father and Rosemary got together, both being dominant in their households, there was always conflict. They would scream at each other, but then they always got along later. I remember once when I was visiting we were going to get pizza. My father forgot his driver's licence so there was a big to-do over it because evidently Rosemary was supposed to pick it up and didn't. So they're screaming and yelling over this stupid thing, then they forgot all about it and were happy the next minute. It made everybody around them tense.

"There was never any brutality when I was a kid. People have said Al Podgis was abusive to his wife but I think you'd find, if you asked my mother, that that wasn't so. Maybe in later years, possibly, but I have no proof."

Twyla Parker (formerly Podgis): "I'd seen him get angry with the kids when we were married, but never hit them. No one can tell me he beat his family and his wife."

After moving to New Jersey, the difficulties between Al and Rosemary Podgis and their children intensified. The eldest girls were either gone or in the process of leaving: Barbara, who was working as a mail carrier for the post office and taking business courses, married Bruce Czacherski in 1972 and was living in nearby Lakewood; Noreen and Rosie had completed high school and were, for the most part, away from home. Of greater concern were Mark and Dawn.

Mark, who had grown his hair long and taken to wearing jeans and tie-dyed T-shirts in the style of the time, was hanging around with the crowd of musicians, drifters and petty criminals that frequented Asbury Park's boardwalk and, at night, cruised the strips along Ocean Avenue and Kingsley Street. At that time, the mid-seventies, drugs were used freely. Once Mark robbed a local gas station and, on another occasion, piloted a stolen car nose first into Deal Lake. He often stole from his mother and stepfather. In 1974, he served eight months in a juvenile detention centre. "We were often at the house looking for him," remembers Chief James Newman of the Allenhurst police department. "He stole a lady's pocket-book once. Another kid finally confessed that Mark had done it. Turns out he spent all the money buying presents for friends." Although Newman admits that Mark may have started out as a boy "reaching desperately out for love," he became, in Newman's view, just another hood. By the time of the Podgis murders, Mark, sometimes using the alias Darrell Bertelson, had a record that included several counts of larceny, breaking and entering, possession of stolen property and possession of dangerous drugs. There were outstanding warrants for his arrest in New Jersey. Although Mark was an initial suspect in the deaths of his parents, his alibi was easily confirmed: he had been in prison in Texas at the time.

Then there was Dawn. After months of rebellion, Rosemary Podgis made an extreme — some family members argue unwarranted — decision in the spring of 1974 to sign a complaint against her youngest daughter for running away from home. Two weeks later, Al and Rosemary signed a second complaint against Dawn for running away and being habitually incorrigible. Dawn, then only fifteen, was placed in the unlocked section of the Monmouth County Youth Detention Centre. Six days later she ran away. Rosemary then filed a larceny complaint against her in order to have her locked up, but a few weeks later she dropped the charges. Terry Rawlinson, who had returned to Florida by that time, tried to take Dawn into her home. After vigorous protests from Rosemary, Barbara agreed to take her sister instead. "I think she got a raw deal," says Terry. "She was like an outcast, real skinny and younger than her three sisters, who were very close to each other. The only one she was close to was Mark, so she sort of followed in his footsteps."

Case workers at the state of New Jersey's Department of Human Services were told that Dawn's stepfather and mother expected her to be in before dark, not to date until she was sixteen, and to tell them at all times where she was going. Dawn added that she constantly bickered with her mother and had to sneak out of the house to see her friends because her mother did not approve of them. She also said she fought with her stepfather over her use of the telephone. A report, suggesting Dawn came from "a family in crisis," stated: "Mrs Podgis is described as being ineffectual in her dealings with her children. She would use verbal threats in order to discipline them and generally found it very difficult to be empathetic or fair as a parent..."

The report concluded: "Her stepfather made her mother choose between his needs and those of her children. The death of their natural father and a natural brother obviously must have been a trauma for this family and each member grieved and suffered in their own way. Mrs Podgis seemed to be overwhelmed with her responsibilities and either unwilling or unable to give her children the stability they needed. Mr Podgis did not integrate well into the family. Dawn reported that she and Scott were physically beaten by him. There were, however, no police involvements with these incidents and we would have to rely on her word that they did occur."

The disputes between Al and Rosemary were equally disturbing. Al moved out a number of times. At one point he was living in a condominium he had bought in Lakewood, in the same development as his stepdaughter Barbara and her husband. There were suspicions that he may have beaten Rosemary, but the only confirmation of this comes from unreliable witnesses: the youngest Franz children, Mark, Dawn and Scott.

By 1976, however, Al and Rosemary had found a suitable property for Al to go into business for himself. It was the Village Drive-In, a fifty-seat restaurant with a take-out window, just outside Stockton Springs, twenty-five miles south of Bangor, Maine. There was even a broken-down motel across the way that came with the bargain. Although it seemed to be a joint venture between Al and Rosemary aimed at reconciliation, it was Al alone who moved to Maine with his youngest son, twenty-three-year-old Tom, who would help him run the enterprise, and his youngest stepson, Scott. Rosemary continued to live in Loch Arbour and work as a postal clerk, a job she had started shortly after arriving in New Jersey, although she made the approximately nine-hundred-mile round trip every few weeks and on holiday weekends.

It was not hard to see why Al was attracted to Maine. After years of partial independence as a salesman, he wanted to be his own boss. The Village Drive-In was typical of the kind of one-man operations that were being replaced by chains throughout most of the country but still predominated in Maine, where small entrepreneurs were considered the backbone of the state. It was, Al imagined, ideally positioned at the inland tip of Penobscot Bay, right on U.S. Route 1, a scenic highway winding from the Maine–New Brunswick border to Kittery and Portsmouth before crossing over into New Hampshire and continuing south to Key West, Florida. Although lumbering and potato farming were major economic activities, Maine's greatest natural resource was its unspoiled way of life; it was a state outside the mainstream of American life, insular, old-fashioned, and therefore a magnet attracting big-city folk who have admired the paintings of Winslow Homer and Andrew Wyeth and want to eat fresh seafood and purchase antiques. During the summers, when most of Maine's five million annual visitors meander along the coast, long-dormant restaurants heat up their grills and motels triple their off-season rates.

The Village Drive-In was also an opportunity for Al to put at least one of his sons to work for him — part of an ambitious project of one day employing all of his children — and to take Scott away from the corrupting influences of Asbury Park before he turned out like Mark.

Whatever promise the Village Drive-In and its motel may have had, a conspiracy of circumstances and Al's intransigence began to sour the venture shortly after Al took over. It was the tail end of the tourist season: the former proprietor made $3,100 during his final week of business; Al earned half that his first week. The motel — an old house with five rooms, five adjacent cabins and a gift shop — had not been winterized, yet Al resisted Tom's suggestion that they offer free accommodation to several transient workers from the St Regis paper-mill in nearby Bucksport in exchange for insulating the motel. The following summer, someone wanted to rent the gift shop for the season. Although it only needed minor remodelling, Tom remembers that his father continued using it as "a giant dog house" for Nanette, his black standard poodle. Another of Al's schemes, acquiring a KOA (Kampgrounds of America) franchise to make use of some of his seven-and-a-half acres of property, was never implemented.

By the second season the business was failing. "He had all different ways he could have made money," says Tom in exasperation. "But he wouldn't take the chance." As Al grew bitter, he alienated his suppliers and the local young people who formed his labour pool. Although Al and Rosemary co-signed a bank loan to help Tom buy a house in Stockton Springs, by 1978 even Tom had quit working for his father and was managing a McDonald's restaurant nearby.

Meanwhile, young Scott was skipping classes at the Roman Catholic school he attended in Bangor. One thing that was never questioned by either the Franz or Podgis children was that Scott was both bright and spoiled. He had always been small and cherubic — Terry Rawlinson has a photo of Scott standing beside her daughter Dana; although Dana is six years younger, the children appear to be about the same age — and the most serious childhood offence that anyone could remember was the morning he dropped an egg from a second-storey window onto the mailman's head. His third-grade teacher at Saint Mary School in Allenhurst, Margaret Dugan, remembers "a handsome, obedient little blond boy who was anxious to please." But Mrs Dugan, perhaps with the advantage of hindsight or drawing on past experience, adds: "But who knows what drastic changes will come upon a child later in life?" As Scott grew into a teenager he became increasingly manipulative and intractable. Tom Podgis, recalling the period he lived with Al and Scott in Maine, says: "He was a loudmouth who'd con anyone he could, although we got along okay." Scott merely had to burst into tears in order to coax ten dollars from his mother, and by all accounts even his stepfather favoured his youngest stepson, although their relationship was stormy.

Scott managed to complete the eighth grade, but a crisis was reached at the beginning of summer 1978. According to Tom Podgis and Barbara Czacherski, Al was having an affair with an eighteen-year-old girl. With the help of his sisters, Scott ran away. He visited Noreen in Oregon and Terry Rawlinson in

Florida — where he was caught shoplifting a pair of shoes — before returning to New Jersey to live with Barbara and begin grade nine at Highstown Junior High School. But Scott soon antagonized his sister. Once, while driving Barbara and Bruce's van in the driveway without their permission, he dented the door. Later he stole the van and was stopped by police while he was picking up several girlfriends at his school.

By that time Al and Rosemary were back living together in Loch Arbour and Al was trying to sell the restaurant. He had recently started a new job as a rural mail carrier, working out of the Englishtown post office where Rosemary was a clerk and his stepdaughter Barbara was operations supervisor. Barbara sent Scott back to live with Al and Rosemary, "to get him out of our lives."

Although none of the family knows how long the Podgises were considering sending Scott away to boarding school, nor how they came upon the name of King's-Edgehill, in Nova Scotia, the decision was not entirely surprising. Sending children to private schools was more common in the U.S. than in Canada because of a perceived erosion in public education in many states. Information on King's-Edgehill was available in certain U.S. markets — including New England at the time Al was living in Maine — to anyone seeking information on private boarding schools. Had Al and Rosemary seen a brochure they would have learned that tuition was $5,500(CAN), cheaper than many similar institutions in the north-eastern states and even more attractive because of an exchange rate that was, in 1978, favouring the American dollar by 14 percent. Furthermore, Al had fond memories of his trips to Canada as a Boy Scout leader, and King's-Edgehill's quasi-military cadet training promised discipline and supervision. Although Rosemary might have preferred a Catholic school, King's-Edgehill's Anglican orientation would ensure that Scott's education included a moral and ethical foundation. In the winter of 1979, shortly after the second semester had started, Scott was sent to Nova Scotia.

Connections

Terry (Podgis) Rawlinson: "After Rosemary's first husband, Norman, died, there was his veteran's pay and social security coming in. The older children felt it should be put toward tuition when they went to college, but Rosemary and my father would never give them any of it; it was used to run the household. So Barb and Noreen had to put themselves through college. But then the younger ones were still getting money from their mother even after they moved away from home. Mark, Dawn, even Rosie sometimes. That was a bad strain on the marriage, Rosemary giving money to these kids all the time.

"Rosemary and my father put every hope they ever had for all the previous children into Scott, the baby. He was smart, but he was very, very spoiled. They paid a lot more for his schooling than they spent on the rest of them altogether."

Ted Podgis: "They spent a lot of money on Scott. They bought him clothes, a stereo system, a moped. They paid for his school in Canada and every time he was home they spent money on him. It was their way of expressing their love.

"My father had some difficulties with his stepchildren when he tried to discipline them. They weren't used to being told what to do and there was a clash there. There was a lot of rebellion building up in the younger boys. Then they moved to Loch Arbour and they were right near a big drug area at the beach and on the boardwalk. Mark kept doing crazy things, stealing my father's coin collection or his baseball cards. Everything my father cared about, Mark would steal. It caused friction between Al and Rosemary because Rosemary would cover up for him and my father would find out. It wasn't a good environment at all."

Mark Franz: "He [Al Podgis] had a very forceful German personality. Almost like Hitler. He used to get mad real quick and real seriously. There'd be more than just yelling, he'd smack you around. He used to hit me like I was his size, like I was a full-grown man. He used to hit me with a force that used to knock my brains silly. On numerous occasions he hit me so hard, he'd knock me out. Every day we'd get into it. Twice he tied me up in a chair and beat me. One time I'd been out late. I came home and he chased me and the girl I was with out the back door with a gun, and he fired it at me. The man was crazy."

Tim Podgis: "I only lived with them [Al and Rosemary] for about a year, in 1969 and part of 1970, but I remember they did argue a lot. It was like a standing joke: about once a week, after they'd moved to New Jersey, Rosemary would tell Dawn to pack her stuff, we're going back to Ohio. So they fought a lot but I never saw any violence. They'd just scream. Rosemary was just as loud, or worse, than my father. Slamming doors, screaming."

Barbara (Franz) Czacherski: "They had many marital problems over the years, but in front of other people they would put on this face. My mother wanted the whole world to think everything was rosy, but it wasn't. I know that. It was not happy for years and years and years. They co-existed, more or less. That's about it. My mother had ulcers off and on, so I know she hid a lot of things inside her that she never let out. She just let them eat her alive."

Tom Podgis: "Starting off, when my father bought the restaurant in Maine, he was hard to get along with. If a salesman raised his price a penny he'd get pissed off and throw him out. It finally got to the point where he had to drive all the way down to Portland twice a week to get his own supplies because no salesmen would drop by. He fired so many different girls from the town too. If they didn't work perfectly, he'd just take a dislike to them. He wouldn't tell them they were fired, he just wouldn't put their name on the next week's schedule and pretty soon they'd figure it out. That wasn't smart. You know, Stockton Springs only has 900 people in it; if you got 8 girls working for you they're probably related to 850 people in town.

"You know his big idea? He had ten kids altogether between both marriages. He figured if he got ten businesses going he could put one of his sons or daughters in to manage each one, give them a good salary, and let them make his money while he retired to St Petersburg, Florida. But he made the mistake of buying the restaurant in Maine at the end of the season, right before the stormy weather. Then when everything didn't go his way he could be like a big kid, an asshole. He'd get so pissed off he'd just stop talking to you. For a year or two."

Ted Podgis: "After my father's divorce, he lost out on everything. He'd put a lot of his life into working at two jobs to make ends meet, so then he was looking to try and make it again. After working in insurance and finally making some money again, he wanted to find a business and settle down. That's when he bought the restaurant in Maine. Then that didn't work out. And he'd had all the trouble with Mark and Dawn. I think there was a lot of hurt built up in him, and some bitterness and resentment toward everything."

Barbara (Franz) Czacherski: "There were times when my stepfather hit my sisters, yes, but never in front of me. I can't tell you that he beat my mother because I never saw it and she would never tell us if he did. But we saw things after the fact that we wondered about. You know, a black eye here or there, a broken arm. One time she broke her back, you know. The stories all covered, the stories she gave to the public, to everyone at work. It was never Al Podgis committing the act, but we wondered just the same. My mother protected Al just like she protected her kids. She wasn't going to tell anyone about anything that went on in that house."

The King's-Edgehill School that Scott Franz began attending in 1979 bore little resemblance to the academy that fathered it nearly two centuries earlier. King's College was the creation of

Nova Scotia's first Anglican bishop and other clergymen who numbered among the thirty thousand United Empire Loyalists from the United States — many of them wealthy, well-educated and branded traitors for their stubborn loyalty to Britain — who fled to Nova Scotia to avoid persecution after the American Revolution. It was not surprising that the college was founded in Windsor. The townsite, fifty miles northwest of Halifax, had been cleared out of forest and built on the banks of a river created by the earliest settlers, French Acadians, who were later expelled because they refused to swear allegiance to the King. Windsor was soon ruled by stern, aristocratic Anglicans who attempted to establish a civilized society modelled after the empire. Temperance Societies outlawed rum-drinking and profanity, and church-going was encouraged by means just short of conscription.

King's College was to provide "a virtuous education, thus diffusing literature, loyalty and good morals among his Majesty's subjects in Nova Scotia." In case the point was missed, no one received their honours or degrees unless they subscribed to the Thirty-nine Articles of the Church of England and swore not to attend Mass or hobnob with Presbyterians, Baptists, Methodists or other dissenters. In 1891, Edgehill Church School for Girls was opened half a mile from the college, as an alternative for prominent Church of England families who refused to send their daughters to the convent in Halifax because of its policy of accepting other faiths.

Both schools were run on Victorian principles. Boys and girls marched to church on opposite sides of the street and sat in segregated pews. Junior masters at King's were instructed not to embarrass a girl by asking her to dance more than once during the strictly supervised semi-annual balls. As recently as 1960, communication between the sexes was conducted via letters furtively dropped in the crack of a tree in one corner of the playing field. But by the time Anne Curtis attended Edgehill, twelve years later, some classes were integrated with those of King's, facilities such as science labs were shared, and most extra-curricular restrictions had been eased.

In 1976, facing severe financial problems, the schools amalgamated to form the co-educational King's-Edgehill. Scott Franz found himself among a handful of "foreign students" that the school attracted from the U.S., Hong Kong, Malaysia, Venezuela and what was then Rhodesia. On his first report, after less than two months at the school during which he tried to make up his lost semester, most of his teachers remarked on his poor effort. His algebra teacher was the most blunt: "I'm not impressed with his attitude. I find him lazy and rather foolish at times. He does have the potential to do well." But at the end of the year, the Housemaster wrote: "Scott fitted well into school-life here; he has made many friends and is popular with almost everyone. He is usually co-operative, well-mannered and witty. We appreciate his presence in residence and look forward to seeing him again in the autumn."

To picture King's-Edgehill, imagine a provincial Nova Scotian town that is noted as the home of humorist Thomas Haliburton — his stories as integral a part of Canada's past as those of Mark Twain are America's — and for being "halfway between the equator and the North Pole." Less frequently mentioned: a local farmer who bred the largest pig in Nova Scotia established his prize in its own house with a dining-room, bedroom, parlour and curtained windows. Follow a quiet road to a long driveway flanked by alders, elms, grey birch that leads to King's-Edgehill. (The former Edgehill has become a luxury apartment complex.) A stately four-storey brick building crowned by six dormers houses the administrative offices, boys' dormitory and, in the basement, the dining-hall. (Girls are boarded separately.) Two, sometimes three, boys share a room. A bookshelf, night-table, desk and closet are provided. So is a bed constructed with three drawers in the rear pedestal and a cupboard in the front pedestal. There are posters of actresses in swim-suits but no nudes.

A grassy quadrangle is bounded on three sides by the back of the main building, a newly built recreation centre, and a building containing classrooms. On the quadrangle, graduation ceremonies are held, and kilted, scarlet-jacketed cadets — they are affiliated with the Black Watch — are put through exercises. Every year students conduct guerrilla raids against Howard Dill's neighbouring orchards where Dill produces apples, pears and award-winning mammoth pumpkins.

Private boarding schools like King's-Edgehill survive because they promise parents things that public schools cannot: a familial environment, rigorous academic standards, limited enrolment that guarantees individual attention, and a highly structured, supervised program. Franz discovered he had to rise at 7:00 A.M., eat breakfast at 7:15, and return to his room for inspection at 7:55. Twenty minutes later there was a prayer service in the chapel and by 8:30 he was in class. After lunch there was "Quiet Hour" at 2:00 P.M., followed by compulsory sports from 3:00 to 5:00. (Franz played tennis and softball in the fall and spring, and during winter he skiied and joined the curling team.) After dinner there were two seventy-five-minute study periods before an enforced bedtime at 11:00 P.M. Once a week, students were allowed to go into town in place of the two-hour afternoon sports period. On weekends, those students who remained at the school were given free time from 3:00 P.M. on Saturday until Sunday evening's chapel service.

A yearbook photo showed Franz seated at a computer terminal, wearing his everyday classroom clothes: a white shirt, dark sweater-vest, corduroy pants. Like all boys, he had to wear a school blazer, tie and grey flannel trousers in the dining-hall. He always carried a battered army surplus knapsack on which slogans and symbols were scribbled in coloured inks. During free time, his favourite uniform consisted of chinos and a T-shirt. He had a stereo in his room and several electronic gadgets that he rigged up by his bed and on his desk lamp.

By grade eleven, the year Bruce Curtis started classes at King's-Edgehill, Franz had established his reputation. Students remember him standing outside the girls' dormitory, at an area known as "smoker's corner" — "where the soap opera of life at King's unfolded" — holding a cigarette and self-consciously striking poses. He encouraged an image of himself as an insider who kept abreast of all developments within the student body and faculty — a claim he supported in part by reminding fellow students that he was the headmaster's private audio-video technician — and as a tactician who could be counted on to spirit marijuana into the dorm or obtain submarine sandwiches from the Kaiser Sub Shop in Windsor late at night. According to legend, Franz could sweet-talk his way out of reprisals when he was caught breaking regulations.

His rhetorical skills extended to self-aggrandizement. Many of his stories contained small accuracies that kept the truth alive. Franz's father was, at various times, said to be the owner of a chain of motels in New England, vice-president of Pan-American Airlines, and affiliated with the Mafia. At one time he was a retired military officer who negotiated the release of Brigadier-General James Dozier after he was kidnapped by Red Brigade terrorists, and at another, "chief lawyer for all of New Jersey." One sister was said to be a lawyer, doctor and former bank president. (Noreen was employed as a loans officer at a bank in Oregon.) A brother was a priest. (His stepbrother, Ted Podgis, had become a born-again Christian and worked in a halfway house for men in Macon, Georgia as assistant to the pastor.) And another brother, modelled in his mind after Mark, was so evil he would "shoot ya, then beat ya for bleedin' on him." Franz also showed photos of a mansion that he said was his home, and of a limousine driven by Jimmy, the family's chauffeur. Once he claimed his father had bought him his own pinball and video-game centre because he was bored one summer. When that story was received doubtfully, Franz produced coupons from a real amusement parlour in New Jersey called "Scotty's Arcade."

That he was an American — Franz occasionally adopted a thick New Jersey accent for effect — and told wildly outrageous stories about his family and past enhanced his reputation because no one was ever sure how much was true. It was his ambition, it seemed, to duplicate F. Scott Fitzgerald's fictional transformation of James Gatz into Jay Gatsby. Despite an unathletic build and unexceptional looks, Franz's waggish antics, easy confidence and apparent worldliness proved seductive.

According to his many female admirers, who called him "Scottie" or "Franzie," he had "an attractive aura that made you want to talk to him." Franz's "aura" was the cornerstone of his reputation: a carefully cultivated persona as the school's resident father-confessor. "He was profound," reports Nancy Wells, one of the supplicants. "He would ask you questions about yourself, very personal questions about your sex life, or your past, or your family. Often you didn't know how to answer, or wouldn't really want to answer, but the manner in which he asked you sort of compelled you to. And if you didn't, he would put words in your mouth. Usually accurate words."

To many girls, Franz presented an alternative to the "A-Starters," a derisive term applied to the boys on the school's first-string sports teams who "thought they were God's gift to women." As a result, Franz was disliked by many of his male peers, who called him "the faggot" behind his back. But within the geometry of student affairs at King's-Edgehill, Franz was skilled at playing angles. His pranks earned him grudging respect, and he used his female friendships as bargaining chips, acting as a go-between when a boy was interested in a girl he knew. By adding intimate details and proposing strategies, Franz recruited allies, or at least collaborators, from the male dorm.

The high point of Franz's three and a half years at King's-Edgehill came towards the end of grade eleven when he began dating Heather Cuthbert. They had become friends after exchanging notes in class and were soon walking together in the hallways, holding hands. Cuthbert, a sensitive, apple-cheeked brunette, told her girlfriends she could talk about "anything and everything" with him.

"Girls liked him because he was empathetic," she explains. "He loved listening to other people's problems. Scott considered himself a psychiatrist and was proud of his ability to help you deal with your problems. He wasn't macho, or even great looking, but he was very understanding, a good listener. Some girls couldn't get through the day without having Scott give them some direction.

"The only thing wrong was that he told a lot of stories that everybody suspected weren't true. It's hard to explain, but people knew that and tended to accept it. I accepted it because he was a nice guy and a nice companion. I mean, I wouldn't have continued going out with him if I hadn't believed he was honest and sincere most of the time. He used to tell me he had problems with his father, that they didn't get along. He said his father had beaten his mother and sisters, and him when he was younger. He'd had a bad past, and I assumed he was trying to make something of himself."

Even Franz's schoolwork improved in the latter half of grade eleven. One teacher commented, "I am finally seeing what Scott is capable of." His highest marks were in algebra and physics, and the one course that genuinely fascinated him was computer science. King's-Edgehill had acquired an elementary home computer that year — a Radio Shack TRS-80 system with 32k memory — and Franz was part of an eager group of students being introduced to its operation. It was in these classes that Franz encountered Bruce Curtis.

Curtis had arrived at King's-Edgehill only that year and, like many teenagers still in the process of discovering themselves, sought to construct a comfortable identity. It was easier for some than others, he noted, not that he aspired to become one of the campus celebrities who were star athletes (Curtis was vehemently opposed to organized sports), active in cadets (he disliked anything military) and popular with teachers (that usually meant acting sycophantic.) But neither was he like some students whose insecurities translated into malleability or self-deprecation. He did not believe there was virtue in weakness, nor would he admit to a need to form unnecessary acquaint-anceships. While not exactly friendless — Curtis got along amiably with his two room-mates and accepted any offer of a chess match — his remoteness struck many of his peers as snobbery.

He read dark, prophetic literature for pleasure, difficult novels like those of Kafka, Joyce, Dostoevsky, and the Gothic poetry of Poe. He read Ursula K. Le Guin's science fiction and the pop mysticism of Richard Bach's *Illusions: The Adventures of a Reluctant Messiah.* He became known as King's-Edgehill's J.R.R. Tolkien expert and eventually, by studying a glossary in one of the books, learned one of the author's Dwarvish languages which he occasionally employed when writing the plot synopses, character sketches and criticisms he recorded for each book he read.

At King's-Edgehill, like most schools and particularly within the self-contained community at a private boarding school, conformity was the norm and anomalous behaviour was regarded as puzzling or unacceptable. Curtis, who was not unaware of the prevailing attitude, was apparently unconcerned. His parents had always solemnly promoted achievement and excellence. He was the product of an isolated childhood and, for the past four years, an unchallenging rural high school. Everything he had experienced had reinforced a sense of his own importance and reminded him that he possessed an efficient intellect.

"There were all these bright people," says Curtis of his first months at King's-Edgehill. "It stunned me because in class they could verbally express all these great ideas, but they wouldn't do any work beyond that. They were as bright as me, y'know, I would never say I was brighter, it was just that they didn't care much about learning. They'd talk in class a lot and the teacher would pass them. I didn't like talking in class. It was a waste of time."

As his parents had hoped, Curtis did become somewhat less withdrawn as the year progressed. "Reach For the Top," a weekly quiz show for students that was televised on the Canadian Broadcasting Corporation (CBC), recruited teams from high schools across Canada. On December 12, 1980, Curtis competed impressively with the King's-Edgehill team at the CBC's Halifax studios. Then he joined the senior debating team that went to the provincial high school championships. While neither "Reach For the Top" nor debating had the cachet of sports, Curtis earned a measure of credibility for his wide-ranging knowledge, and his social life slowly expanded. With two new friends, Andrew Chodakowski and Mark Brennan, he played Dungeons and Dragons and Top Secret, fantasy role-playing games that were then the rage on high-school and college campuses throughout North America.

A friend, and one of Curtis's room-mates, was John Leefe. He says: "I knew him as well as anyone could know the guy because he was pretty secretive. He was really quiet, socially awkward, a total bookworm. Very knowledgeable. Totally passive and non-violent with regards to everything. He just went about his day-to-day work, his reading and studies. He wasn't disliked, but I don't think you could say he was liked either. He never really got to know anyone that well."

Curtis's teachers praised him, especially Colleen Smith, the mathematics and computer-science teacher who was impressed by his quick grasp of programming and his willingness to spend free hours in her classroom. At the end of the year, Jim and Alice Curtis were sure they had made the right decision for Bruce when they saw him receive three honours: the King's Gavel, for debating, the Old Boys Gold Ring, for the highest overall average in grade eleven, and the Chancellor Harris Prize for mathematics. Everyone agreed Curtis exemplified King's-Edgehill's reputation as a breeding ground for scholars.

In grade twelve Curtis was among an "elite group" (their choice of words) of honours students that were accorded special privileges. One of these was accompanying Colleen Smith on trips to the Radio Shack computing centre in Halifax. Smith, a plump woman in her early twenties with a tightly curled perm, felt she enjoyed a special rapport with the students because she was younger than the rest of the staff. She liked to make the point by taking her favourite students away from the campus, sometimes to the bookstore at Acadia University in nearby Wolfville or to restaurants in neighbouring towns. On the Halifax trips, she usually stopped at Pizza Hut for lunch. Of course, only the keenest students were invited, which meant that Scott Franz, despite an otherwise modest academic record, was frequently included.

Curtis had not said more than half a dozen words to Franz

before the first semester of grade twelve. One afternoon, while playing Diplomacy, the World War I strategy game, Curtis, holding England, and Franz, with Italy, entered into an alliance. Up to that time, Curtis knew of Franz only as a braggart and mythomaniac, not that he necessarily disapproved. He didn't care so long as a person had sufficient wit to keep the game interesting. But Franz was also a curiosity. He had a glib way of speaking, yet he charmed both teachers and students alike. The headmaster, Tom Menzies, relied on Franz as a confidant who would keep him attuned to the goings-on of the student population. Curtis was struck by how Franz could play both ends off the middle. That tickled the rebellious side of Curtis's nature. Franz also made jokes at Miss Smith's expense, especially about the way Smith was forever jokingly mussing Curtis's hair and teasing him. Curtis and Franz discussed ways of sabotaging her computer programs, just for a laugh.

Soon they began playing marathon backgammon tournaments together. Curtis noticed that his friends Chodakowski and Brennan were uncomfortable around the American boy, and his best friend and room-mate, Rory Kempster, didn't like Franz at all. That amused Curtis because he found Franz absurdly transparent. It wasn't that he disbelieved everything Franz said, he was just less impressed than others. Besides, there was something attractive about Franz's dark side, even if most of it was posturing and over-statement.

"Scott was a schemer and a hustler, one of the smokers who was always with the in-crowd," Curtis would later say. "But he was also intelligent and had an interest in computers. He sort of ignored that side of himself for a long time because he always had to present this big image, like he was a rich kid who could get anything he wanted, y'know. But he knew I didn't care how much money he had, or whether he had a car. He realized he didn't have to put on this big front with me. He could just sort of be himself."

The trouble with Franz's image was not its intricately detailed façade but the strength of its underpinning. During the second term of grade twelve, in March 1982, it began to collapse. For weeks Heather Cuthbert, Nancy Wells and other girls who were Franz's companions had been remarking on discrepancies in his stories. One of Cuthbert's friends was Al Sebastian, a sarcastic, slightly built teenager who also knew Franz. "He was real good with females," Sebastian recalls. "He was always hanging around them, eating with them at dinner. Then he'd come back, as guys are prone to do, and tell all the other guys he had them under his thumb, that he was getting skin off all of them. Anyway, he told so many stories they started getting mixed up."

Whether offended at Franz's indiscretions or for other reasons of his own, Sebastian finally told Cuthbert about Franz's locker-room braggadocio. Cuthbert was incensed. "He was talking about people, saying we girls had done things we'd never done. I broke up with him. Afterwards I started talking about things he'd said to me, and pretty soon everybody realized he'd been lying about everybody. That definitely ruined most of his friendships with the girls and a lot of the guys too. He lost just about every friend he'd ever had."

Franz's efforts to repair his relationship with Cuthbert were a failure, even when he sent her a dozen long-stemmed roses and a note pledging his undying love. Suddenly ostracized, he began spending most of his free time with Curtis. It was during this period, as spring came to Nova Scotia in the last few months of the school year, that students and teachers recall Franz and Curtis's behaviour becoming increasingly erratic. Sitting together in the dining-hall, winking at each other and exchanging coded gestures, they would repeat the phrase: "It doesn't matter any more. Everybody's going to pay." One day Cuthbert approached Franz, holding a tiny gold necklace he had given her.

"I'd like to talk to you, Scott."

"It doesn't matter."

Cuthbert winced. "Why are you talking like this, Scott? You always wanted to talk to me before. I'd just like you to take your necklace back."

Franz stared at her mockingly. "It doesn't matter any more. Everybody's going to pay."

One Saturday, in the middle of the night, Rory Kempster was

awakened by a noise in the room he shared with Curtis. Lifting an eyelid cautiously, he was able to make out two figures in the darkness. He heard Franz whisper, "I think he's awake," and Curtis reply, "No, he hasn't made a move." A few moments later Franz and Curtis began waving their hands and either whispering or chanting. Then Kempster felt a drop of water on his face. Suddenly convinced he was being hexed, he sat up in bed, thrashing his pillow around and yelling invectives. When he confronted Curtis later he was told they had been conducting an experiment to determine whether a person would wake up when liquid was dropped on his face. As for a hex, Curtis told Kempster his imagination had been excited by a recent screening at the school of the movie, *The Exorcist*. Although Kempster dismissed the incident as a stupid prank, he remained annoyed. He told Curtis, "I never want to see Scott in our room again."

Both Kempster and Mark Brennan, concerned about Curtis's bond with a boy they called "a sneaky, shady character," advised their friend to stay away from Franz. No one could explain why Curtis had taken up with Franz, although some combination of rebellion, loneliness and boredom seemed the likeliest explanation. Several students pointed out that both were "loner-type personalities." On one weekend trip to Halifax, Franz even induced Curtis to get drunk for the first time, a spectacle vividly recalled by two other students. Not everyone sympathized with Curtis. Kurt Scholz, Franz's room-mate during the first semester of grade twelve and a student well liked by both teachers and his peers, felt Franz was often undeservedly maligned and considered Curtis someone who "didn't fit in and didn't try to." Yet he conceded that "Scott went out of his way to break rules. Bruce never did that until he started hanging around with Scott."

But years later, Heather Cuthbert remains adamant in her views on the two boys. "I don't think Bruce was a sweet, innocent little boy. He wasn't the perfect little parents' boy. No one really knew him, no one could get inside him. He and Scott got into black magic and talked about strange things. Scott had some problems, but he was never like that before he started hanging around with Bruce."

Curtis began speaking out in certain classes, reacting impatiently and with scorn when classmates asked for an explanation of a concept that he considered elementary. First his teachers thought he was studying too hard, suffering from stress and fatigue. That wasn't uncommon at a competitive school like King's-Edgehill. But Curtis's marks had been slipping that term. Once, when his sister Anne was visiting, Curtis told her that his teachers had chosen him as a "star pupil" to be displayed as an example to parents considering sending their children to King's-Edgehill. Anne, whose tendency had always been to fulfil other people's expectations of her, was surprised at her brother's response. "He'd decided his objective was to maximize his computer time. He couldn't understand why they were disturbed when he was getting marks in the high 70s. He felt he wasn't doing demonstrably well enough to suit their needs."

Soon his teachers began to speculate that the shy scholar was developing an unpleasant streak of arrogance. Several agreed he seemed to be mocking them, acting as though he were smarter than anyone else in his classes, including his teachers. He once threw a tantrum when he was told he had to participate in the physical education program, and on other occasions he was hostile towards teachers who caught him breaking minor regulations or trying to avoid the rest of the school at the Thursday evening hockey matches at the arena in Windsor.

"He was a really complicated boy," comments John Naugler, a biology and science teacher who also taught an introductory philosophy course called Theory of Knowledge. "On one hand he was a quiet, demure fellow who rarely seemed to be in any kind of trouble. But he also displayed a contempt for authority that was rather surprising."

Andrew Chodakowski, who, along with Mark Brennan and Curtis, fancied himself one of the school's "philosopher-intellectuals," liked and respected Curtis even though he sometimes felt that his friend treated him as "a slight inferior." Chodakowski suspected Curtis was cut from more exceptional cloth than he, and envied his cool detachment, his powers of logic. He recalls Curtis as "having some sort of problem with power. In no way was he weak-willed. Intellectually he had a superiority complex. He told me once he liked the idea of an elite body controlling the masses."

Chodakowski smiles, then adds: "But you could never tell whether he meant anything by the things he said."

Although Jim Curtis stopped at the school twice every week — on Friday night, on his way home from Halifax, to pick up Bruce's laundry, and again on Sunday, on his way back to Halifax, to return the laundry and deliver a care package of food — he reports that only once did a teacher comment on Bruce's behaviour. (Bruce was reportedly skipping some gym classes.)

One night, Rea deBoer and his wife, Heidi, walked across the campus and into the classroom building. DeBoer, who taught science and chemistry, unlocked the chemistry lab door and switched on the light. Since Heidi, a part-time teacher, wanted to clean the salt-water fish tank in the biology lab, her husband unlocked the door leading to a connecting storeroom. The biology lab was in darkness so Heidi took several steps towards the light switch on the opposite wall before freezing. There were two figures next to the door, less than five feet away. Heidi screamed as they dashed out the door leading to the hallway. In later discussions, she would explain that she had seen two silhouettes, one short and one tall. The shorter one had curly hair and was wearing light-coloured painter pants, a detail she remembered because most students wore jeans. When her husband rushed into the lab, she told him: "I think it was Scott Franz and Bruce Curtis."

The deBoers reported the incident to John Naugler, who was the duty master that evening. Naugler was concerned without being alarmed. At twenty-six, he, like Colleen Smith, was not so far removed from adolescence that he couldn't appreciate the sorts of activities that constitute pranks. The science labs were obvious targets. Beakers and test-tubes often turned up as furnishings in student bedrooms. Naugler wondered whether someone was going to discover a preserved frog in their bed one night. But Naugler also knew that Franz, Curtis or whoever had been in the lab might have been after chemicals. Naugler chuckled to himself. They were probably intending to manufacture a stink bomb, although that presumption would be a poor defence if the headmaster's residence was blown up one night. On a more serious note Naugler wondered whether any ethyl alcohol was missing. Some kids might be stupid enough to try getting drunk on that and end up dead.

When Franz and Curtis were located, both boys could account for their whereabouts. Franz was convincingly indignant that he was being accused, although Naugler noted that he was wearing white painter pants. Later Naugler recorded the incident in his duty report, although he knew the evidence was tenuous. Heidi deBoer had not seen any faces and neither Naugler nor deBoer could detect anything missing from the storeroom. (A few days later, an empty chloroform bottle was found in Curtis's room, but there was no evidence to suggest it had been stolen that night.) Still, Naugler was reminded of the peculiar incident in which Rory Kempster claimed Franz and Curtis had tried to put a spell on him.

A few weeks later, Colleen Smith was in the girls' residence when she was told she was wanted downstairs. She wasn't entirely surprised to see Franz and Curtis. She had taught both of them mathematics for the past two years and was their computer-science teacher. She liked both boys, particularly Curtis. In fact Smith, who was lonely, had decided she liked Curtis a lot. She was a local girl — born and raised in Windsor, attended Acadia University twenty miles away — and felt her life was unfulfilled. Curtis was an overly intellectual boy whose ideas she found challenging and unorthodox. She often kidded him and made innuendos, hoping for a response. She thought of him as enormously clever but repressed, an inhibited young man to whom Smith could offer an untapped spring of passion.

For a while Smith was wearing Curtis's ring on a chain around her neck. ("I only wore it for about a week," Smith would later explain. "He said he didn't want it so I said I'd wear it and he gave it to me.") Soon gossip about Smith's pursuit of Curtis —

of all people — had earned its place as the oddest ribald tale in the collective memories of the graduating class of 1982. Finally, aware that Curtis was becoming increasingly uncomfortable, Smith backed off. She then wrote him a letter on pink stationery.

Bruce —

I really must apologize for my behaviour. It's just that I find you attractive — you're intelligent, witty and have some interesting ideas and beliefs. I wish we could spend some time together away from the school — just to talk, play some games and get to discuss more of our disagreeing beliefs (i.e. God, Jeffery). However I also realize that I have been creating an awkward situation and am really going to try to behave myself in the future. Please destroy this or I'm sure it could be used as incriminating evidence — a chance I'll take. I do trust you.

many thanks,

CES

P.S. If you ever want a friend or
more — you know where to look.

(Curtis did not destroy the letter. It was found among his possessions by his parents after his arrest in New Jersey. Smith would later explain: "I can't excuse it because it was inexcusable. It was my own weakness. I was searching for somebody then, and I found him interesting. He expanded my horizons a bit, and suggested some books for me to read. I regret it. It was a mistake, bad judgement.")

Franz and Curtis told Smith they were bored and wanted to leave the campus. Would she take them out for dinner? Smith was sympathetic. It was a warm, early summer Saturday, the school year was nearly over, and Curtis had just written his International Baccalaureate exams. May was a busy month for many students — a camping trip, the dance group performing in Halifax, the boys' rugby team competing in Prince Edward Island — so it was hardly surprising the boys were restless. She agreed, signed them out, and they climbed into her little black Acadian. After dinner at Burger King in New Minas, the boys suggested getting ice-cream for dessert. Smith hesitated. There was a fruit stand on the way back to King's-Edgehill that served cones, but Franz wanted to go to a nearby Dairy Queen. Smith and Curtis sat in the car and talked while Franz got their order: a chocolate milkshake for Smith, a strawberry shake for Franz, a banana split for Curtis.

Smith had no sooner swallowed her first mouthful before she was making a face. She thought it was some exotic flavour for a second, then realized it tasted like cigarette butts. She told the Dairy Queen attendant to get her a glass of water before she was sick all over his counter. After tasting the milkshake, the attendant agreed there was something wrong and dumped it into a sink. There were no cigarette butts, he reported. Then he tasted the chocolate syrup and the ice-milk. Finally he made her another shake, which tasted fine. Franz and Curtis expressed amazement that that was all he had done. "You could've sued," Franz told her, offering to drive back to the school. Smith felt queasy but had no intention of letting a student drive her car.

Smith still felt ill later that evening but decided to go to a party at the home of fellow-teacher Art Jamison, as planned. Jamison, who taught geography, was going to show the slides from a trip to Cuba that he and Smith and three other teachers and twelve students had taken the previous March. But by the time Smith reached Edgehill Estates and climbed the four flights to Jamison's apartment, she could only stagger into the bathroom and throw up. She was sick several times throughout the evening. Later she told Jamison about the taste of cigarettes in her milkshake.

"Maybe those kids poisoned you," Jamison suggested with a grin.

"No," Smith answered. "They're two of my best students. Why would they?"

The first real tragedy in Curtis's life occurred at the end of May 1982, when he learned of Patricia Hirtle's death. Hirtle, a tiny, slender girl with brown hair and dusky, hazel eyes, had been a member of the quartet of friends at the high school in Lawrencetown that included Valerie Milo, Donny Llewellyn and Curtis. An A-student fiercely committed to her schoolwork, Hirtle was a perfectionist with a troubled soul. Milo remembers her as a sympathetic listener who rarely opened up herself, a student "the class didn't warm to because she didn't lend an aura of warmth or compassion." Hirtle often spoke of suicide to Curtis, who would "always talk her out of it, convince her there was no point to it." Later Curtis received tortured letters from her at King's-Edgehill, although he rarely saw her. The last time had been five months earlier, after a production of *A Christmas Carol* at the school. She had wanted to talk to him but Curtis, for reasons that he later chose to bury deep inside, did not make the time for her.

On May 17, a few weeks after she had received an uncharacteristically low grade in physics, yet around the time she was awarded a scholarship to an agricultural college (she intended to become a veterinarian), Hirtle walked into her family's barn and shot herself in the head with a .22-calibre rifle. Curtis, who heard about his friend ten days later, was filled with anguish and an incoherent rage at the senselessness of her death. He was convinced that he could have saved her life had he spoken to her beforehand. That night he made the first entry in a journal that would have an unimagined impact on circumstances in the near future.

Friday, May 28, 1982*

Today I found out about the death of Patricia Hirtle. She shot herself. Very memorable occasion. On Monday, 17 May. I do hope it was not an attempt at a very

*Note: All letters, journal entries and poems written by Bruce Curtis are reproduced verbatim, including errors in spelling and grammar.

old cliche. Was not like that. Sunset rather nice. I am afraid Rory goes tonight. Very stunned (big question why? answer Aker? probably). I shall phone Ruth tomorrow for details. I have to know where, very important. Get all the details, reaction etc, mood before whatever that would cause her to waste her life. I hate the waste. I told her if you go go in a big way. Dumb. I talked to her only that Christmas, at Scrooge. From what I heard she was doing okay though a hint of Aker (I know, I know). Did not live up to her quote or other discussions. Very disappointed. I have no mouth and I must scream. But that is not true, correct. Wonderful outlets present themselves. We shall see. Very pink. I really wished I had been there, could have save her. Too late everybody got to go, got to leave behind the slow. Everything we had crumbles to the ground, though we refuse to see. Dust in the wind, all we are is dust in the wind. This certainly resolves it. I close my eyes only for a moment and the moments gone, swirling into madness, whirling twisting, to the sight of demons robed in black. Revenge is very necessary. Goodbye Patricia.

I am afraid Rory goes tonight.
A plan had been devised to "kidnap" Rory Kempster — "because he was a prefect and ... for being too goody goody" — and tie him to a tree beside the girls' dorm late one night. It was, according to Curtis, a prank to bring a little school spirit onto the campus.
Did not live up to her quote ...
The quote, often discussed by Curtis and Hirtle, was "Better to reign in hell than serve in heaven," Satan's line from Milton's *Paradise Lost*, the epic poem based on the fall of Adam and Eve, the rebellion and fall of Satan, the redemption of mankind through Christ. Milton's Satan, far from the loathsome devil of popular lore, was eloquent, strong, proud, symbolic of the rebellious soul, a noble opponent of God.

*Everything we had crumbles to the ground, though we refuse
to see. Dust in the wind, all we are is dust in the wind.*

"Dust in the Wind" was a pop song that rang from radios
throughout the dorm that year. Apparently Curtis found the
lyrics significant, although he disliked most pop music with
the exception of the group Rush, whose lyrics spoke of a future
in existential conflict, dominated by machines.

His thoughts were pouring out of him, black streaked with red.
He continued, in his cramped, tightly looped script, to write:

> Blue feathers rest gently on sunken features. Have fun
> though where is not known. I do not believe before or at
> the last moment you had religion. Rot in the ground,
> you have disappointed, shocked me. I shall not ask again.

That entry was inspired by Richard Bach's *Illusions: The
Adventures of a Reluctant Messiah*, a book Curtis particularly
enjoyed. So compelling was this mystical tale that Curtis was at
a loss to fathom how the same author could have written
Jonathan Livingston Seagull. Curtis thought about the premise
"What if a Siddartha or a Jesus came into our time, with power
over the illusions of the world because he knew the reality
behind them?" Hadn't he and Patricia discussed ideas just like
this? In the book, the messiah explained how to bring anything
into one's life by imagining that it was already there. The story's
narrator chose to imagine a blue feather.

> From childhood's hour I have not been
> As others were — I have not seen
> as others saw — I could not bring
> my passions from a common spring.
> From the same source I have not taken
> my sorrow; I could not awaken
> my heart to joy at the same tone;
> And all I lov'd, I lov'd alone.

These were lines from Curtis's favourite poem, Edgar Allan Poe's *Alone*. There was something of Poe in Curtis: a romantic temperament, an attraction to fantasy and mysterious, dreamlike, macabre forces. Spiritual questioning. As J.R. Hammond noted in *An Edgar Allan Poe Companion*, "Poe saw himself as a coldly analytic reasoner, solving problems by the dispassionate use of intellect." As a young man, Poe attended a school in England where his imperious intelligence and aristocratic superiority failed to win many friends amongst teachers or fellow pupils. *Alone*, written when he was only twenty, expressed feelings of alienation and an awareness of the strengths and weaknesses of his character that together conspired to form a personal "demon."

Addressing Hirtle, Curtis wrote:

> Not true Patricia, I loved too. But you are gone, I still here ready for my destiny. Why you did not come bothers me. I shall reign supreme, not for you but I shall devote some to your mind and memory. Memory is all we ever really have, perverted and twisted to our own desires. All that we see or seem is but a dream within a dream. I hate the world, we both did, but the idea is to have fun, sweet red revenge over the earth. Get back and take as much and more, much more, from the earth as it has taken from you. Nothing should stop you certainly not your own hand. Was it pleasant as the bone cracked, flesh flying. Enjoyable!, God, I hope so. Hope you got something, to make it worthwhile.

Curtis offers his own explanation of this passage. "The point was it bothered me a great deal that someone like this, who was a very sensitive, very intelligent person, could be driven by society to commit suicide, to go through all this pain and suffering because she didn't *fit* in, and couldn't *conform* to what other people *thought* she should be *like*. For me, this was exceptionally upsetting."

The line, *I shall reign supreme, not for you but I shall devote some to your mind and memory,* Curtis explains, was also inspired by *Paradise Lost.* "To get into that, you have to go into the conflict that has always existed in me. I went through stages; from age five to about ten or eleven I was into facts. I had a huge appetite for every single fact, no matter how strange. I wanted to know everything about the entire universe. Then from age eleven to fifteen, I read nothing but fiction, mostly science fiction and things like that. When I went to King's, both parts of the world, the totally scientific and the totally fictional, and the aspects of emotion in society, came together. I had to resolve them. I could go two ways, because I was very good in English and History and all that garbage, and very good in sciences too. I didn't know whether I wanted to become a scientist or an archaeologist or even a librarian that would spend the entire day locked away in some little room, poring over some obscure volume of forgotten lore — again from Edgar Allan Poe.

"The point is, I didn't know what to do. I still had the conflict, whether I should devote myself to empirical knowledge, and learning about the universe and stars, or whether that was totally trivial and of no importance to my life. I believe in extremes. I don't believe in half-measures. At King's, the Reverend [John Ford] asked me whether I wanted to be confirmed or not. I thought about it and I told him very sincerely that I didn't think I could make the commitment. He said 'Well, that doesn't matter.' He said it very sincerely too, that to be part of the Anglican church we really don't care whether you believe in God. But me, if I wanted to believe in God, it meant totally, like being Christ, believing you can move a mountain just through your belief.

"So I couldn't take this giant leap. For most people, they have religion and don't take that leap. For me it's a question of which leap I take, whether I devote myself totally to science, and enter that world and refuse to accept anything that has to do with emotion. If I accept science, then I must accept I have no free will whatsoever and that I'm just a collection of electro-chemical impulses and become a computer-like figure. That is the extreme of science. The other extreme is to become immersed in the mystical thing, such as Buddhism, Hinduism, and things like that, to totally ignore the world and enter into the subconscious of one's personality. I was being driven or I was tending towards becoming I didn't know what, and still don't know which world I want to enter totally."

And "...*the idea is to have fun, sweet red revenge over the earth.*"

"That was one way of trying to sustain her," Curtis continues, "to show her that by killing herself she was achieving nothing but showing that they had done to her exactly what they wanted to do.

"When emotional things happen, your mind fills with a lot of garbage and a lot of connections, with sensations and emotions that should not exist because they are illogical. So the point is to get rid of all those dumb connections. So what you put down is usually not exactly what you come to. You distill, you get rid of all the vapours so what you're left with in your mind is not what you put down."

The following weekend Curtis added another entry to the journal, a poem he said was included in a letter Hirtle sent him while he was at King's-Edgehill.

June 4, 1982

purple skiens replace limbs
coins clange as madness rises, screaming
silent, building
trees away, silence cries, cries, cries to wind, shut
up.
Darkness peaceful, walls around, I long to be
dead under while worms chew and mutilate
my shrunken pale skin.
I am nothing but dirt contributing to well
being, plants grow upon me. I rejoice, nature
reigns supreme in the hollow of my chest.

for nothing have I been and nothing I
will become.
all illusions, visions and ghosts before my
eyes dancing to a deadly rhyme.
Peace exists never, chaos always, throwing
us about. Pieces fly off, blood dims our sight
and we walk like a drunkard, stumbling
over our dead friends.
Magots rise from their eyes and stomachs,
we caress them, partnerships in deception.
Red filter, green filter, Blue filter, white.
Doors vast, inumerable, stretching on into
infinity.
We choose, always wrong, never close
but distant. Vision is now clear
for what is seen is hell (life)

Graduation Day. Friday, June 18.

Sunlight, filtering through a hazy sky, casts an appropriately reverential glow across the quadrangle at King's-Edgehill. Several hundred students, staff, families and friends — including Jim and Alice Curtis with their daughter Carol, and Al and Rosemary Podgis — were listening to Arthur Andrews, a retired career diplomat and former Canadian ambassador to Israel, Sweden and Greece, tell them that "while a flag must represent an idea, a person must represent a principle if either is to command respect and affection." Then Andrews, who graduated from King's in 1933, presented the grade twelve diplomas. Later, when the prizes and special honours were dispensed, a student from Hong Kong was awarded the Governor-General's Medal for being the best all-round citizen in the senior school. Rory Kempster also accepted an award and gave the valedictory address.

Jim Curtis had driven the Honda up from Halifax. Carol, who was living in the city by then, had arrived with a friend, and Alice had brought the station wagon from Mount Hanley to transport Bruce's belongings back to the farm. They were surprised and a little disappointed that Bruce hadn't won any prizes, especially since he'd been awarded three the previous year. They had hoped his marks would have been high enough to earn him a scholarship to Dalhousie. Anne's scholarship had helped offset the cost of textbooks and the University of Toronto's expensive tuition. But the Curtises shoved the thought from their minds. Perhaps they had built their expectations too high; after all, they had attended Anne's triumphant graduation and marriage in Ontario just a month ago. Children are different, not to be compared.

Actually, the Curtises had received a foreshadowing of their son's performance a few months earlier on a mid-term report. On average his marks were respectable, but he had dropped 12 percentage points in Chemistry, one of his strongest subjects. And although he scored 94 percent in physics, his teacher, John Collins, commented: "Bruce has an excellent grasp of the material covered this term. He is, however, somewhat hampered in his ability to participate in the classroom by a certain degree of academic arrogance." It would be several weeks before the Curtises would receive Bruce's final report. Had they but known the news it contained, that might have affected their enthusiasm for their graduation present to him, a trip to New Jersey. His physics mark had plunged 14 percentage points; this time Collins wrote: "Bruce's final mark dropped significantly due to a failure to hand in any lab work during the final term." And his chemistry teacher, Rea deBoer, observed: "Bruce's attitude has steadily worsened throughout the term which has caused his grade to fall."

After the graduation ceremonies, Alice helped Bruce clear out his room and together they loaded the station wagon. Bruce stayed at the school to attend the graduation party that night. He planned to return home by bus late the following afternoon. At no time did Jim and Alice Curtis meet Scott Franz or his parents, nor would they have expected to. Bruce had never mentioned his name.

Later that afternoon, Curtis and Franz drove with Nancy Lyons out to her parents' cottage on Coxcoombe Lake, south of

Windsor. Lyons, the gregarious youngest child of a local optometrist, was following a tradition established by her older siblings by hosting the party. By 6:00 P.M., most of the students and staff who were planning to attend were present. Champagne bottles were uncorked and there was plenty of wine and beer. Dinner consisted of buckets and buckets of Kentucky Fried Chicken, and it was Franz's stereo system providing the beat for dancing.

During the final weeks of school, Franz had managed to at least tenuously re-establish himself within his former circle of friends. Teenage grudges tend to be short-lived, especially amongst a graduating class preparing to disperse, but that only partly accounts for Franz's comeback. He hastened the process himself by introducing to the campus an exclusive diversion called "Franz's Mystical Mind Fuck." The clear liquid — chloroform believed to have been obtained from the school lab — was stored in a mayonnaise jar in his knapsack. Soon the appetite for cheap thrills common to teenagers facing high-school graduation proved irresistible to many of Franz's former friends, who were happy to set aside past feuds for the opportunity of poking their noses above the open lid of Franz's jar.

Lyons was happy Franz had come to her party. They'd been close friends for three years, often going together on ski trips or to curling matches and organizing excursions to Halifax. Although he was "a real bullshitter," Lyons considered him "a good friend who'd be there when you needed him." They'd had many "really good chats about all the society bullshit, you know, child abuse, alcoholism, this and that. Never once did he say his father had hit him or that he came from an unhappy home." Lyons was ambivalent about Curtis's presence. As soon as he'd arrived he'd sat down on a couch in the living-room and begun staring out the picture window that overlooked the lake. Lyons brought him a glass of wine and asked him to come outside and join the party. She deduced from the coolness of his response and from past experiences — once, when she had asked him why he was sitting alone in the dining-hall, he had told her, "I'm here to eat, not voice my opinions" — that he might come outside later, but probably wouldn't. "I don't think he was shy," Lyons says, "because he never seemed uncomfortable when you talked to him. If you were up in the computer room and needed any help, he'd go to any lengths to show you what you were supposed to do. But the rest of the time it was like he wasn't interested. I don't think many people did anything for him."

Given the unreliable nature of high-school reminiscences, and a tendency for the King's-Edgehill graduating class of 1982 to create — and embellish upon — a durable folklore surrounding Franz and Curtis, fact and fiction gradually merged. What occurred the day after the graduation party, however, remains an open file at RCMP headquarters in Halifax.

That morning, Kurt Scholz drove Franz and Curtis back to King's-Edgehill from Lyons's cottage in his father's Mercedes-Benz. Scholz parked in front of the school and ran up to his room to get his luggage. When he returned, Franz and Curtis were gone. As he left the campus, the car's hood ornament fell off. "I knew Scott or Bruce did it," Scholz would insist angrily.

Sometime later the two boys made their way to Franz's room to collect the last of his things. The hallways were nearly deserted and most rooms had been vacated. Only a small group of Chinese students remained in the dormitory, awaiting flights home the following week. Since Christmas, Franz's room-mate had been Antonio Maher, a slight, soft-spoken boy of Chinese descent whose home was in Portugal. It would be difficult to imagine more dissimilar individuals. During the semester Maher, who studied prodigiously, wore ear plugs to counteract Franz's stereo, a move that inspired Franz to jack the volume higher. At one point a strip of masking tape on the floor divided their respective sides of the room.

Curtis had also roomed with Maher during the first term that year. "He was very interested in physics," Curtis recalls, "so we were put together so we could discuss physics all day. Only it didn't work out that way because Antonio studied all the time. I mean constantly, never a break. He was a very good student, he spoke five languages and wrote better English than most Canadians do, but all he did was study."

At noon, Al and Rosemary Podgis met Franz in front of the school. After the two boys had loaded Franz's steamer trunk into the van, Curtis was invited to join them for lunch. They ate at a Chinese restaurant in New Minas. It was at this time, Curtis told his parents a few days later, that Mrs Podgis invited him to visit Scott in New Jersey. The Podgises dropped Curtis off at his home at approximately 2:00 P.M. and continued on their way to catch the ferry that connects Yarmouth, Nova Scotia with Bar Harbour, Maine. Again Jim and Alice Curtis missed meeting the Podgises; since they weren't expecting Bruce until the bus arrived in Middleton at 5:00 P.M., they had gone out for the day with visitors from Winnipeg.

At approximately 10:00 P.M. that night, Antonio Maher and his friend Steven Ho became violently ill. The housemaster, D'Arcy Walsh, telephoned the school nurse, Ann Mayer, at her house on the campus grounds. Mayer, who was pregnant at the time, asked Walsh to drive them to the hospital. She also determined that the boys had eaten the same dinner as their friends that evening, but had been drinking a bottle of cream soda later. "D'Arcy, if the pop's the only thing they've had that's different," she said, "you'd better take the bottle with you. There might be dirt or something in it that made them sick."

At 10:26 P.M., Maher and Ho were admitted to the out-patient department of Hants County Community Hospital. A nurse noted on the report: "Drinking cream soda tonight — sudden onset of vomiting sometime later." Both boys were diagnosed as having a gastritis attack and were given 50 mg of Gravol to take through the night. The cream soda was kept and sent to Halifax for analysis the following Monday. The two boys were discharged at 11:20 P.M. When Walsh returned to King's-Edgehill, he stopped at Ann Mayer's house. Mayer tried to convince the boys to spend the night in her small infirmary so she could keep her eye on them but they insisted on going back to the dorm where their friends were sleeping.

"Where did you buy the pop?" she asked them. "I'll have to phone the store and tell them not to sell any more until we find out if something's wrong with it."

Both boys shook their heads. "It's not the pop, Mrs Mayer," Antonio told her. "We drank half the bottle yesterday and felt fine."

Upon further questioning, Antonio explained that the bottle had been left sitting overnight and all that day in his room. When he drank from it earlier in the evening, it had tasted "funny." He had asked his friend Steven to taste it.

"It didn't taste funny yesterday?" Mayer persisted.

"No," Antonio replied. "Tonight it tasted different. It sort of burned our tongues."

Mayer glanced at Walsh. "Antonio, could there be anybody in there playing a nasty joke on you? Would anybody put something funny in your pop?"

Antonio shook his head again. Both Mayer and Walsh knew that the Chinese students remaining in the dorm were all close friends. None of them were known as troublemakers.

"Who did you room with?"

"Scott Franz."

Suddenly Mayer was suspicious. She knew Franz to have been mixed up in all manner of shenanigans over the past few years at King's-Edgehill. She had also heard stories of how he tormented Antonio, who was regarded as a pleasant, hard-working boy by all of his teachers. She also knew Franz "lived in daydreams. There were all these far-fetched stories that you knew couldn't be true about his father being in the CIA, and having loads of money, Cadillacs, chauffeurs."

"Could Scott Franz have put something in the pop?" Mayer asked. "Was he back today?"

Antonio nodded. "He was back this afternoon to pick up his things. He and Bruce Curtis came into the room."

Mayer was shocked. During the last semester Curtis and Franz had been inseparable. They had been involved in a prank played on Curtis's roommate, Rory Kempster, and were suspects in an unsolved break-in at the chemistry lab. Furthermore, it was said there was animosity between Curtis and Antonio over Antonio's winning of the year-end physics prize.

"Was the pop there when they were in your room?" Mayer asked.

Antonio said that it was.

At the end-of-the-year staff meeting held the following morning, the Antonio Maher and Steven Ho incident was the topic of conversation before the meeting began and became the first item on the agenda. The headmaster, Tom Menzies, listened to various opinions, weighed them and ultimately decided not to contact the parents of either boy. But a number of teachers remained concerned. Colleen Smith, for one, was horrified by the similarities between the symptoms she had experienced after drinking the milkshake and those of Antonio and Steven. It was a disturbing coincidence, she felt, that Franz and Curtis had been present on both occasions. Others maintained that it was the school's responsibility to notify the respective families.

Although the essence of the opposition to Menzies focused on the headmaster's alleged desire to protect his school from scandal at all costs, it was complicated by a resentment, shared privately by several teachers, of Menzies' autocratic administrative style. One teacher, who asked not to be identified, recalls: "His [Menzies'] position has always been that the boys left the school before we could put together all the information about them. There were a number of us who felt strongly that there was enough evidence surrounding all the things that had taken place that something should have been communicated to the family."

One day, shortly after the staff meeting, a thought occurred to John Naugler, the biology teacher. He had searched the storage room between the chemistry and biology labs at the time of the break-in and found nothing missing, but high-school labs weren't run like pharmacies, with strictly controlled inventories and a master stock list. All this talk about poisoning made Naugler think of that package of commercial pesticide, Black Leaf 40, that a former biology teacher had kept in the lab to use on his rose bushes. It had occurred to Naugler that a pesticide wasn't the sort of thing that should be accessible to students so he had put it at the back of a shelf in the storage room and promptly forgotten about it. Naugler unlocked the storage room door and looked on the middle shelf. The pesticide was missing.

The following Monday, the school's physician received the analysis of the cream soda from Halifax. He immediately called Menzies. The report indicated the presence of nicotine.

Used primarily as an agricultural insecticide, nicotine sulphate — an alkaloid derived from tobacco — is a colourless and almost odourless oil soluble in alcohol, water, chloroform, kerosene, ether and most oils. It has a sharp, burning taste, and the symptoms of nicotine poisoning include nausea, vomiting, diarrhea, mental disturbances and convulsions. Under "Hazards of Nicotine" in the *Encyclopedia of Occupational Health and Safety*, it is described as "a very toxic substance, and serious or fatal poisoning may occur as a result of the ingestion, inhalation, or skin absorption of only very small amounts." Nicotine sulphate is present in a 40 percent solution as the active ingredient in a popular gardening product, Black Leaf 40.

By the time the revelations about the missing pesticide and the presence of nicotine in the cream soda had sunk in at King's-Edgehill, it was July first, Canada Day. The RCMP had already been notified but no complaints had been made by either of the victims involved. Antonio Maher had returned to Portugal and Steven Ho was in Hong Kong. Scott Franz was in New Jersey. None of the boys would be returning to the school in the fall. It was not until July 8, after RCMP officers in Windsor visited King's-Edgehill to gather background information on Franz and Curtis for authorities in New Jersey, that all the details about the incident were revealed — rather belatedly, as one senior officer in Halifax would later observe. A file was opened that day — although no charges were ever laid — under the heading: "Maher/Ho — Suspected Poisonings."

Misgivings remained amongst the staff at King's-Edgehill. There was circumstantial evidence to link Franz and Curtis — to what?, they asked each other. A macabre prank? It was certainly difficult, prior to the news they would soon be hearing from New Jersey, to seriously entertain the notion of attempted murder. Criticism of Menzies could still be heard, although the most widely held view was probably represented by John Naugler, who admitted to having strong suspicions about Franz and Curtis, yet appreciated the awkwardness of the school's position. "Most of what we knew was hearsay," he says. "Do you call the parents of a boy near the top of his class and tell them we think he may have planned a murder? The parents would obviously say, 'Well, God, you'd better have evidence.' But it never reached a point where we could say he'd done any specific thing."

Today, Menzies defends his decision. "We had no proof of anything, and we'd been wrong about such things before. Curtis's academic arrogance was not particularly significant, and though I'm sure Scott Franz had been in some trouble before, we had no specific evidence. We thought we acted in the best interests of all concerned."

At 8:38 P.M. on Wednesday, June 23, Scott Franz phoned Bruce Curtis from his home in New Jersey and the boys talked for seventeen minutes. The next morning he called again and they talked for half an hour. Then, at 3:19 that afternoon, Franz called back a third time and they talked for eleven minutes. Alice had already taken her son to Halifax to pre-register for his courses at Dalhousie that fall — she would later recall that Bruce met Antonio Maher there and the two boys talked amiably — and she and Jim had been discussing what to give him for a graduation present. Alice overheard him saying unenthusiastically: "It's too far, and too hard to get down there," to Franz on the phone. Later, when she found out that Bruce had been invited to visit his friend, she said: "You know, Bruce, it's not impossible to get down there. That could be your graduation present, if you'd like to go."

After conferring with Jim in Halifax, Alice began to make the arrangements. A one-way ticket — to Newark via Boston — was purchased because Franz was planning to drive back to Canada in order to register for classes at Mount Allison, a university in the neighbouring province of New Brunswick. The Curtises did not contact Franz's parents to verify these details. "We put ridiculous blind trust in that school," says Alice angrily. "We figured that anybody who went to the school would be reasonable. Bruce had spent a number of weekends with various people at different times. We never knew about that but it was always okay. They were all families from the school, so we figured this family would be okay."

The Curtises did not know — nor would they find out until much later — that Franz had made several fantastic offers to other classmates over his four years at King's-Edgehill. One boy was asked to join him at his sister's wedding in Hawaii, with the assurance that his plane fare and hotel accommodation would be taken care of. At the last moment, Franz announced that his mother had fallen down the stairs and the trip was cancelled. (None of Franz's sisters had been married in Hawaii.) He also invited Rory Kempster to join him for an all-expenses-paid vacation at his family's chalet in Switzerland. But when Kempster's father asked for Franz's home phone number, the boy was evasive. "I had no doubts," explains Frank Kempster, "but you don't accept a free ride like that without calling up the parents and thanking them. Rory finally got a name and a city, and when I found the number and called it, it was some kind of relative who told me to call someone else. After a ludicrous number of phone calls I still hadn't reached the boy's father and no one could conceive of what this trip was all about. I asked Rory later what it was all about and he said Scott was just playing a joke. I said, that's a hell of a game to play."

On Sunday, June 27, the day after Alice was hospitalized with a blocked bile duct, Curtis was alone in the farmhouse. Franz called from New Jersey three times that day — the boys talked for a total of an hour and a half — and Curtis called him back once. In two days, Curtis would arrive in New Jersey to begin his holiday. That night, he made his final entry in his journal:

Sunday June   1:00 A.M.

Hymn to the Moon

A choice, the simple, the kind, the tedious, the complex, hard, adventurous. Have you chosen. I believe so. Mother got sick and went to the hospital yesterday. I had to make and bake the bread. Went through Ann's memory books 12, 13 a few interesting selections. She is very conceited, as are you. Are you normal, I do not think so. I am mad, insane as I always wanted to be, I have achieved it. A difference however. I am fully aware of my madness and thoughts, my intellect still reigns supreme, obsessions do not become fixed for I know them as such. My insane qualities are controllable. I want power, or more specifically I wish to occupy a large chapter in future world history texts. That way I achieve immortality, something I shall also strive for in a physical sense. I do not want to die. I want to do it but the thought grows more frightening by the hour. However it makes sense, freedom, money a start on my life. I must carry it through.

Of this entry Curtis says: "The thing was again about conflict. One day I'd taken a walk with Anne, through the snowy woods around Mount Hanley, and revealed to her that I wanted to become an astrophysicist. She thought it was rather a dumb idea, that there wasn't much of a career in that. So I should devote myself to being a careerist and not to the pursuit of knowledge."

When asked whether the phrase "Have you chosen" referred to Anne or to himself using the second person, Curtis replied: "Myself." He refused to discuss the journal further.

The final entry, made the same night, was a graphic homosexual fantasy that Curtis maintained was included in one of Patricia Hirtle's last letters to him and simply copied out verbatim into the journal:

they embraced. Paul's coke, hard and long pressed against Bill's stomach lightly covered with brown curly hair. Bill's mouth moved downward, his hot wet tongue his thick lips licking, caressing Paul's body the curve of his throat, his erect nipples, the supple hard abdomen and finally his straining throbbing cock. At the same time, one hand caressed his own cock while the other felt Pauls inflamed anus. Pauls hand moved in rhyme, with his squirming body, over Bill's handsome face, his thick brown silky hair, his tender ears and that wonderful neck. With his tongue flecking across Pauls purple cock head, circling it and enticing it he caused the owner of the erected cock to wither with ecstasy and pain, his hips moving trying to force his long 9 inch hard cock into Bills steaming mouth. Finally Bill consented and impaled his oral cavity on Pauls sex organ, tasting the velvet sweet tang of sweat running down the hard rock cock as his mouth and throat swirled about it, rubbing, sucking it as the cock pulsated with pleasure. Pain rippled through the straining vien as Bill bit the cock repeatedly. Paul moaned, his back arched, his tongue wetly rolled about his opened mouth. He could feel it coming, his climax, his hips moved faster, sweat coursed over his straining muscular body as he forced his cock deeper into Bills mouth, in and out till it was all in. Bill sucked harder, his tongue moving fast over the shaft as he shoved his middle finger up deep into his partners anus, Paul came with a tremendous moan, his whole body shuddering, straining, rocking as his engorged cock exploded semen, shooting it hard against Bills throat. Again and again his powerful rod twitched with pleasure.

Well what were you expecting.

These final entries would prove to be the most damaging, prejudicing the New Jersey authorities investigating the Podgis murder case against Curtis, creating an indelible impression of a misfit too intellectually domineering, rebellious and unstable to fit comfortably into society, a boy who could have been a co-conspirator in a plot to kill two people and dispose of their bodies. James Newman, the Allenhurst police chief, loudly advocated the theory that Curtis and Franz had been homosexual lovers; he likened them to Nathan Leopold and Richard Loeb, the teenagers convicted in 1924 of the "thrill-killing" of a Chicago millionaire's son.

But the journal could also be viewed as the reflections of an overly cerebral teenager suffering through a turbulent adolescence, a boy whose intellect was at war with his emotions. Curtis was agonizing over the violent suicide of a close friend and may have been experiencing a period of confusion over his sexual identity. That his journal indicated a "murderous" state of mind was a tenuous connection at best, yet it was destined to become a significant element in the judicial proceedings to determine Curtis's guilt or innocence.

Years later, his friend Valerie Milo would remark: "Both Bruce and I always turned to writing for release. After Patricia's death I wrote reams and reams of stuff that was in my handwriting but wasn't me. Now I can't comprehend what I wrote, I can't relate to the state of mind I was in. It was turmoil, depression.

"I destroyed it all later because of the circumstances of Bruce's diary. I certainly didn't expect anything like that to ever happen to me, but who would have expected it to happen to Bruce?"

III

August 22, 1982
Monmouth County
Correctional Institution

Dear Aunt Lorraine:

I have enjoyed your letters very much. It is good to hear from people who care at any time and especially now... I am on the grand jury wing in a tier with ten other people. It is a caged area with eight cells all facing a common hall recreation area about ten feet wide. That is where I am on a mattress in the hallway... It is all a very bland shade of yellow. We eat in another section of the building at very odd hours, breakfast 5:30, lunch 10:30, and supper 3:30. The food is not to bad, you just have to get used to it. My time is occupied by sleeping, reading and writing. There is a television but I do not watch it very often, the whole experience having changed my perception of most television. They all seem so fake and unimportant. There are cards of course, but much of the play is gambling.. Recently we got a chess set and I play but

there is not much competition. So I read alot ... I plan
to take one course, since this is all they recommend for
first timers, either a philosophy course discussing the
major philosophical questions like free will or deter-
minism or a psychology course outlining the basic
principles or a history course on the evolution of
Europe.. Mom also sends in every letter some math
puzzles and brain teasers and provides the answers in
the next letter. I phone home on Saturday night so as to
catch both of them in. It is very good to hear their
voices, extremely good. Once I caught Carol home to
from the big city of Halifax. She had lots of plans for
me in September with both of us in the city. I have
also talked to Anne. Mom and Dad are coming down
again soon.

I hope you had fun in Holland. It sounds very enjoyable bicycling through the countryside. I wish I was
anywhere else but here. It is all very depressing but I
am sure it will turn out. I will keep my mind occupied
till then and my thoughts to myself. I really must finish
this now so I can mail it at 3:30.

Love Bruce

On September 9, 1982, Curtis met with Dr Harry Brunt, a
psychologist engaged by his lawyer, Michael Schottland.
Curtis's version of the events during the week before the
shootings followed the general outline of Scott Franz's statement
to the police. According to Brunt's report Curtis added that
Franz had told him that his stepfather was "very dangerous." He
wrote: "Scott told Bruce all the stories about his father and what
he had done to Scott's sister. He said that he hit the sister with an
encyclopedia and she had to go to the hospital and have
stitches.... He told him about his older brother always fighting
with his father...."

Curtis also mentioned to Brunt that on Saturday night, July 3,
when he and Franz were hiding from the rain under the porch
at 401 Euclid Avenue, he heard loud quarrelling. Brunt's report

continued: "All the time he [Al Podgis] was standing on the porch he was swearing and cursing Scott and then they heard him go into the kitchen and argue with Mrs Podgis, telling her how much of a pain Scott was and that if he could get his hands on him he would beat him or 'something like that.' They were arguing back and forth about how much trouble Scott was and how much he was like his brother who ran away. Then Mr Podgis hit Mrs Podgis and she started crying and went upstairs."

Finally Brunt summarized Curtis's chronology by writing: "Bruce [said he] had never shot a gun before in his life and he was upset by the Podgis home which was 'messy' and by their lifestyle. It was a lifestyle that he never imagined existed, everything was disorganized. Bruce describes himself as a loner."

Psychiatric examination: "Bruce was a thin, asthenic male who appeared very dejected.... Although for the most part his affect was dejected, at times he appeared to be silly.... He was able to think abstractly. Hallucinations were denied and no delusions or any paranoid thinking could be elicited. His judgement was defective at the time of the incident."

Diagnosis: "Although in my opinion Mr Curtis was not insane at the time of the act, he certainly was thrown into an environment and situation which could prevent him from carrying out a commission of an act resulting in the death of Mrs Podgis. In my opinion he fired the rifle in a startle reaction and the report of the autopsy and the path of the bullet as well as the fact that he was not used to firearms makes me feel that the shooting was certainly unintentional.

"The flight after the act indicated a panic reaction. Certainly the shooting was an additional stressor. I think that Bruce was in a situation where he was totally at sea and he reacted to his friend's actions as a follower. I feel he was suffering from an Adjustment Disorder at the time of the shooting, brought on by the foreign environment in which he found himself."

Schottland and his partner Charles Uliano studied Brunt's report. It supported an important element of their defence: Curtis's state of mind at the time of the shootings. Although the two boys had brought the rifles into the house the night before, there was no mention in Franz's statement that indicated they had discussed murdering the Podgises. Weapons and ammunition had been found in the house, lending credibility to the potentially life-threatening environment Curtis and Franz had described.

After reviewing the state's progress to date, the two men knew that the prosecutor, Paul Chaiet, had not yet come up with a very strong case. Chaiet would probably move to sever. A 1968 Supreme Court decision, *Bruton v United States*, had ruled on the admissibility of incriminating statements in cases involving more than one defendant charged with participating in the same crime. Although Franz's statement was competent evidence against Franz, it amounted to inadmissible hearsay against Curtis. If Franz and Curtis stood trial together, the state would not be able to use its only solid piece of evidence: Franz's statement.

Schottland and Uliano felt the statement was none too solid to begin with. It occurred to them that Franz had confessed under questionable circumstances; the *Miranda* rule, based on a 1966 Supreme Court decision on the rights of an accused in custody, might have been violated. "We had some indication that Franz told the local police in Texas he wanted to consult an attorney," Schottland explains, "just like our client did. He was given some number for a Bar Association or something like that but nobody got back to him. Then the Monmouth County detectives conducted an interrogation over a long period of time, seven or eight hours, I think. Under *Miranda*, if an interrogation goes on too long, or the police use trickery or deny someone their constitutional right to an attorney, the courts can step in and say that it wasn't a voluntary confession.

"Besides," Schottland continues, "Franz never confessed to committing murder. I felt a forceful attorney could argue that his client was guilty of some kind of killing-in-hot-blood form of manslaughter, precipitated by a week of domestic violence and threats."

"Franz's statement actually helped our client," adds Uliano. "A boy, Franz, who's just killed someone, was holding a gun and standing over his mother who's lying on the floor with blood running out of her. You would think rage would dictate blowing his friend's head off. Instead, when Curtis tells him it was an accident, he accepts it."

The autopsy report indicated that the bullet that killed Rosemary Podgis entered on a steep downward angle. Schottland accompanied his private investigator, Dennis Fahey, to 401 Euclid Avenue where the two men re-enacted Curtis's actions, with Fahey playing Curtis to Schottland's Rosemary Podgis. Fahey would rush towards the entranceway leading from the dining-room into the kitchen, jumping back each time that he nearly collided with Schottland. After trying it several times, Schottland satisfied himself that it was possible for Curtis to have accidentally shot the woman in the way he had claimed. Fahey was also following up a possibility that the firing mechanism on Curtis's rifle was faulty.

"Not only did it look like a defensible case," recalls Schottland, "it looks like I could win it. They were going to try Scott Franz first. If Tommy Smith didn't do a deal with the state, and I had been assured by Mr Smith right along that he was going to defend the case, then I was in a good position. Let's assume his client was found guilty of manslaughter. There would be no incentive for Scott to testify against Bruce, and without Scott I don't even think the state can place Bruce at the house at the time of the shootings. It was just a lot of circumstantial evidence that didn't add up to a very strong case against my client.

"So I'm sitting back, more or less smiling, and watching to see what happens."

Outside the window of Piedmont Airlines Flight 306, Investigator William Lucia stared into a cloud bank. He and his companion, Bill Duerr, had left Newark an hour earlier and now felt the plane descending into Boston. It was a warm fall day: Monday, September 13.

The Podgis murder case had presented a number of bizarre twists that gave it an intriguing character. It was hardly surprising that Lucia found it difficult to view the case as anything but murder, followed as it was by the deliberate efforts of two boys to conceal their deeds. Since it was Duerr's first homicide, Lucia ran off a checklist for his benefit: Consider the condition of 401 Euclid Avenue; walls wiped clean, bloody evidence and rifle shells placed in garbage bags in the basement. Consider the transporting of bodies — "Jeezus, Billy, they were the Franz kid's *parents*" — across the state where they were unceremoniously heaved into a ravine in the dead of night. Franz had admitted that he and Curtis returned to the house on the morning of July 6, twenty-four hours after the shootings, but fled at the sight of a police car. Those boys, Lucia suggested, intended to complete the cover-up right then.

Consider the rifles discarded in a storm drain, and Franz's admission that gloves used during the commission of the crime were thrown into a dumpster in a nearby mall. Then the five-day journey diagonally across the south-eastern United States — with stops at a gambling casino in Atlantic City and the World's Fair in Knoxville, Tennessee — before they were discovered in Texas. When the local police first questioned Franz, he denied any knowledge of his parents' deaths. It was only later, when Lucia and Duerr arrived, that he admitted his involvement.

"Not like any accident I've ever seen," concluded Lucia. "And if it was self-defence, why wouldn't Franz have called the police?"

One week away from his thirty-eighth birthday, Lucia prided himself on retaining the instincts as well as the physique of a street hustler. Franz and Curtis may have been a couple of teenagers — and Curtis, "some kind of brain" — but Lucia figured he didn't have to relate to them in order to "read" their characters. "It's just a sense you develop when you deal with people," he explains. "Call it experience, I guess, although some people never comprehend it and others do. Sometimes a person don't have to say a word. It's their actions, their movements, the way they look at you or don't look at you. The way they carry and handle themselves."

After landing in Boston, Lucia and Duerr connected with Air Canada Flight 608 bound for Halifax, Nova Scotia. When they were aloft, Lucia let his mind wander over what he knew of the boys thus far. Franz was easy: a dime-store punk with eyes that lied. He could be counted on, Lucia felt certain, to tinker with his story to his advantage; the challenge would be determining how much truth they were getting. Franz had told something at least vaguely like the truth in Texas, and Lucia remembered saying to him: "Listen, I may have to live with what you're saying, but I don't believe your little ass."

Duerr had told Lucia about some kind of scam involving A-1 Specialty Services and Supplies Inc., where Franz worked. Its owner, Suresh Khosla, said he had given Franz $1,000 last January to buy scrap automobile mufflers in Nova Scotia. ("What the hell for?" Lucia asked. "They extract platinum from the catalytic converters, or something like that," Duerr shrugged, and both men rolled their eyes.) According to Khosla, Franz had come to work on June 28 and told his employer he had stored mufflers in a garage at the home of a schoolmate, Bruce Curtis, in Nova Scotia. Two days later Franz again appeared, this time with Curtis, and told Khosla that he and his friend would return to Canada over the Fourth of July weekend with his parents' van to collect the mufflers. But on Friday, July 2, three days before her death, Rosemary Podgis called Khosla and told him she was opposed to her son going away over the holiday weekend. Lucia was certain there were no mufflers stored at the Curtis home; he suspected Franz had been bilking his boss.

Frankly, Lucia didn't much care. Franz's small-time embezzling had no connection to the homicide investigation except insofar as it revealed a side of Franz's character. Lucia also wondered whether Rosemary Podgis might have confronted her son about Khosla's money. Domestic disputes had been ignited over less.

Lucia was less certain about Curtis. There was something he thought of as "not right" and "strange" (his favourite expression) about the boy, although he was at a loss to define it. After returning from Texas in July, he had told first-assistant prosecutor Paul Chaiet: "The first time I laid eyes on him I thought he was strange. Even with minor adjustments here and there, this was not your normal, social, everyday type of person." Lucia admitted he was influenced by a past experience. "I've seen these types before," he continued. "I can go back years ago to when I was a detective on a local police department. I ran into a guy like this. Very, very much like Curtis. I said to my partner, 'we're gonna see him again.' And we ended up tear-gassing him out of a house."

There was also a disturbing report from Nova Scotia that was one of the justifications for this trip to Canada. The RCMP, while making routine inquiries at King's-Edgehill School on behalf of Lucia, learned of two poisoning incidents allegedly involving Franz and Curtis that had occurred at the end of the school year, less than three weeks prior to the Podgis shootings. No charges had been laid, and the outcome of this avenue of investigation was unlikely to be of direct use in court, but Lucia knew it might provide important evidence of the mental state of the boys.

"One thing people don't understand about doing this job," Lucia explains, "is that it's not a one-way street. We're not just looking to discredit someone. If we come up with information that substantiates a person's story, that's fine. Whatever we found in Nova Scotia, good or bad, that's the way it would have went."

After landing in Halifax, Lucia and Duerr drove directly to Windsor. The next morning, at 11:15 A.M., accompanied by Constable Bernie Corrigan of the RCMP detachment in Windsor, they interviewed Colleen Smith. Later, Lucia wrote in his report:

> Ms Smith described Bruce as a loner, very lazy, not into sports. She stated Bruce did not believe in God. She stated that Bruce liked the book, *Lord of the Rings*, and often used a dwarfish [sic] language associated with that book.

> Ms Smith described Scott as somewhat of a storyteller. She said Scott told her that his sister was a doctor or lawyer. He also told her that he had been shot in the neck and she was led to believe it may have had

something to do with his father's business. She said
Scott organized a few weekend parties in Hallifax [sic].
She mentioned an incident where Scott told her he
did not want his father's name on the home mailing
list.

Ms Smith stated that Bruce and Scott spent a lot of
time together on computers. She said that toward the
end of their last year Bruce and Scott developed a feeling of superiority.

At 12:20 P.M., Lucia and Duerr spoke to the headmaster, Tom
Menzies, in his office.

Regarding Scott Franz, Mr Menzies advised that Scott
attended the school for the better part of four years. He
described Scott as an ordinary, bright teenager.
Nothing unusual about him one way or the other...
Scott used to do some recording for him. Only remembered one discipline problem when Scott was caught
with liquor. He said Scott was not liked by some of
the others.

Regarding Bruce Curtis, Mr Menzies advised that
Bruce was there for two years. He described Bruce as
very clever and quiet. He said that Bruce was very into
computers. He stated that during his last year, Bruce
developed an attitude that he was superior to others.

Curtis's friend, Mark Brennan, a pale, blond-haired boy of
seventeen, was ushered into Menzies' office at 1:15 P.M. Several
years later, Brennan would recall his session with "Bill-and-
Bill" contemptuously. "They were typical cops, sitting there
with some RCMP guy. They were asking outrageous questions
to see how I'd react. They asked me if Bruce and Scott were
homosexuals. I said, 'No way.'"

The interview, reduced to Lucia's minimalist prose, read:

Mark stated he met Bruce and Scott at the school, but said he did not know much about Scott and was more friendly with Bruce. Mark described Bruce as being interested in computers and chess. A typical brain. He said Bruce showed no interest in girls at the school. Said Bruce enjoyed reading "Lord of the Rings." He said Bruce was an alright guy. Mark stated that Bruce mentioned the existence of Satanic worshipers [sic], but told Mark he did not believe in the devil either.

Over the next three days, Lucia and Duerr interviewed a number of students and teachers. Reverend John Ford, an English and Latin teacher and the school's chaplain, told them that Curtis was "a first rate student, very quiet and conscientious." He remembered that when he discussed confirmation with him, Curtis said he "couldn't make the committment. [sic]"

After interviewing John Naugler, Lucia wrote:

Mr Naugler stated that he never taught Scott and could not think of anything out of the ordinary about him. He found Scott to be quick-witted.

Regarding Bruce Curtis, he advised he taught Bruce for two years. Mr Naugler advised that first he thought of Bruce as a quiet, shy fellow. Nothing out of the ordinary. Then in the twelfth grade Bruce seemed to be ignoring him. He said he rather ignored Bruce because Bruce ignored him.

Mr Naugler stated that he once spoke to Bruce's father and told him he was trying to get Bruce to get out of his shell. Bruce's father reportedly said good, because that was one of the reasons Bruce was there.

Mr Naugler advised that he and another teacher, Mr Nimmo, together taught a course titled *Theory of Knowledge*. Bruce was enrolled in that class. He said that one thing that stuck in his mind was that once Mr Nimmo asked students for definitions of the words "body," "mind," and "soul or spirit." In response to a definition of soul or spirit, Bruce stated that he couldn't give one because he didn't believe it existed.

One afternoon, Constable Bernie Corrigan took Lucia and Duerr to the Bridgetown RCMP detachment, where they spoke to two officers about their investigation into Patricia Hirtle's death on May 17. It had been ruled a suicide. The principal and vice-principal of the high school in Lawrencetown said that although Curtis and Hirtle had been in grade ten together, "they knew of no special relationship between them."

The longest section of Lucia's report was devoted to a meeting with Curtis's former room-mate Rory Kempster that took place on the evening of Wednesday, September 15 at his home outside Halifax. His father was also present.

Rory described Bruce Curtis as a unique type of person, not normal. He said that Bruce dreamed that computers would take over the world. Rory said that Bruce told him he did not believe in God. He said that Bruce was out of the norm with most people. Bruce thought of himself as the number one person in the world. People had to meet his standards. Rory said that Bruce changed from grade eleven to grade twelve concerning his attitude toward teachers. He lost respect.

Rory stated he recalled Bruce telling him one time that his dad had called and told him someone had died. Bruce looked through the obituaries in the newspapers and when he found the name in the paper he showed it to Rory. Rory recalled the name to be Patricia Hirtle.

Rory also informed us of an incident that he said took place around 4:00 A.M., on a Sunday morning in May.

Rory said he was laying on his bed with his eyes closed. Bruce and Scott were over by Bruce's bed, apparently unaware that he (Rory) was actually awake. Rory said it sounded to him like Bruce and Scott were chanting. Bruce then came over to Rory's bed. Bruce had a black glove on his hand and made some motions with his hand and then went back over and talked to Scott some more. Then Bruce and Scott got under Rory's bed. Scott then got out from under the bed and was holding something over Rory. Rory stated that he was scared during the whole thing and at this point he swung his pillow at Scott and told them both to get out and not come back that night. Rory said that Bruce told him the next day that it was an experiment they were doing. It involved seeing whether someone would wake up if drops of water were dropped on the head of a sleeping person.

Rory said that Bruce told him on more than one occasion that he had attended devil worshipping meetings when he lived in Toronto.* Rory advised that Bruce received Communion even though he did not believe in God, because he liked the ceremony. He also liked the ceremony of the devil worshipping. Rory said he roomed with Bruce from 1/82 to 6/82 and knew Bruce for the two years he attended the school. Rory stated that Bruce did not talk about his family too much. Bruce told him he did not like his younger sister.** Bruce mentioned that his parents were both in the Army at one time or the other. Bruce told Rory he wasn't scared of death. Rory advised that Bruce told him his parents had already served their purpose in

*This may have been an error, since Curtis never lived in Toronto.

**The reference to a younger sister was probably either misunderstood or incorrectly typed into the report. It may have referred to Carol, the younger of Curtis's two older sisters.

life, which was to raise and educate him. Bruce said he would not sacrifice his life to save his father's. Rory said that Bruce liked Steven [sic] King Books - 2001 Space Oddessy [sic].

Regarding Scott Franz, Rory said he didn't bother much with Scott because he didn't trust him. He said you could never tell when Scott was telling the truth. Rory said that Scott once invited him to go to Switzerland with Scott and his family. Scott said they had a cottage there and his father was a big shot in Pan Am.

Rory advised that when Bruce and Scott were together they didn't want to bother with anyone and no one wanted to bother with them.

When asked about his comments three years later, Kempster said: "The Bruce I knew was agreeable. He had no problems obeying rules no matter how petty. It wasn't that other students didn't like him, they didn't know him. We'd discuss our classes and do labs together because we both liked to learn new things. We played chess and read the same books. I'd read *Lord of the Rings* three or four times so I knew all the characters and, yes, I knew the Dwarvish language.

"He did have a superior attitude and was incredibly stubborn. We often had discussions, and I can only remember winning one of them. If he wanted to he could talk rings around anybody but it wasn't in his character to do that. He didn't act evilly or destructively, but he was one type of person when he was with Scott. It's not that he became a bad person, but I chose not to be around in Scott's presence. Did I know Scott's inner workings? No, but I didn't like him. I found him a sneaky, shady character. I think Bruce began to develop some of Scott's sneaky, secretive traits, although he hadn't really changed. In June, on Graduation Day, he was just as nice as he was at the beginning of the year as long as he wasn't with Scott.

"Why did he spend time with Scott? I'd be the smartest person in the world if I knew that."

On Friday, September 17, Lucia and Duerr flew back to New Jersey with a lot of information about Franz and Curtis and an invitation from Bernie Corrigan to come back for some moose hunting some day. Lucia felt they had assembled reasonably accurate portraits of the boys. While it was not clear that either of them had done anything illegal, and it was even less clear whether Curtis's role was that of a participant, an observer or a dupe, Lucia was convinced that together Franz and Curtis were responsible for the deaths of Al and Rosemary Podgis.

"What we're digging for, to be perfectly honest, is to find out exactly what happened. I believe in my mind that those boys killed those people. We'd confirmed a profile of Curtis as a super-intelligent loner. He was strange, to put it mildly. With Franz's street-sense — and that's what he was, a con artist — and the other guy's intelligence and weird outlook, they were a very dangerous combination. No question about it."

An initial motion to reduce Bruce Curtis's $250,000 bail was denied on October 6, 1982.

Five weeks later, on Friday, November 12, Charles Uliano appeared with Joe Dempsey before John Ricciardi, the trial judge assigned to the case, in Freehold, New Jersey. First assistant prosecutor Paul Chaiet represented the state. Uliano intended to request that bail be reduced to 10 percent of the total: $25,000.

Since the only evidence against Curtis was Scott Franz's statement, and according to *Bruton* that statement was inadmissable if the two boys were tried together, it seemed likely that the state would move to sever the cases and try Franz first. Chaiet was supposed to have made a motion for severance by November 19 but hadn't notified the defence team yet. It was Chaiet's position that the delay was caused because "I haven't received one shred of discoverable evidence from the defence." (Under New Jersey law, both sides are required to exchange information gathered in preparation for trial, including statements given by witnesses, photographs, the results of forensic or other scientific tests, and the intention to call expert witnesses to testify.) In the meantime, Curtis had spent four months in the Monmouth County prison.

Uliano began by pointing out to Judge Ricciardi that investigators with the prosecutor's office had a statement from Barbara Czacherski verifying that her brother had said Bruce described the shooting of Rosemary Podgis as an accident. Uliano also reminded the judge that Franz's statement was inadmissable evidence.

"It's only inadmissable today," Judge Ricciardi said.

"That's right," Uliano admitted. "That's what we're doing at this juncture."

"Maybe Mr Franz is going to plead guilty tomorrow. Maybe they're going to cut a deal with him. That may happen fifteen minutes from now, for all I know. Then it becomes admissable, wouldn't it?"

Uliano nodded. "That would be true."

Changing his tack, Uliano informed the court that if the bail was reduced to a more manageable sum, Jim Curtis would place his property in escrow and allow the Clerk of Monmouth County to hold it. In addition, an RCMP officer from the Bridgetown detachment, ten miles from the Curtis home, would keep in close contact with the family. In conclusion, Uliano gave his personal assurance that Curtis would be present to stand trial.

In handing down his decision, Judge Ricciardi touched on three bothersome elements: the seriousness of the crime, the possibility that the defendant might flee and the fact that he was not a resident of New Jersey, nor even of the United States.

"We have, from what has been outlined to me, a statement by a co-defendant indicating that this defendant, Bruce Curtis, committed a murder," Judge Ricciardi began. "You can read it any number of ways that you want to, but it certainly can be interpreted to indicate that Bruce Curtis picked up a gun and blew his mother away, or blew the woman away. Scott Franz makes that statement.

"I do not, and cannot, take from my mind the fact that it is indicated by the state that they were tracked to Pennsylvania and finally caught in Pennsylvania, or was it Texas?, not sitting around waiting. We have a situation where they were on the road fleeing when they were apprehended. There is no reason to believe Mr Curtis would not do the same."

Judge Ricciardi addressed the issue of Curtis's nationality. "Canada is right above the United States, you know, right above the border," he observed, "and we have a tendency at times because of our relationship with our friends to the north to think that it is merely an extension of the United States...but it is a foreign country...."

"I don't think that the sanctity of his parents' farm, the fact that his parents are putting up a farm, or somebody putting up twenty-five thousand for him if 10 percent were allowed, is going to deter Mr Curtis under the circumstances of this case, and knowing what he is facing if he is convicted, and knowing that his co-defendant has fingered him...I don't think that's going to deter him from grabbing a sleeping bag and an overnight tent and off he goes. I think the likelihood of fleeing is great, particularly if he is in his own familiar territory, his own familiar corner of Canada."

Judge Ricciardi glanced up at Uliano and Chaiet. "Accordingly, I deny the motion for reduction of bail."

The following Monday, November 15, Uliano wrote a memo to Mike Schottland. After summarizing Ricciardi's decision, he added: "I'm convinced that Chaiet has now examined this file and knows he has a problem. He is going to have to sever. He is giving, as an excuse to why he hasn't moved for severing, that the discovery hasn't been completed... If Chaiet severs, that is when we will make a renewed application for reduction of bail for this kid since he is going to have to linger in jail for a while while his co-defendant is being tried. I am pretty certain, though, that the court is going to be reluctant to lower the bail unless we can assure them that the kid is going to be in this jurisdiction."

Uliano appealed the decision to the Appellate Division of the New Jersey Superior Court on December 6. The motion was denied. Three weeks later, he filed an appeal with the New

Jersey Supreme Court. Jim and Alice Curtis prepared an affidavit in support of the appeal. In it they stated: "We saw him [Bruce] in August of 1982 at the Monmouth County Jail. On Tuesday and Wednesday, December 28 and 29, 1982, we had the opportunity to again visit with him. We were both shocked by the change in his appearance. He is lethargic, pale, unkempt and we are very concerned for his continued welfare.

"While we are not able to raise $250,000 to post bail for him, we would be able to provide our own personal guarantee and recognizance plus $25,000 cash payment to the Clerk of Monmouth County if the Court alters his bail status to permit payment of ten (10%) percent. In addition, we can both personally guarantee he will remain in the Monmouth County area and Mrs Curtis will temporarily change her residence and remove herself to a location in Monmouth County, of which she will advise the Prosecutor and the Court.

"There is a trial date which is fixed for February 14, 1983. Bruce's condition has deteriorated to such a point that we actually feel there will be a deleterious effect on his ability to testify and assist in his defense at the trial. When he was arrested, he had just graduated from a private academy and had been accepted to college. He was a bright, articulate young man. After five and one-half months at the Monmouth County Jail he has changed considerably and if at trial it is necessary for him to testify, his witness value has been severely encumbered by the conditions at the jail and their effect upon him."

The appeal was denied.

Jim and Alice Curtis, accompanied by Lorraine and Bob Peever and Jennie Curtis, visited Bruce at Christmas. They learned that the Salvation Army had made its rounds but the Monmouth County jail did not offer church services. Since they were not permitted to leave gifts of any kind, Jim and Alice put money in Bruce's commissary before they left as usual. Alice remembers that her son appeared subdued and that it was difficult to idly chat with him at that time. "We didn't stress Christmas. It's difficult to know what will make a person feel bad, you see. You endeavour to avoid saying, 'Oh, you missed this,' or 'Wish you could have seen what so-and-so did at the Sunday School Christmas concert.' "

Three weeks later, Peever received a disturbing letter from her nephew:

January 19, 1983

Dear Aunt Lorraine:

I am feeling quite depressed. I am very sick of this place and all its stupidities. I hope it is only a month till this ordeal is over, I can stand that. I don't feel like doing anything except reading and more reading, entering a book, and not coming out, to ignore anything and everybody. My corresspondence with people has fallen, I feel loathe to write, nothing new to say, not wishing to enter upon their lives, a shell, a wall, the escape mechanism. To have seen part of my family was a contradiction of emotion and thought, that brought on a slow building yearning and longing and a swirling of feelings that left the mind cluttered with trash. Only a book, a novel of profound importance or the inner workings of a great mind, can mask such things and cover them effectively, a retreat from confusion into logic and another person. I feel weird, and this must all sound weird to, since I found a way to release conflicting emotions, by mirroring them on paper whether they are what is truly felt. This lessens the whirling the torrent that must be sorted. Often in dwarvish I write what I suppose could be called, or likened to stream of consciousness, what flirts through my brain and stays long enough to utter its speech to the empty crowd. It goes then, maybe returning, maybe not, making room for the next unbidden thought. Some of these writtings, along with some of your letters, grandmas and some friends letters, are gone, stolen. I had them in fourteen unmarked, self-stamped envelopes. I wanted to keep them so I had intended to mail them home, but before I could, the envelopes plus all the letters were taken. They left my pictures and twelve other envelopes filling with letters. Also missing was a large amount of commissary. I know who took them and I know why, to pay another inmate for some marijuania. They threw the letters in the garbage. I can do nothing, except depress myself by thinking of what is lost, part of me, part of my mind and development, and parts of other people speaking across the gap. I can do nothing except sit here and play cards with the person that did it, being joyous and jovial to maintain the tenuous relationship I have with these people of nothing. I am in despair, I am in agony, I am overdramatizing. I should shut up and go to sleep. I will write tomorrow. It will be better then, more distant and closer, the metronome continues.

Next day. I am feeling much better. I doubted whether I should send what I wrote above, but it illustrates that at times my spirits sink....

On Wednesday, January 12, 1983, a bitterly cold evening, Schottland's private investigator, Dennis Fahey, met with Barbara Czacherski at 401 Euclid Avenue in Loch Arbour.

"Would you describe Mr Podgis's attitude and disposition?" Fahey asked.

"He was stubborn and quick-tempered," Barbara answered. "He was verbally violent. He displayed physical violence towards his children when they were little. He stayed to himself, didn't have any friends and never socialized except for parties from work at the post office. He never went out to dinner or dancing. There were hardly any family gatherings during the last ten years. Often he would not speak to his own children, let alone his step-children, for years at a time without any reason. We would have no idea why all of a sudden he decided not to talk to us."

"Do you know where the late Alfred Podgis was employed?"

"He was employed by the United States Post Office, English-town, New Jersey."

"Who was his immediate supervisor?"

"I was his immediate supervisor."

"Could you tell me what Mr Podgis's work habits were," Fahey asked, "and his attitude towards work?"

"Al was a Rural Carrier," Barbara told Fahey, choosing her words carefully, "which means he drove his own car and delivered mail from the right-hand side of the car. Recently he was taken out on street supervision with the Post Master and the Post Master's comments regarding Alfred's behaviour for the day were that" — Barbara read from a piece of paper — " 'Everything in the morning seemed to go along smooth, but as the day wore on his temper got shorter and shorter and any little thing and every little thing seemed to bother him, like garbage cans in front of mail boxes or parked cars, or kids asking him for rubber bands.'

"We have a file at work on the complaints that we had received about Mr Podgis's attitude towards the customers, things he had said to them that were off-colour. The customers would call and complain to either myself or the Post Master."

Fahey pursued this line of questioning. "How many complaints have been lodged against Mr Podgis at the post office within the last year?"

"We have on file at least ten to twelve written complaints not counting the number of phone complaints. We started a file on Al in order to initiate action to terminate his employment."

The implication of this statement would be noted by Schott-land and his defence team later. He thought it extraordinary to hear a stepdaughter calmly describe her participation in an effort to have her stepfather fired from his job. There was clearly no love lost in their relationship.

"Are you familiar with any violent actions on the part of Alfred Podgis towards his family?" Fahey continued.

"At one time, after an argument over my curfew on a Sunday morning, he heaved the kitchen table at me with all the breakfast goodies all over it. They splattered on the walls and floor. I moved out of the house the next day."

"Do you know of any other instances of violence displayed by Alfred Podgis?"

"I was here one time when Al hit my sister Dawn with a baseball bat on the leg. Many times he had physical confrontations with Mark, and I remember him chasing Scott, but Scott was always too fast for him to catch."

"Would you describe the relationship between your mother and stepfather?"

"They constantly, constantly fought. My mother worked at the same post office as my stepfather. At work they put on airs that they were friendly. They would take coffee breaks together, but at home they were constantly fighting. My cousin Patrick took a trip with them to Canada. He said all they did was fight with each other from morning to night."

"Did you ever observe any physical injuries to your mother that you considered suspicious?" inquired Fahey, following up on a point he had established with Barbara during a preliminary conversation.

"Yes, many times. One time, when she came home from a vacation in Florida, she had a black eye. She broke her back on another occasion. She said that the dog had pulled her down the back steps, but we didn't believe that. She also had her arm broken twice."

"Would you describe the temperament of your stepfather in the house in regards to your mother and the children?"

"They were constantly screaming at each other. Neither one of them would give in on their point of view."

"Do you know of any instances in which your brothers or sisters ran away from home?"

Barbara nodded. "Mark, Dawn and Scott, the youngest three children, all ran away from home. Scott was living with Al in Maine, and he ran away from Al. My mother wasn't even living with them at the time. Dawn and Mark both had arguments with Al and ran away. They were so frightened, they wouldn't come back home."

Fahey focused his last questions sharply. "Were these children afraid of Al verbally abusing them or physically abusing them?"

"They were afraid of him both physically and verbally."

"Were there any threats made against the children?"

"Yes," Barbara said. "Numerous times he said: 'If you do that again, I'll kill you.' It ended up with pushing and hitting the children."

Michael Schottland was pleased with Fahey's interview. Barbara Czacherski confirmed the impression given in Scott Franz's state-ment — and echoed by his client — of a violent, frightening household. It somewhat mollified his anger over the surprising turn the case had taken eight weeks earlier: the autopsy report on Al Podgis, prepared the previous July by Dr Halbert Fillinger, had given no estimate of the distance from which the fatal shot had been fired. Then, on November 22, following a meeting with Fillinger in the Philadelphia Medical Examiner's Office with Paul Chaiet, William Lucia and three other investigators, Fillinger agreed to testify that Podgis had died of a contact wound to the head. When Chaiet called Schottland to inform him, Schottland exclaimed: "That's ridiculous, Paul. It's not in his report. Where are you getting that from?" To which Chaiet replied: "I met with the guy, and he really feels that way." Schottland wondered how long Franz's lawyer, Tommy Smith, would remain inclined to plead self-defence in the face of an expert witness's testimony implying that Franz had held the muzzle of a rifle against his stepfather's head — probably while he was asleep — and fired.

Schottland did not have to wait long to find out. The follow-ing week, Smith requested that the body of Al Podgis be exhumed. Smith wanted an independent pathologist to examine the wound to determine whether it had been caused by a bullet fired from close range or at a distance of several yards, as his client claimed. Smith's motion was denied. Although Smith had not yet called him to confirm it, Schottland smelled a plea bargain in the air. He instructed Fahey to find out more about conditions in the Podgis house.

On January 20, 1983, Dennis Fahey interviewed Mark Franz at his former home, 401 Euclid Avenue.

"Can you describe to me the relationship between your mother and Alfred Podgis."

"They fought often. He once broke her arm by pushing her down the stairs. We had to take her to Jersey Shore for treatment."

"Did you personally observe Alfred Podgis place his hands on your mother and push her down the stairs?"

"Yes."

"How did your mother get to Jersey Shore Medical Centre?"

"We called an ambulance."

"On any occasions, did you observe your mother crying?"

"Yes, I saw her crying a lot of times. On many occasions I could hear my mom crying in her bedroom for long periods of time. She would cry herself to sleep."

"Could you describe the relationship between Alfred Podgis and the other children in the house?"

"The other Franz children all despised him. They really did."

"How did he treat these children?"

"Starting with Barbara in 1969, he threw a completely loaded breakfast table on her. Rosie, he broke her pinkie on her right hand. He gave me numerous beatings."

Fahey pursued the extent to which domestic tension was present in the home. "How often would Alfred Podgis assault you on a weekly basis?"

"Every day we'd get into it."

"What do you mean by 'get into it'?"

"It would start up verbally and then he would come after me and beat me up."

Mark then admitted his stepfather had fired a .22-calibre rifle at him. Fahey asked him how often.

"Twice that I can distinctly recall."

"While living with Alfred Podgis, were you ever in fear of your life?"

"Yes," Mark answered. "He put me that afraid of him."

A week later, Fahey spoke with Charlotte Pierce, a former girl-friend of Mark's who was around the Podgis home in the mid-1970s, when Mark was in his late teens.

"Could you describe the interaction between Alfred Podgis and his family?" Fahey began.

"I observed violent interaction."

"Would you describe this violence which you observed?"

"One time I saw Mr Podgis chase Mark with a metal object which I believe was a poker from the fireplace. I believe that if Mark didn't run, Mr Podgis would have hit him with it and hurt him or might have killed him."

"During this period of time, was there any conversation between Mark and Mr Podgis?"

"Yes," Charlotte replied. "Mark was trying to sneak upstairs to make sure he was asleep so we could sneak up to the third-floor bedroom to go to sleep. Mark said 'Wait here.' I was between the kitchen and the dining-room. A few minutes later I heard a bang and Mrs Podgis screaming, 'Get the hell out of here, you son of a bitch.' Then I heard Mr Podgis scream, 'What the fuck are you doing here?' Mark said, 'All I want to do is go to sleep.' Mr Podgis said, 'I don't want you here. You had better get the hell out of here before I kick your ass up and down the stairs.' I heard more banging, yelling and screaming and people running down the stairs. Mark was first, Mr Podgis was right behind him.

"By the time Mark had gotten to the end of the stairs, Mr Podgis had grabbed him and punched him in the chest. Mark doubled over and Mr Podgis grabbed him by the hair, pulled his head back, grabbed him by the throat and jacked him up against the bannister. Mr Podgis said, 'I'll kill you, you mother-fucker.' Mark finally got away. Running through the dining-room he tripped over a chair and fell with Mr Podgis behind him all the way. Mr Podgis went behind the TV and grabbed a metal object, I believe it was a poker. He had it in his hands raised like he was going to hit Mark with it. We both ran out the back door, falling over each other. We just ran like hell."

Fahey asked Charlotte about other incidents.

"On another night," she told him, "Mark and I wanted to go

into the house to sleep. This time I was waiting outside by the back door. Mark went inside the house and a few minutes later I heard the same kind of things which I heard the last time: yelling, screaming, running and banging. Then I heard a 'pop' noise, like someone would step on a paper bag and it would go 'pop.' I heard more scrambling and yelling. The noises were getting closer so I ran to the gazebo in the backyard and hid behind it.

"Mark came running out of the back door, running towards me. He was calling my name: 'Charlotte, where are you?' I said, 'Mark, wait for me,' and I started running with him. He was out of breath and obviously scared and had a look of horror on his face. He said, 'That son of a bitch tried to shoot me. He tried to blow me away.'"

Fahey interrupted. "When you say, 'He shot at Mark,' who were you referring to?"

"Alfred Podgis."

"On any subsequent day, was there any conversation between yourself and Mark Franz or any other person regarding this shooting incident?"

"The next day Mark called his mother. He started yelling at her, 'Why did you let that crazy bastard shoot at me? Don't you care if he shoots me, are you as crazy as he is?' Mrs Podgis said to Mark, 'I wish he did shoot you, you son of a bitch. Too bad he didn't.'"

Fahey was uncertain how much of these breathless tales to believe, but even taking into account the likelihood that the girl was exaggerating, there would certainly seem to have been something very wrong at 401 Euclid Avenue.

"How would you describe Mr Podgis's disposition?"

"He was very violent. Super-violent, malicious. I never heard him say a nice word towards the kids. He didn't have any regard for anyone but himself."

"What type of language did Mr Podgis use in the house towards the children and his wife?"

"Filthy language."

"Did you ever observe any physical or tell-tale marks on Mark Franz?"

"Yes, I did," Charlotte said. "Mark had black and blue marks around his face, eyes and nose. It looked like someone had given him two black eyes. Mark said that Mr Podgis had punched him in the nose."

"Did Mark Franz ever relate to you any stories of abuse at the hands of Alfred Podgis?"

"Mark told me that before they moved to New Jersey, they were living in Ohio. He told me that Mr Podgis had tied him to a chair, beat him and left him there for a couple of days."

"During the period of time that you were familiar with the Franz family, did you believe that these children were victims of child abuse?"

"I believed it from the very beginning when I met Mark. They were definitely victims of child abuse."

"Did you observe at any time a confrontation between Alfred Podgis and Rosemary Podgis?"

"Yes, I did. They were screaming back and forth at each other like maniacs. They were in the bedroom, I was in Dawn's room. I heard him yelling and screaming, and Mrs Podgis crying. They were arguing violently, like the roof would fly off any minute. During these times I was afraid they would come after me and hurt me. I was scared to death."

One question Fahey and Schottland had posed to Curtis was why, when he had heard shots on the morning of July 5, 1982, he hadn't run out the *front* door of the house, which was adjacent to the living-room. Curtis had explained that during his entire visit to 401 Euclid, he and Scott had always used the kitchen door. He had understood Scott to say that the front door was not used.

"Do you know if the front door to the Podgis house was operable?" Fahey asked Charlotte.

"The front door was never used. One time, when Mr Podgis was chasing Mark, Mark tried to open the front door but couldn't."

"Is there anything you would like to add or delete to this statement?" Fahey concluded.

Charlotte nodded. "Those children were abused and mistreated. Those people did not care about their kids."

When Schottland read transcriptions of these interviews, he was even more convinced that his client had become involved in a domestic dispute with a long history. He wondered what course of action Tommy Smith would take. Certainly Smith couldn't complain that Schottland hadn't been sharing his defence preparations with him.

"I still felt Scott had a good shot at manslaughter," Schottland recalls, "what with the build-up of tension over the days the boys were hanging around that house."

As first-assistant prosecutor for Monmouth County, Paul Fred Chaiet had been acting as legal adviser to William Lucia and the other investigators on the Podgis case since July 1982, and for the last few months he'd been more actively involved in shaping the case for trial. In the fall he had rebuffed Michael Schottland's offer to plea bargain. Schottland wanted manslaughter, but that would mean that his client, Bruce Curtis, would end up serving a three-year sentence. Although Chaiet had told the judge at Curtis's bail hearing in November, "I don't accept the fact that the killing of the mother was an accident in any way, shape or form," that was by no means the only reason he had declined to horse-trade with Schottland. Frankly, there was nothing to be gained by it. Chaiet didn't believe Curtis's story, and he was confident he could get a murder conviction if given half a chance. If he cut a deal with Curtis, he still had a fight on his hands with Franz. But Halbert Fillinger's willingness to testify was like being dealt an ace in an otherwise unpromising poker hand. Fillinger provided leverage against Franz, a witness to support the forensic data that showed blood, bone and brain tissue blown *down into* Al Podgis's pillows. Chaiet knew that this suggested Franz had not fired from across the bedroom while his stepfather was sitting up in bed. Now Chaiet was working on Tommy Smith, trying to convince him that his client's best move was a guilty plea to the murder charge. Chaiet would promise to recommend that Franz receive a reduced sentence so long as he testified against Curtis. (Although a prosecutor cannot provide any guarantees to a defendant entering into a plea bargain, judges routinely follow such recommendations.) Chaiet, who enjoyed assembling tidy, complex strategies, had a very good feeling about this one.

Chaiet, who turned thirty-eight on Valentine's Day, was particularly fired up in the winter of 1983. He had experienced a health scare a few months earlier when doctors diagnosed *acromegaly*, chronic hyperfunction of the pituitary gland, usually associated with middle age, that results in excess production of growth hormones. Although the symptoms were gradual, they included elongation and enlargement of the feet and hands, nose and lips, and certain facial bones. He had entered NYU Medical Center in December where they had removed what turned out to be a non-cancerous tumour in his pituitary gland. Doctors described the condition as "life-shortening" but not "life-threatening," although Chaiet tended to regard the two as somewhat the same. An experience like that, Chaiet could attest, made you think about things.

But Chaiet didn't feel bad about his life. He was born in East Orange, New Jersey to parents of Russian-Jewish ancestry. He attended Asbury Park High School where he was an average student who excelled at sports. He was captain of the football, baseball and swimming teams there and later, when he attended Albright College in Reading, Pennsylvania as a history major, he was a star offensive guard. He'd dreamed of turning professional but, as he would wryly explain, "I was short on talent, size and speed. All the essential ingredients." He'd never thought about becoming a lawyer, but since he enjoyed a pre-law course he decided to use his National Collegiate Athletic Association post-graduate scholarship to study at Villanova Law School. He graduated from the law school at Rutgers University in 1971 feeling as though he'd found his calling. Chaiet had enjoyed acting as a child, but had given it up because of peer pressure by the time he reached high school. Suddenly he realized the courtroom, like the football field, was a forum in which he could be the centre of attention, a performer.

After an internship in county legal services followed by a

judicial clerkship and a stint with the city attorney for Asbury Park, Chaiet knew he was attracted to public service. He liked the idea of being "a servant of the law." In 1973, he became an assistant prosecutor in Monmouth County.

County prosecutors are the chief law enforcement officers in each of New Jersey's twenty-one counties. Unlike district attorneys, their elected counterparts in most states, they are appointed by the governor with the consent of the senate. Which is not to say the role of county prosecutor is not profoundly political. At one time, a change in the state's governing party led to a wholesale housecleaning of the prosecutor's office as soon as the previous administration's appointee completed his five-year term. Although prosecutors still use the office as a stepping-stone to a political career or high-profile appointment, by 1973, the year Democrat Brendan Byrne became governor in a landslide victory and Chaiet was hired, many assistant prosecutors were beginning to see themselves as career officials.

In 1978, at a time when Monmouth County was becoming increasingly urbanized and its population was growing, an ambitious and politically adroit lawyer named Alexander Lehrer was appointed county prosecutor. Lehrer, a broad-shouldered, fair-haired man with handsome features, was called "Hollywood Al" after his flamboyant personality and fondness for publicity. If Al ever died, his colleagues joked, it would be from overexposure to flash bulbs. While he was also called "an egomaniac" and "a totally political animal" by friends and foes alike, he modernized the prosecutor's office by requesting that a state-organized task force overhaul its operations.

While Lehrer was not personally responsible for every change — "Al would take credit for a sunny day if you let him," one observer noted — it was generally accepted that he transformed the prosecutor's office from a local operation into a sprawling, efficient bureaucracy during his tenure. Policy and politics were his domain; he entrusted the most important prosecutorial duties to his skilful, competitive and apolitical first assistant, Paul Chaiet.

"Guys like Lehrer need a guy like Chaiet to watch the store while they get their picture taken," explains one former assistant prosecutor who respects Chaiet. "But Paul would never become county prosecutor. There's a lot of discretion and political decision-making, and Paul's pure prosecutor. He lives in a world of black and white. No grey. He's a straight shooter who loves the system, the pristine system. That makes him a good lawyer and a really good prosecutor."

On Tuesday, March 1, 1983, at 10:25 A.M., Chaiet and William Lucia met with Scott Franz, Barbara Czacherski and Tommy Smith. They sat around a large table in a conference room in the Monmouth County Prosecutor's Office, on the third floor of the County Court House in Freehold. Smith outlined the circumstances facing Franz: the forensic evidence, Fillinger's testimony, the opportunities Franz had to leave the house. Lingering beneath the surface of the discussions was another issue: a trial would be expensive. Barbara was financing her brother's defence, but she lacked the resources to mount a drawn-out campaign. No decision had yet been reached on Scott's claim to his share of his mother and stepfather's estate, although he was named in their will along with the other Franz and Podgis children. That added a dimension to what Smith apparently felt was a shaky case at best. Chaiet and Lucia discussed with Franz his status in jail with other inmates if he were to plead guilty to murder and testify against Curtis.

After Smith recommended a plea bargain, Franz agreed to co-operate with Chaiet. At first he did not venture far from his original statement. He repeated to Chaiet and Lucia that his mother had asked him to buy .30-.30 ammunition for his stepfather. He also told them that on the morning of July 5, his stepfather had sat up in bed and fired a shot at him, and that his pillows had been behind him. He again confirmed that Bruce had told him he had heard shots and was running out of the house when the gun went off.

But further questioning produced several revelations. Regarding the poisoning incidents at King's-Edgehill, Franz denied any knowledge of what had happened to Colleen Smith's milkshake, but Lucia wrote in his report: "Scott said that Bruce said he would probably try and make Antonio sick. Bruce was mad because Antonio was first in physics and Bruce had helped Antonio with the work." Franz also told them that Curtis had said Al Podgis "would have to pay for what he did." He added that Curtis wanted to break a window in the Scout in order to get the guns because they "shouldn't go into the house without protection," and that he, Scott, had loaded but not cocked the weapons. Franz claimed that after the shootings he picked up the phone to call the police but, according to Lucia's report, "Bruce shook his head 'no.' Bruce said they would have to get rid of the bodies and he would take care of everything." Lastly, Franz told Chaiet and Lucia that he did not believe the shooting of his mother was an accident.

"Wha-at!" Schottland exclaimed angrily when he heard the news. "I was very happy Tommy was defending the case," he told Fahey. "But look at this. It's a shitty plea" — Schottland's eyes popped like a minstrel singer's — "*Shitty!* Even if he'd tried the case and Franz was found guilty of murder, the kid wouldn't have got hit any harder. The case could have gone for murder, or aggravated manslaughter or manslaughter or not guilty. Copping that plea was a lay-down."

For some reason, Schottland thought, Tommy hadn't prepared the case with his customary vigour. Nowhere on that autopsy report had it mentioned a contact wound. Where was Tommy Smith's expert witness to counter Fillinger? After he'd cooled down, of course, Schottland considered the possibility that Franz had told Smith something that made a plea bargain the most sensible alternative. One thing was for sure, it looked as if it was he, Schottland, who was going to need the expert witness now. After setting up a time for Fahey to interview Franz, he sat down with his detective to discuss the areas he wanted Fahey to cover.

At 1:00 P.M. on Thursday, March 3, Fahey sat across a table from Franz in an airless room in the Monmouth County jail. Fahey switched on his tape recorder.

"Scott, uh, have you been told by Mr Smith or Mr Chaiet that they would be unable to make a case against Bruce Curtis without your testimony?"

"No," Franz replied sullenly.

"You were never told that?"

"No. They said it would be hard to make a case."

"Who said that?" Fahey asked.

"Mr Smith, I believe."

"And how did he say it?" Fahey persisted.

"They said that they needed me. That the prosecution needed me."

"When did he tell you this?"

Franz mumbled a reply.

"Pardon me?"

"The other day."

Fahey stared at the boy. "Was this the day that you pled?"

"Yes, or the day before."

Fahey then asked Franz about the rifles. "When we talk about the weapon that was used, did you see Bruce Curtis cock the gun in question?"

"No."

"You didn't," Fahey said. "Who loaded that weapon?"

"The weapon?" Franz repeated. "Bruce had to."

"Why?"

"Because they were not cocked when they were brought into the house."

"What does Bruce Curtis know about guns?"

"I don't know for sure."

Fahey moved on to the shootings. "Okay, after the incident had taken place, who suggested calling the police?"

"I did."

"You did? Why?"

"Because of what just happened."

"What was Bruce's response to it?"

"He looked at me and shook his head, 'no.'"

"Did he say, no?"

"No."

"Did he physically try to stop you from taking the phone?"

"No."

Fahey closed in. "So what actually happened was you reached for the phone, and you decided you weren't going to call."

"I picked up the phone," Franz said firmly. "I looked at Bruce. He shook his head, 'no,' so I put the phone down."

Fahey moved on to the question of purchasing the ammunition. Franz, who kept his head lowered, peering up occasionally from under his eyebrows, maintained that it was his mother who asked him to do it.

"Did you think it was unusual for your mother to ask you to go out and buy ammunition for your stepfather?"

"Yes."

"Why did you think that was unusual?"

"Because she never asked me to do it before."

Franz lit a cigarette. He smoked nervously yet defiantly. When Fahey asked him about the poisoning incidents, he said he wouldn't discuss it while he was being taped, on the advice of his lawyer.

"Okay," Fahey told him. "So what you're saying is that you don't want to commit yourself to the situation on tape. Let me ask you this then, do you know who was involved with this?"

"Yes."

"Can you tell me who it was?"

"Bruce."

"Are you telling me that Bruce Curtis poisoned that teacher?" Fahey probed.

"Not the teacher, no."

"Did Bruce Curtis poison someone?"

"Yes."

"And you have knowledge of that?"

"Yes."

"Did you poison anyone?"

"No."

Fahey then tried to establish the planning and execution of events after the shootings. "After the incident, when you were driving, did Bruce Curtis ever drive the van?"

"No."

"At no time did he get behind the wheel and drive?"

"No."

"Whose idea was it to get rid of the bodies?"

"Bruce's."

"What did Bruce say?"

"I said, 'What are we going to do?' and he said, 'We have to get rid of the bodies.'"

"Let me ask you another question in that regard," Fahey said. "When you were driving down the road, whose idea was it to stop near that Interstate and get rid of the bodies?"

"We stopped at a rest stop," Franz replied "and there was a map for a State Park where there was a lot of woods. So we both looked" — Franz paused — "I looked at it, more or less, and I said it was there. Both of our ideas, really."

Fahey knew it was important to nip at Franz gently, in the hope that some of his admissions could be used to trip him up in court.

"You looked at the map and then what happened?"

"There was a wooded area the next exit up so we just drove up through there and we looked for a spot."

"And you were driving at this time?"

"Yes."

"Okay," Fahey said. "What was the conversation going back and forth between you and Bruce?"

"I can't remember the exact words, more or less."

"Who finally came to the decision that you were going to put the bodies there?"

"Bruce finally agreed that that was a good spot because we drove further down and he goes, 'No, let's go back to that spot.'"

Fahey sought an opening. "Now, when he said he agreed, then you started the conversation? He agreed with you, with what you said?"

"He agreed at the rest area, more or less."

"Okay, so the conversation was going back and forth between the both of you," said Fahey. "He agreed, then you initiated the conversation, if he agreed with you?"

"I don't remember who initiated it, to tell you the truth."

"Did Bruce Curtis" — Fahey shifted direction — "Did you intend to kill Alfred Podgis when you were going upstairs?"

"No."

"Did Bruce Curtis know, have any idea, that you were going to kill Alfred Podgis when you went upstairs?"

"As far as my knowledge, no."

"Was there any conversation between you and Bruce Curtis concerning the death of Alfred Podgis prior to you going upstairs that day?"

"Yes."

Fahey paused. "There was. And what was that conversation?"

"It varied from time to time where, you know, Bruce said we'd have to pay Al back for making us stay out in the trailer when it was raining and stuff."

"Was it your understanding," Fahey inquired carefully, "that 'pay back' means that you were going to kill Alfred Podgis?"

"No."

"What was your sense of idea at that point? What did he mean, 'pay back'?"

"I don't know."

"Were you in fear that Bruce Curtis might kill Alfred Podgis in that regard?"

"He goes on like that a lot," Franz explained. "So, no."

"So he's exaggerating a point?" Fahey asked. "He was exaggerating a point?"

"I don't know."

Fahey decided it was time to pursue the actual moment of the shootings. He knew that Franz had never deviated from his account of the events upstairs but that now, since the plea bargain, he was implicating his friend.

"What was said and by who when you went upstairs that morning?"

"When I went upstairs," Franz said, "I went in and I was standing in front of my stepfather and he said... I asked him, you know, why did you shoot at me the day before? He just started to yell, saying I was no better than Mark and I was stealing everything in the house. Then he lifted up his rifle and I said, 'That's only going to give me a limp and this will finish you.' Then he started to shoot."

"How many times did he shoot at you?"

"Three or four times."

"Up until that point, did you have any intention of killing Alfred Podgis?"

"No."

"Did Bruce Curtis have any intention of killing your mother, Rosemary Podgis?"

"Not as far as I know."

"Did you and Bruce Curtis ever discuss the possibility of ever killing your mother, Rosemary Podgis?"

"No."

Fahey softened his voice. "Did you love your mother?"

"Very much," mumbled Franz.

"Were you very close to your mother?"

"Yes."

"Why did Bruce Curtis shoot your mother supposedly?"

"I don't know."

"Did you think he wanted to see her dead?"

"It's a possibility. I'm not sure."

"Why do you say it's a possibility?"

"Because I found out a few things."

"At that time?"

"At that time? I don't know."

"In your statement you state that Bruce was afraid," Fahey reminded Franz. "What was he afraid of?"

"Maybe what was going on upstairs."

"What did Bruce tell you in regards to the shooting of your mother?"

"That he shot her."

"Why," Fahey asked. "Did he say why."

"He said he was running out of the house and his gun went off. That's what he told me."

"Did he indicate that the gun went off by accident?" Fahey asked, knowing that Franz's sister said that he had.

"No."

Later, Fahey again addressed this subject. "Did Bruce say anything to you regarding the shooting of your mother?"

"Only that he shot her."

"And he said that he was afraid."

"I don't know like when you're saying that he was afraid," reacted Franz angrily. "When did he tell this like?"

"You have it in your statement that he said that," Fahey told him calmly. "That you stated that Bruce Curtis said he was afraid."

Franz stared down. "Yes."

"Is that what he said to you, that he was afraid?"

"Afterwards, yes."

"We're talking about after the shooting?"

"Yes."

Franz took a drag from his cigarette and exhaled. Fahey continued.

"Whose idea was it to hide the guns?"

"Bruce's idea, my spot."

"So it's both of your ideas?"

"Yeah," Franz replied. "He said we'll have to hide the guns and we were going to throw them in the woods and I said, no, because somebody might be drinking beer or whatever. So I threw them down the storm drain."

Schottland had told Fahey that he thought there may have been a *Miranda* violation when Franz gave his original statement in Texas the previous July. Franz told Fahey the interrogation had started around dinner-time and lasted until two in the morning.

"Did they feed you during this period of time?"

"They gave me a soda."

"Did they give you any food?"

"Some crackers."

"Nothing other than crackers?"

"No."

"Prior to giving this statement, do you recall requesting to talk to an attorney?"

"Yes."

"Did you make an attempt to make a telephone call to an attorney?"

"Yes."

"Could you tell me what happened?"

"I asked to call a lawyer, an attorney."

"And what was their response?"

" 'There's the phone and the Bar Association number is on the wall right next to it.' "

"Did you call the Bar Association?"

"Yes."

"And what happened?"

"I phoned and they asked for the name and phone number of a relative. So I gave them my sister's."

Fahey nudged the tape recorder towards him. "Did a lawyer contact you after you made the call?"

"No."

"Were you expecting one to contact you after you made the call?"

"Not really."

"Why?" Fahey asked.

"Because she sort of gave me a snotty," Franz said, referring to the woman who had taken his call at the Bar Association.

"Did you want to be represented by counsel at that time?" Fahey asked.

"Yes."

Although the officers may have been treading a fine line in Texas, Fahey was unsure Schottland could make a *Miranda* case — based on violation of an accused's rights during an interrogation — out of Franz's interrogation. He returned to the evening before the shootings. "Why do you think Bruce wanted to get the weapons out of the Scout?"

"For protection I guess."

"Did he say anything to you in regards to that?"

"He said, 'We have to get the guns before we go back into the house.' He didn't say why."

"And what was your response to him?"

Franz shrugged. "'Alright. I guess so.'"

"Did you think it unusual for him to be taking a gun into your home?"

"It would be now," Franz admitted. "But at the time I was going along with anything he said."

"Why?" Fahey asked.

"I don't know."

Franz told the detective that he had been frightened because his stepfather had taken a shot at him the previous day. When Fahey asked him if he'd ever heard of his stepfather shooting at any of the other children, Franz said he hadn't.

"Describe for me how Alfred Podgis came to putting the weapons into the Scout, please."

"We were out in the back cutting the grass," Franz told him, "and he came out in his bathrobe with four guns, four boxes, four rifle boxes. He put them in the back [of the Scout], went back into the house, got two more and then went back in the house and got some towels and put them in."

"Did you ever ask your mother why he put the weapons out there?" Fahey asked. Franz shook his head.

"Did you and Bruce discuss why he put the weapons out there?"

Franz shook his head again.

"And you didn't think it was unusual for him to take such an action?"

"Well," Franz said, "he looked like he was hyper at the time. That's why I said [to Bruce], 'He looks hyper, we better leave before he goes off.'"

"When you say hyper, what do you mean by that?" Fahey asked.

"Hyper is mad about something. He was upset."

Fahey asked Franz a few general questions about his friendship with Curtis and the private school in Nova Scotia. Then he returned to the original interrogation in Texas.

"Going back to the statement that you had signed and given in Texas, did at any time anyone say to you, 'Stop what you're giving me, what you're giving me is foolish. I can get a better statement from a baby or a child'?"

"No, not quite like that," Franz replied. "It was how I would remember things before, and he said, 'a ten-year-old,' he said, 'I could get a better chronological statement from a ten-year-old,' or something to that effect."

"Were you tired?"

"Yes."

"Were you frightened?"

"Basically, yes."

"And you stated prior that you wanted an attorney present? You had called an attorney and were hoping to get one?"

"Yes."

"And what was their response?"

" 'Did he show up?' And I said, no. And then they said, 'Are you willing to talk to us?' and I said, yes."

"Going back to Mr Smith and Mr Chaiet," said Fahey, "or rather Mr Smith's conversation with you in the Court House the other day, the day that you pled, would you just tell me again how the conversation went?"

"They were saying if I, they were saying the prosecution's offering a thirty-year maximum with a fifteen [year] stipulation before eligible for parole. And Mr Smith said he would try to work fifteen down and he can only go as far as ten. So after a conversation with my sister, whatever, I agreed."

"Okay," Fahey said. "And did at that time Mr Smith mention that the State would be unable to make a case against Bruce Curtis without your testimony?"

"He did not say that exactly. He said it would probably be a bit difficult."

Fahey decided to throw out one sensitive question now that the interview was nearly over. "Have you ever been sexually involved with Bruce Curtis?"

"Never." Franz answered firmly.

They had been sitting in the tiny room for eighty minutes.

Fahey asked whether Franz would be willing to sign the interview once it had been typed up and he had had a chance to read it.

"No."

"Why?" Fahey asked.

"Because I'm not signing anything else."

By March 1983, a few weeks before he would have written his final first-year examinations at Dalhousie University, Curtis had been in prison for eight months. Shortly after his incarceration, in July 1982, Curtis's family bought him subscriptions to a newspaper, *The Toronto Star*, and a national newsmagazine, *Maclean's*, so he could read news about Canada. By late 1982, his family had enrolled him in an introductory philosophy course offered as part of a correspondence program at Queen's University in Kingston, Ontario. Curtis exchanged rambling philosophical discourses with his aunt, Lorraine Peever, who would later comment: "It was obvious to us that unless we established some kind of rapport with Bruce he might disintegrate completely and suffer a breakdown." Among the books they discussed was Plato's *Apology*, which deals with, among other things, concepts of justice and the trial of Socrates.

Peever photocopied resource material for him to use when writing his required ten essays. Twice, after mailing essays to Queen's, he was notified that they had never been received. Finally, after laboriously reconstructing them from rough notes, he mailed them to Peever who forwarded them to the university. The family suspected officials at the Monmouth County jail of sabotaging Curtis's mail. By March, when he should have been preparing for his final examination, Curtis was too distracted to study.

March 2, 1983

Dear Aunt Lorraine:

Things are really happening now. I have been moved again. On Monday I went over to the court house with Scott to go in front of the judge. It was to be decided whether the trials were to be separate. The outcome was that the judge could not decide until it was decided whether some of Scott's statements were admissable as evidence. So they were going to decide about the evidence on Tuesday. On Tuesday morning both of us go over. Scott goes up and I stay downstairs in the "pen" waiting to be called up. I wait all day until four when I go back to the jail and discover that I have been moved again. My new residence is now Civil 1 or C-1 in one of the isolation tanks. It is a fairly big stone room about twelve by six with a raised platform for the mattress, a sink and toilet, a shelf, a mirror, a light cage and a ventilation duct. Also a window which is unfortunately covered over by a sheet of metal. The entrance to the room is by way of a steel door with a small square window the same size as that in the visitor's area. It is quite spacious compared to what I am used to.... The people themselves are a collection of the strange and weird, the ones who are not locked in. This is the wing where the "crazies" and "shot-out" people go and the ones who can not get along on a normal wing. It is seen as punishment to be sent here. I feel much safer here....

Anyway, all Wednesday I waited here for news but no one came. On Thursday, my lawyer came over and told me what was happening. Scott plea bargained. The judge, Arnone, can give him up to thirty years and must stipulate that Scott remain in prison between one third and one half of the sentence he gives him. So if the judge gives Scott thirty years he must set a period between 10–15 years before Scott is eligible for parole. The catch is that the time Scott gets depends on his performance in nailing me to the wall. So he is going to make up alot of lies and twist everything to make me look bad, in hopes that the judge and the prosecution look kindly on him when it comes time to sentence. It is all very ridiculous and barbaric. I have read several articles in magazines condeming the practice of plea bargaining which is very widespread. Only a small percent of cases go to trial, most people pleading guilty to a less crime. If you go to trial and are found guilty the court almost always goes for the big sentence when deciding. One example given in one of the articles about the stupidity of the system was the one concerning Jean Harris, the former headmistress of a prominent private school who killed the author of the Scarsdale Diet. She was offered a plea bargain of manslaughter which meant she would be eligible for parole in 3–5 years. Instead she decided to go to trial and tell her story which she felt excused her. She was found guilty and under New York law must serve 15 years before eligible. The court traps alot of people this way but some of the criminals get off to. The lawyer also said my trial is this month, March 14. I keep on thinking it is April but it is March. Only ten days to go before the start. I very much doubt if there will be any delay now since the prosecution too was anxious to go ahead. He wants to get it over with before Scott has to be sentenced. The lawyer will be up every day next week for final preparations. The next few weeks are going to be extremely nerve racking and hectic. But it will also be a delight to have things finally moving, deciding my fate. All this is most likely why I am here cut off from the rest of the jail. I am sure they do not want me to talk to Scott or influence him in any way....

I had a dream a few days ago which was filled with people and locations that would not mean anything except maybe for the ending. The whole dream took place at my old school at Lawrencetown. I was walking around the school building to get to the main door, the one I usually went into. When I went into the building from this door I was in a small store, the size of a classroom. The walls were packed with all things imaginable, it was very new and the owner was still putting things on the shelf. He asked me if I wanted to buy anything. I replied no and hurried through to the back entrance which lead into a twisting passage lined with glass cases filled with all sorts of candy. When I turned the corner I came into another classroom sized store filled with stationary supplies. I thought to myself this is where I want to be. The store became a classroom with a nice old lady teacher to one side. She was packing papers into a cardboard box. I went up to her and asked eagerly whether she had read my paper yet. She said no, she was packing them in the box to take them home and read them at her leisure. Some of the remaining essays were tacked up on a bulletin board from which she was taking them. I reached up and got mine and discovered to my horror that someone had replaced my essay with evidence from the case. I was upset because I thought I had done a good job on the essay and now it was lost forever. I explained this to the nice old lady and she seemed to understand and she knew that I had passed in an essay because I had given it to her myself. The end. I guess the most obvious explanation is that I feel my academic work has been replaced by my involvement in this case.

March 6/83

Dear Bruce:

I think your parents are somewhat puzzled by Scott's plea, and so am I. Do you have any insight? What does your lawyer say? Could it possibly be related to his financial situation? I'm glad that you have a good lawyer because I think there may be some plea bargaining going on. I hope that your lawyer will be able to attack Scott's character if he testifies against you. I think you will feel badly about that but if others play dirty, you have to do all you can to defend yourself. You have already suffered too much. I think that under the circumstances your lawyer should certainly be able to prove that his testimony is unreliable. The trial is going to take a lot of energy and be a test of your patience and endurance....

Grandma and I are very pleased that you got the parcel from McMaster [University bookstore] and hope that these books will help you through these difficult days. We are still thinking about what we will do in regards to the trial. I am definitely coming for most of it. Expect me about Wed. of first week. We haven't decided about Grandma. She wants to come but your parents think she shouldn't, because of her age and diabetes. I think that she should phone Anne and Blake and ask their professional opinion. If they think it's O.K. then I think Grandma would be happier to come because she worries a lot about your mom and dad.

Regarding the trial itself, I know your lawyer will be giving you lots of coaching but just in case he forgets, there's a couple of things I want to tell you. The prosecutor will be trying to make you contradict yourself and get you confused and flustered. To counteract this I would suggest that you go over your rules of debating, know your facts, anticipate questions etc. Try to maintain a calm, composed aire [sic] at all times and through your manner, speech etc., let the jury know that you are a person of integrity. Remember, always, to say 'Sir' or 'Ma'am' to the person addressing you. It's one of those things that has a strong psychological effect on the jury. If you have to talk about what happened in Scott's home, always refer to his parents with respect. I know that you know all these things but, since I know this next week will be hectic, I thought I'd remind you.

Well, I must go now. It's midnight. The essay is

finished! Bravo. See you soon. Much love (and some hugs), Aunt Lorraine

On the afternoon of Thursday, March 3, after Franz was interviewed by Fahey on behalf of Michael Schottland, he was taken to the Monmouth County Prosecutor's Office where Chaiet and Lucia awaited him. He related several examples of his stepfather's brutality towards his brother and sister, Mark and Dawn, as well as himself. On one occasion, when he was living in Maine and his stepfather was having an affair with an eighteen-year-old, he told them, he had been beaten up. Podgis had struck his mother on the Friday before the shootings as well, he said.

Chaiet had the rifle that killed Al Podgis brought into the room. Franz stared at it. "Show us what you did with this gun after taking it out of the Scout," Chaiet instructed him. Franz demonstrated the way he had unloaded eight shells from the weapon and reloaded it with four. Then he had loaded the remaining four shells in the other rifle and given it to Curtis. Again he insisted that the rifle had not been cocked when he handed it to his companion.

"What did you intend to do after disposing of the bodies?" Lucia asked.

Franz told him that he and Curtis had planned to retrieve the remaining evidence and pick up their personal effects. It was Curtis, Franz said, who wiped the rifles with a sheet before they were dropped into the storm drain behind the Hilton Inn, and then wiped the bullets before throwing them out the window of the van. When Franz reviewed a copy of Curtis's account of the events that was included in Harry Brunt's psychological report, he pointed out certain parts that weren't "truthful."

Franz then provided the prosecutor with another addition to his story. In his report, Lucia wrote: "Scott advised that he had something to tell us that he had not told us before. The reason that his stepfather brought the guns out to the Scout was because Al had found guns of his [Al's] under Bruce's mattress. Scott said that when Al brought the guns to the Scout, Bruce said, 'He must have found it.' Scott said that during his late night-early morning discussion with his mother, she told him the guns were found under Bruce's mattress. In jail, Bruce told him they were under the mattress, referring to the guns."

Five days later Franz was led painstakingly through his story again. It remained essentially the same, although his additions had now taken up permanent residence in the narrative. Finally he admitted to Chaiet that he had not told Fahey about the guns under Curtis's mattress. Chaiet and Lucia had been easy with him thus far; Franz's own presentation proved that. There was a crispness to his words and his eyes darted furtively.

Suddenly Chaiet said: "Are you telling us the whole truth? I'm not so sure you're telling us everything you know."

Franz stared down and chewed his lip.

"Look, Scott," Lucia told him sternly, "truth is truth, facts are facts, common sense is common sense. It'll go better for you if you tell us."

Eventually Franz told them he had more to say, but wanted an opportunity to talk to Curtis, to warn his friend that he would be testifying to "the whole truth." Chaiet was perplexed, but he decided he had nothing to lose by letting Franz and Curtis meet. At nine the next morning, Franz was ushered into a room at the Monmouth County jail. Schottland and Fahey stood outside the door. Later, Franz jotted down notes from their conversation in a nearly illegible scrawl for Chaiet and Lucia.

s[cott]:
> Bruce, I just wanted to tell you that when I testify that I'm going to testify to the whole truth.

b[ruce]:
> I thought your statement was the truth.

> s: I'm just saying that when I testify I'm going to testify to the truth and I told Mr Smith the truth.

> b: Mr Smith knows the truth?

> s: I told him the truth. You're facing two 25's [years] and I believe Mr Chaiet will offer you the same plea as he did

with me, a 30–15. Do you have anything you want to tell, or ask?

B: Are you prepared to get up on the stand and testify to the real truth?

S: Yes. Anything else?

B: Are you going to be out on bail?

S: I don't know. Yes, sometime this week I believe.

M. s[chottland]:

Are you guys almost finished? I'm getting dirty looks out here.

S: Yes.

B: So you're going to testify with the truth, but which one?

S: I have to be very pesky about what I say and I can only say that I'm testifying to the truth. Schottland is giving me the evil eye so I better leave. That's all I wanted to tell you.

B: Yea. OK.

M.S.: Did the prosecutor ask you to talk to him?

S: No.

Mr F[ahey]:

Could you unbutton your shirt.

S: Yes.

M.S.: You see we're in a lot of trouble and I'm not supposed to be doing this.

S: [scratched out]

M.S. and Mr Fahey searches me.

Mr F.: I'm sorry about this.

S: It's o.k.

M.S.: All I can say is Good Luck again.

S.: Thank you. Goodbye.

Later, Chaiet and Lucia pondered Franz's evidence. It was clear he was carefully measuring everything he told them, but both men were accustomed to deception when dealing with witnesses entering into a plea bargain. "How often do we know 100 percent?" Lucia asked. "I'm satisfied he's telling us pretty much what happened."

Chaiet frowned. The many holes in the case bothered him.

The "magnetic point," as Oliver Wendell Holmes had described the hub around which the evidence in a criminal investigation clusters, was weak. Although some family members indicated there had been a history of problems at 401 Euclid, Chaiet could not find a clear motive for either boy to have shot either of the parents. Yet when he considered their actions afterwards — concealing the crime, dumping the bodies, attempting a getaway — he was absolutely certain of their complicity.

"Pick any one of Franz's stories," he said to Lucia. "Supposedly the stepfather found guns under Curtis's bed. In any case, he carries these weapons out to the Scout on Saturday morning. The kids say they saw him while they were cutting the grass. The next morning, Sunday, Franz says his stepfather takes a shot at him that ends up in the hallway door. That night they break into the Scout and get out two rifles. But the bullet found in Podgis's pillow and the one dug out of the moulding around the hallway door match."

Lucia nodded. "So the rifle that killed Podgis is the same one that he used to shoot at Scott, if that ever happened."

"That make any sense to you, Bill?" Chaiet asked. "Why'd Podgis lock his guns in the Scout anyway? Probably because somebody was messing with them. So Scott wants us to believe that his stepfather put them in the Scout on Saturday, went out later to get one that he uses to shoot at Scott on Sunday, then locks it back in the Scout in order for it to be the same gun that kills him Monday morning."

Chaiet had no doubts about Franz's cunning. The previous fall, an RCMP officer had informed Lucia that Franz had telephoned Colleen Smith, his computer-science teacher at King's-Edgehill School, saying he was out on bail. He'd wanted to know what had been said to the New Jersey investigators. But Franz had never been released on bail: the call had been made from the Monmouth County jail. Chaiet suspected his chief witness was probably not telling "the whole truth," but trials themselves were just forums to get something settled. When that mechanism became too costly and time-consuming, around the 1960s the legal system adopted a marriage of convenience called plea bargaining. It was neither inherently good nor evil; it was simply accepted as workable and, for the most part, equitable. It was a prosecutor's job to present as much of the evidence as possible in court; the jury would decide its veracity.

"Our case depended on Franz," Chaiet admits years later. "Without Franz we didn't even know who shot who. We had the physical evidence, but that's like having all the dots with only a few of them connected."

"To begin with, I was somewhat surprised he pled. Certainly the self-defence issue could have been raised with respect to Scott Franz. But personally, even if we hadn't had Fillinger, I think that any attorney would have had a difficult time squaring Scott's testimony with self-defence. He had all kinds of opportunities to leave that house, yet he brought guns inside himself. When you take into account going to Sears to buy rope, packing up the parents, running off to Texas, we had a pretty good case. And I still think Curtis was more active in what happened afterward than we know. I never believed he was any bumpkin going along for the ride.

"That's another funny thing. I found Scott reluctant to say things that were incriminating towards Bruce. It was like pulling teeth. If he'd wanted to come in and bury Bruce he could have, but he seemed to be trying to protect him in a limited sense."

With the trial of Bruce Curtis only a few days away, Michael Schottland sat at his desk staring at an elaborate, five-page chart outlining the inconsistencies in Franz's statements.

During Fahey's interview with Franz on March 3, 1983, Fahey asked about the rifles. "Fahey: Do you have a reason why you think he would have put them in the Scout? Franz: No." But in Bill Lucia's report four days later, the following statement appeared: "The reason that his stepfather brought the guns out to the Scout was because Al had found guns of his [Al's] under Bruce's mattress." Elsewhere in the report he wrote: "Scott said that when Al brought the guns out to the Scout, Bruce said 'he must have found it.'" And in Lucia's March 11 report, he wrote: "Scott stated that in jail, Bruce told him that he had the guns under his mattress just in case."

In Franz's original statement, given to Lucia in Texas on July 11, 1982, he said: "I went to the Scout and opened the door with a piece of wire." Eight months later, after agreeing to plea bargain, Lucia's March 7, 1983 report quoted Franz as saying: "Bruce wanted to break a window in the Scout to get the guns."

In his original statement, when describing the confrontation with his stepfather on the morning of the shooting, Franz said: "My stepfather was laying in bed." Yet on March 7, 1983, Lucia wrote: "He said his stepfather was sitting up when he shot at Scott. The pillows were in back of his stepfather."

Franz's account of the moment of shooting also varied. In his original statement, Franz said: "I ran towards the door and fired." In Lucia's report of August 22, 1982, after talking to Barbara Czacherski, he wrote: "She stated Scott told her that he felt this was his chance and he pointed the rifle, closed his eyes and fired." In his report of March 7, 1983, Lucia wrote: "Scott said he cocked his gun after his stepfather took a shot at him."

In his original statement, after discovering his mother had been shot, Franz told Lucia that Curtis screamed, "What are we going to do?" "At first I said I didn't know, and then I said we got to get rid of the bodies." But on March 3, 1983, two days after signing his plea agreement, Franz told Fahey: "I said what are we going to do and he [Curtis] said we have to get rid of the bodies." Then on March 7, Lucia's report read: "Scott said they had to get rid of the bodies."

In Lucia's report of August 22, 1982, he wrote: "Scott told her [Barbara Czacherski] that Bruce said he shot accidentally." Yet on March 3, 1983, when Fahey asked Franz why Curtis had shot his mother, he answered: "I don't know." In Lucia's March 7 report he wrote: "Scott stated that he does not believe that Bruce's shooting of his mother was an accident." And on March 11, after a telephone conversation with Dawn Franz, Lucia recorded the following conversation: "She said that Bruce said to her, 'I'm really sorry, I didn't mean to do it.' Dawn stated that she spoke to Scott on the phone before talking to Bruce and Scott told her that it was an accident."

Franz vacillated wildly, Schottland thought. The details of his account changed with the wind, producing a muddle that aided the defence as much as the state. The inference Schottland favoured was the obvious one: that Franz had changed his story only *after* the plea bargain. That was in keeping with the profile of Franz as an opportunist and a schemer with a history of deceitfulness. One could argue that the most accurate version of the truth was likely to be his original statement, made just six days after the shootings and favouring Schottland's client. (Of course, Schottland was not unaware that a jury might conclude Franz had initially lied to protect his friend.)

When Schottland reviewed his case it looked strong. There was ample evidence that the week Curtis spent at the Podgis home had been filled with tension, threats and at least one assault. He began jotting notes on a yellow legal pad. First, there was the nature of Rosemary Podgis's wound, which indicated that a bullet had entered at a steep downward angle consistent with a rifle that was being carried loosely, rather than aimed, when it discharged. He also had, thanks to Fahey, some evidence indicating that Curtis's rifle was faulty. The location of the shooting, at a sharp U-turn between the dining-room and the kitchen, supported Curtis's claim that he had collided with the woman. Despite his rural background, Curtis had had no experience with firearms. (Lucia, Schottland knew, had tried to enlist the testimony of Ed MacInnis, a teacher who conducted a hunter safety course Curtis had attended when he was thirteen. MacInnis informed Lucia that the course did not involve the firing of any weapons, and, of the rifles he brought into the class, none were lever actions. He added that Curtis was an introverted, studious boy who had never displayed the slightest interest in guns or hunting. "He wouldn't know whether a gun was cocked or not," MacInnis said. "Bruce Curtis was capable of having an accident with a firearm, but not capable of killing anyone deliberately.")

There was no motive for Curtis to have shot Rosemary Podgis,

Schottland scribbled, and furthermore, Franz had said — and his sisters corroborated — that his first reaction after discovering that Curtis had shot his mother was that it had been an accident.

Schottland then wrote the word, "flight," and listed two points. First, the judgement of a terrified eighteen-year-old in a state of shock and confusion would be understandably poor. Secondly, Curtis, the retiring boy whom his parents described as "not a leader," would have yielded the decision-making to the assertive Franz because he knew how to drive, and was familiar with both the geography of the area and the bizarre workings of his family. Franz had every reason to lie: he doubtlessly harboured some anger towards Curtis for killing his mother, whether it was accidental or not, and by currying favour with the state he would end up with a lighter sentence.

The plea bargaining irritated Schottland. Franz was more like an agent of the state than a confessed murderer. "He became one of the detectives on this case," Schottland complained angrily. "He was working with the state almost like he was on the fucking payroll of the Monmouth County Prosecutor's Office. Chaiet and those detectives were living with the guy. I was getting another supplement to the Discovery almost on a daily basis. He was there almost every day. Without an attorney! Tommy Smith wasn't even there most of the time. They exceeded the bounds of propriety. I think they enlisted his support in an unholy cause."

Schottland did know Chaiet's strategy. "Paul told me how he was going to try the case. He was going to put in all the garbage about the shooting upstairs. He was going to throw all that crap up against the wall and hope that it would drip all over my client."

Al and Rosemary Podgis

The Curtis farmhouse, Mount Hanley, Nova Scotia

Left to right: Anne, Alice, Bruce and Carol Curtis, 1965

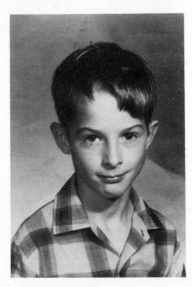

Bruce Curtis, 1971

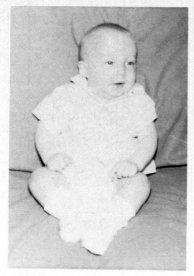

Scott Franz at 16 months

Scott Franz c1970

401 Euclid Avenue

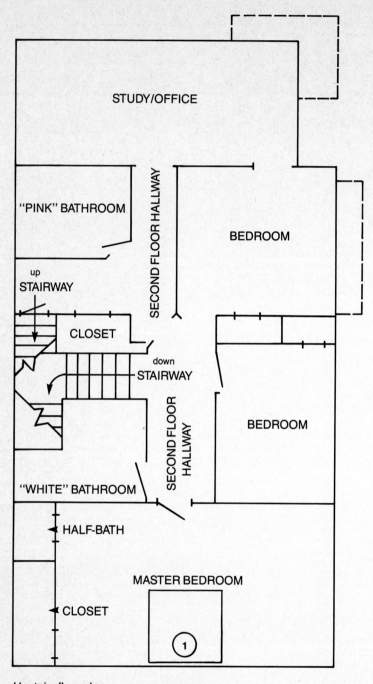

Upstairs floor plan:
SECOND FLOOR OF 401 EUCLID AVENUE
1. Probable position of Al Podgis when he was shot

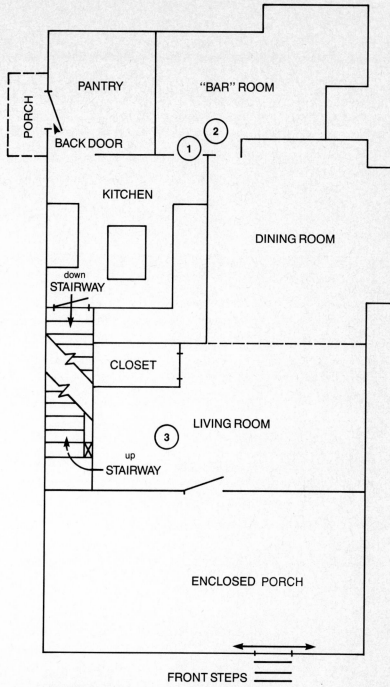

PANTRY

"BAR" ROOM

PORCH

BACK DOOR

② 1

KITCHEN

DINING ROOM

down
STAIRWAY

CLOSET

LIVING ROOM

③

up
STAIRWAY

ENCLOSED PORCH

FRONT STEPS

Downstairs plan:
FIRST FLOOR OF 401 EUCLID AVENUE
1. Scott Franz's first estimate of position of Rosemary
   Podgis's body
2. Franz's second estimate of position of Rosemary
   Podgis's body
3. Franz's estimate of Bruce Curtis's position when Franz
   came downstairs after the shootings

The rifles that killed Al and Rosemary Podgis (Curtis was carrying the longer gun)

Detective William Lucia

Bruce Curtis (left) and Scott Franz in court

Defence lawyer Michael Schottland

Prosecutor Paul Chaiet

Jim and Alice Curtis in their kitchen

Bruce Curtis, Bordentown

IV

"What I have been listening to in Court . . . is not my life.
It is the shape and shadow of my life. With all the
accidents of truth taken out of it."

Enid Bagnold, *The Chalk Garden*

[*The Chalk Garden* by Enid Bagnold printed by special
arrangement with Brandt & Brandt Literary Agents Inc.]

On the morning of Monday, March 14, 1983, the trial of Bruce
Curtis began with the selection of a jury. It had long been
believed that factors such as education, occupation, religion,
race, income, ethnic background and political affiliation could
be used to identify an "ideal" pro-defence or pro-state juror. Certain standards had gained acceptance over the years: a defence
attorney, for example, usually sought to avoid anyone with
strong church connections, prior experience as a witness or
juror, exposure to news accounts of the case, or relatives working
in law enforcement. Previous victims of crime were thought to
identify favourably with the police and prosecutor. Rigid
mannerisms could reflect harsh, inflexible personalities. An
ideal defence juror, based on a number of widely accepted

characteristics, would be a female member of an ethnic minority who was also a white-collar worker, under thirty, voted Democrat and had little or no religious preference.

These data, however, were of little use to either Michael Schottland or Paul Chaiet. Unlike some states, New Jersey law did not permit attorneys to interview each prospective juror. The courts were already backlogged with cases, so in the interests of efficiency the judge posed a few general questions and both attorneys were given a limited number of challenges they could use to reject individuals not to their liking. However precise the science of jury selection had become, the procedure followed that morning left room for little more than educated guesswork.

Nine men and five women were chosen, a full jury complement of 12 plus two alternates. Schottland would later explain: "Even though there were some pretty technical, scientific issues in the case, a jury was going to find it a lot easier to relate to all the emotional crap, the blood and guts. I was looking for technicians, people who'd like to get a little detail, and I was also looking for outdoorsmen, people who looked a little tough and probably had handled guns. They would know Bruce didn't know what he was doing with a gun.

"There were a couple of engineers up there, but I also got stuck with some housewives, and I was afraid they might kill me."

" 'Truth will come to light; murder cannot be hid long,' " began first-assistant prosecutor Paul Chaiet. "So said Shakespeare in *The Merchant of Venice*."

Chaiet scanned the jurors with a gaze at once sorrowful and stern. "Well, we are a long way from Shakespeare and this isn't any play. What we are talking about is the real-life story of two murders. The murder of Alfred Podgis by his stepson, Scott Franz, and the murder of Rosemary Podgis by Bruce Curtis" — he nodded towards the lanky boy in the blue blazer who sat at the defence table with his head bowed — "a friend of Scott Franz's."

At seven that morning, Monday, March 14, 1983, Bruce Curtis

had been taken from the Monmouth County jail to the County Courthouse. It was a four-storey, brick-and-limestone edifice that presided over a fifteen-acre tract of parkland in the centre of Freehold, New Jersey, a sleepy town of 10,000 that is the county seat. Like so many government buildings, it was modelled after Greek architecture, in this case the Erechtheum Temple on the Acropolis in Athens. Four towering Ionic columns crowned the top of a broad flight of steps, an effect designed, today as then, to humble ordinary citizens.

Curtis was taken in through a back entrance and left for two hours in a holding cell in the building's basement. He tried to read a book — a biography of Sigmund Freud — but it could not relieve his tension. Shortly before 9:00 A.M., he was led into a second-floor courtroom and seated at the defence table with his attorney, Michael Schottland, Dennis Fahey, and co-counsel Joe Dempsey who, although he was undergoing cancer treatment, chose to be present for the first few days of proceedings. Before turning his back on the spectator's gallery, Curtis saw his parents, Jim and Alice Curtis, sitting in a front row.

"Scott Franz has already pleaded guilty to the murder of his stepfather," Chaiet was saying, "and he will testify in this case. You will hear what he has to say. Obviously his testimony will be critical because he was there."

Chaiet began outlining the state's case by describing a chronology of the events preceding the deaths of Al and Rosemary Podgis. One of the reasons for the delays in Curtis's trial, apart from the prosecutor's courtship of Franz, had been the need to replace the assigned trial judge, John Ricciardi, who had suffered heart problems during the winter. The case was now before the Honourable John P. Arnone, a fifty-five-year-old father of six and son of a Red Bank, N.J. grocer. Arnone's dream of a career in law earned him the boyhood nickname, "Judge." A graduate of Georgetown Law School in Washington, D.C., Arnone returned to Red Bank, after a two-year stint in the air force, to set up a private practice. His roots in that community, twenty-five miles north-east of Freehold, ran deep: he was credited with revitalizing the local Republican party and was mayor of Red Bank during the mid-1960s, an achievement he attributed in part to active support from thirty-five close relatives living in the area. He was a churchgoer and member of the Knights of Columbus, Red Bank Elks and the Loyal Order of Moose. An avid gardener, Arnone's main departure from fellow community leaders of his generation was a disinclination to learn golf. He had been a Superior Court judge for twelve years.

Judge Arnone's first duty that morning had been to dismiss, at the state's request, two of the charges named in the indictment against Curtis: conspiring with Franz and aiding and abetting in the murder of Al Podgis. He was to be tried for the murder of Rosemary Podgis and theft of the van. Arnone's reputation within Monmouth County legal circles was that of a tough but fair adjudicator who gave both sides latitude to present their cases. When it came to sentencing a convicted offender, however, Arnone's philosophy of severely punishing wrongdoing had earned him two nicknames: "Johnny Max" and "Never-Go-Home-Arnone." In this case Arnone, who had experienced the sorrow and dislocation of his own mother's death when he was a child, could hardly regard lightly the shooting of a mother of six and stepmother of four. He listened attentively as Chaiet summarized the state's case.

Chaiet, hoping to soften a potentially contentious issue, addressed the nature of the state's plea bargain agreement with Franz. "I bring it to your attention," he told the jury, "because it is important for you to weigh the credibility of Scott Franz. Is Scott Franz telling us the truth, or is Scott Franz attempting to curry favour with the state? That is your unique province, to look at and analyze his testimony against everything else and make that decision."

Using information provided by his star witness, Chaiet moved on to the events following the shootings. "This shooting incident is alleged to have occurred at 8:30 A.M. on that fateful Monday morning. They spend a number of hours in that house cleaning up. Bruce Curtis does most of the clean-up in the master bedroom. Bruce Curtis puts the mother in a sleeping bag.... Scott will tell us that during the course of the clean-up Bruce seemed to enjoy it."

"I object to this, Judge," cried Schottland, rising quickly to his feet.

Although Judge Arnone's first impulse was to sustain the objection, he permitted Chaiet to discuss it with him at the sidebar, beyond the jury's hearing. "Scott is going to testify that while he was doing this he was smiling," Chaiet explained, "and based on that smile he seemed to enjoy it. What's wrong with that?"

"So what, Judge?" Schottland protested. "How is it relevant to this case?"

"Actions," Chaiet said before Judge Arnone could answer. "After his state of mind."

"Don't interrupt me, Mr Chaiet."

"You interrupted me during an opening statement."

Schottland turned to Judge Arnone. "I am going to interrupt if I feel I have to object. I will if it means counsel is seeking to inflame this jury, and I resent it. He has gone into great detail in his opening. He has consumed about forty minutes. I think that an opening statement has to stay within the bounds of fairness and candor, and these comments are seeking to inflame the jury against my client."

Judge Arnone turned to Chaiet. "Instead of saying he enjoyed it, why can't you say what his expression was?"

Chaiet resumed his opening statement. "He said that Bruce Curtis had a smile on his face..."

"Note my objection, Judge," Schottland said.

"...and at one point he was playing with the congealed blood of Alfred Podgis."

Schottland leapt to his feet. "I object again, Judge. I would like to make it clear...I think these comments are outside the proper bounds of an opening. He is seeking to inflame this jury against my client, and I think it is highly improper. These statements are emerging day by day from Mr Franz."

Judge Arnone overruled Schottland's objection.

"And in addition to that," Chaiet continued, "at one point in jest he came out with a piece of gum and said, perhaps this is Mr Podgis's pituitary gland."

"Note my continuing objection to this line, Judge," Schottland repeated.

"Now the central issue," said Chaiet. "The state has the burden to prove that Bruce Curtis murdered Rosemary Podgis beyond a reasonable doubt. To reach that determination I will ask you to look at the testimony of the witnesses. Obviously, you will have to consider the testimony of Scott Franz and the physical evidence in the case. You will have physical evidence in the courtroom. You will see a videotape of 401 Euclid Avenue. You will see a lot of pictures. You will see diagrams, all with the idea of giving you as clear as possible a picture of the scene...

"Above all I am asking you to apply your good, common sense and the reasonable inferences from what you hear and see in making your determination in this case. Are we talking about a reckless act on this defendant's part, thus giving rise to aggravated manslaughter or manslaughter? Or are we talking about something more, to give rise to murder?

"Now, on the one hand you will hear from Scott Franz that Bruce Curtis told him that he was running out of the house and the gun went off. Based upon that description, Scott Franz related to his sisters — or some of them — that the shooting of his mother was accidental... Or on the other hand, in making your determination, do you consider the purchase of the bullets, the resentment of the treatment they were receiving, the anxiousness of Bruce Curtis to go back into that house, his desire to bring the guns in, the conversations they had between them before the shootings and the actions of cleaning up, of the flight that occurred after the shootings?"

Chaiet paused. "Was it an accident? Or when the shooting started did it trigger an inclination to seek some revenge for the real or imagined slights that Bruce Curtis received in that Podgis household?"

In conclusion, Chaiet brought his opening statement back to Shakespeare. "'Truth will come to light; murder cannot be hid long.' Don't let the convenient cloak of accident hide the truth in this case."

After the jury was excused for a short recess, Schottland approached the bench. First he argued that Chaiet had not presented any evidence in his opening statement to support the sixth count against his client: theft of the van. Judge Arnone denied the motion for dismissal. Next, Schottland moved for a mistrial on the grounds that the prosecutor's opening statement "exceeded the bounds of propriety." He pointed out that the references to a smile on his client's face and jokes about a pituitary gland might have been ruled improper had Franz made them on the witness stand, let alone forming part of an opening statement. The state's opening statement was supposed to be confined to the facts elicited in evidence and should not be argumentative. Schottland added that the prosecutor had intimated his own chief witness might not be trustworthy.

"There is a constitutional limitation that a prosecutor has in a case," Schottland said, "a law limitation as to the use of an accomplice in terms of perjured testimony or knowing use of testimony which the prosecutor doubts the verity of. Now, it is not simple enough to just say, well, ladies and gentlemen of the jury, here it is. This version or that. You pick it. Because the prosecution has a function that transcends the function of a mere adversary or a mere jouster at a sporting event. This isn't sport."

Then Schottland addressed the issue he suspected would prove crucial to the state's case. "He is the one, Your Honour, that in his opening introduced into this case the details and the circumstances of the shooting that occurred upstairs, even though my client is not charged with any participation or having anything to do with that shooting upstairs."

Schottland asked Judge Arnone to either grant a mistrial or direct the prosecutor not to use Scott Franz's testimony in the case.

"I am not so sure what Mr Schottland is saying," Chaiet said to Judge Arnone, "but obviously in my opening statement I am allowed to comment on what facts I think will be presented during the state's case... As far as the truthfulness of my witness, that is a dichotomy that I have. Scott Franz says one thing, the expert says another thing.... I think I have an obligation, and it is part of the state's case, to bring both of those facts, both of those positions, to the jury and let them make their determination. That is their basic function."

Judge Arnone agreed. He denied Schottland's motions.

Schottland stood in front of the defence table facing the jurors and began to speak. When a defence attorney exercises his option to make an opening statement, he usually begins, as Schottland did, by reminding the jurors of the presumption that every defendant is considered innocent until proven guilty, and of their responsibility to remain objective. Next Schottland focused his attention on the testimony of the state's key witness, Scott Franz. He pointed out the nature of a plea bargain and its advantages to anyone charged with a crime. After testifying, Schottland noted, Franz was scheduled for sentencing before Judge Arnone with an assurance that the prosecutor would make an appeal on his behalf.

"I am saying that to you," Schottland told the jury, glancing from face to face, "so you understand that Scott Franz has a lot to gain and a lot to lose in terms of his testimony at this trial against Bruce Curtis. It is not simply that he is going to come in here and tell the truth and that is the end of it.... The state needs him, they think, to make a case against my client. Now, that means Franz knows in his own mind that if he can help the case against Bruce Curtis, that may have some impact upon the sentence...."

"And I say right now in my opening that he is a liar. He has never told the truth, he is still not telling the truth, and he will not tell the truth because he doesn't know the difference between what is true and what is not true. He doesn't know. All he is doing is trying to save his own neck."

Chaiet rose to object. Judge Arnone sustained the objection.

Schottland devoted the rest of his opening to telling the jury that the state's other important witness, Dr. Halbert Fillinger, had conducted autopsies that were sloppy and incomplete, and that the household into which an unsuspecting

Curtis had arrived as a guest was "an environment of guns, bullets, threats."

Schottland rested his hand on the railing of the jury box in a fatherly gesture. "Now let me close by saying this to you. I again ask you about keeping an open mind in the case. . . . A defendant in a criminal case comes before you presumed innocent. And Bruce Curtis may choose to sit at that counsel table and never testify, or I may not put one single witness on that stand, because the defendant doesn't have to prove he is innocent under our system. The defendant can sit, and it is up to you after you hear the evidence, even if the defendant sits and never testifies, to say to yourself: has the state sustained the burden of proving beyond a reasonable doubt the guilt of Bruce Curtis? I submit to you now, and I will submit to you at the end of the case when I come back before you, that they will not, and they have not. Thank you very much."

Juries in New Jersey were rarely sequestered in non-capital cases. (The death penalty, thrown out on constitutional grounds in 1972, had been re-enacted one month after the deaths of Al and Rosemary Podgis.) In any case, Judge Arnone, like many judges, disliked compounding the inconveniences of jury duty by isolating jurors from their families and friends. Another consideration was cost: putting up fourteen people in a hotel for what might be weeks was expensive for the county. The men and women empanelled to decide the outcome of the Curtis case would be permitted to go home each evening. Mindful of the notoriety surrounding the case, however, Judge Arnone gave the jury instructions he would repeat at the end of every day: "Don't discuss the case with anyone. If anyone attempts to discuss it with you, let me know about it. Don't discuss it among yourselves. Should there be any newspaper accounts or any radio accounts, don't read them and don't listen to them."

As Jim and Alice Curtis were walking towards the parking lot located behind the courthouse, they saw Bruce stepping into the paddywagon that would return him to the Monmouth County jail. They stood and waved as it drove away.

On Tuesday, March 15, the state began building a foundation for its case. John Foley, who worked with the Podgises at the Englishtown post office, recounted Rosemary's brief appearance at his Independence Day picnic and her explanation that she and her husband would not be attending because there were "either problems, or trouble, at home. She seemed upset and embarrassed, like she didn't want to tell me this."

Maurice Orlando Jr., the Podgises' next-door neighbour, testified that he and his wife knew the couple well and had had dinner with them less than two weeks before their death. He said he heard them arguing "approximately once or twice a month."

"And when you say you heard them," Chaiet said, "could you give us a sample of what you would hear?"

"Well," Orlando replied, "I couldn't really make out too many of the words, except every once in a while Rosemary or Al would raise their voice and say, 'I'll kill you, you SOB,' or something like that."

Orlando added that the Podgises had never argued in front of him, nor had he observed any arguments between Scott Franz and his parents. He did recall seeing Franz and Curtis during the week prior to the shootings, and his children had seen them hiding in the bushes at the back of the property the day before the shootings.

"Did you have occasion to see the van on Monday, July 5, 1982?" Chaiet asked, referring to the day of the shootings. Orlando said that he had seen the van backed against a seldom-used side door that led to a cellar stairway. "This was very unusual, as far as I thought," Orlando added.

Chaiet also called several law enforcement officers to the stand. Patrolman John Stillwell, of the Allenhurst police department, told of his discovery of the blood-stained mattress, and the court heard from a Pennsylvania state trooper who had investigated the ravine in which the bodies had been discovered. Bill Duerr narrated a videotape of the interior and exterior of 401 Euclid that included footage of the blood-soaked mattress. Diagrams and photographs — many of them depicting bloody evidence from the upstairs killing — were also introduced. Then Captain Frank Tenbroeck described the various weapons and boxes of ammunition recovered from the house, and the bullet, removed from a hole in the doorway leading into the second-floor study, that matched the rifle used to kill Al Podgis.

Having failed in his bid for a mistrial and the exclusion of Franz's testimony, Schottland realized he would have to raise a continuous series of objections in order to preserve issues in the court's record that could later be argued on appeal. At one point, when many of the goriest photographs were being circulated to the jury, Schottland turned to Judge Arnone. "They saw the videotape," he complained. "Why do they have to see the pictures? Do they [the state] have to dwell on it? Isn't it a little cumulative?"

"There is nothing in here that is going to terribly upset anybody," Chaiet remarked. "People get shot in the head, they bleed."

When Chaiet produced the .22-calibre rifle discovered under Al Podgis's bed, Schottland protested vigorously. "I am saying to Your Honour, respectfully, I just think we are going to get involved in something. I am being forced to defend a murder that the defendant in *that* case has already admitted he has done in order to defend my client. It's sort of like a guilt-by-association type of thing."

To which Chaiet countered: "My position is that everything found in that house, everything concerning the double homicide, is relevant to the murder trial of this defendant. I think I have said before, I don't know how the state could try this case without the evidence found in that [bed]room coming into play . . . .

"All of this is intertwined in the murder trial of Bruce Curtis, and you can't separate them."

After listening to both attorneys, Judge Arnone made his ruling. "As I said earlier, and I indicate again, the court is of the opinion, in spite of the argument made by defence counsel, that the jury is entitled to know everything that took place at this

particular time . . . so they can make a determination on this case.
I'm going to overrule the objection."

The next morning, after dispensing with some unfinished
details carried over from the day before, the state called Sergeant
James P. Wambold. A fifteen-year veteran of the New Jersey State
Troopers, Wambold had, for the past three years, been assigned
to a ballistics laboratory in Sea Girt, N.J., where his duties
included the receiving and storage of firearms evidence,
examining and test-firing firearms, and identifying and testing
ammunition. By his own count he had test-fired more than five
thousand weapons, and had testified as an expert witness on
many occasions.

Chaiet led Wambold through the ballistics evidence. It was
determined that the metal bullet casing taken from the doorframe on the second floor of 401 Euclid Avenue matched the one
buried in Al Podgis's pillow. Both of these matched a discharged
shell found in a box of ammunition in the garage and a second
spent shell casing recovered from the side of the highway near
the Hilton Inn in Tinton Falls. They had all been fired from a
Winchester model 94 .30-.30 rifle, serial number IS29924. This
weapon, the shorter of the two .30-.30s entered as evidence in
the trial, was the one Scott Franz had taken upstairs on the
morning of July 5, 1982. The bullet that was recovered from
Rosemary Podgis's left hip matched the second weapon, a
Winchester model 94 .30-.30, serial number NRA24538. It was
this longer-barrelled carbine that Bruce Curtis had been carrying on the same morning. But Chaiet also established that the
second spent casing found beside the highway had come from
Curtis's rifle.

"Now, I believe you have already testified to it, when you fire
the .30-calibre Winchester would the shell automatically be
ejected?"

"It will eject only when you lever the firearm," replied
Wambold. "It doesn't come out automatically. You have to push
the lever forward for the discharged shell to be ejected."

Wambold went on to describe the firing test patterns of both rifles — at thirty-six inches, for example, the rifle that killed Rosemary Podgis no longer left powder residues on a test fabric — and the respective "trigger pulls" of the two weapons, a measurement of the force required to discharge a firearm. Franz's rifle measured a three-and-one-half-pound pull, and Curtis's measured three pounds.

"Is there a scale of 'trigger pulls'?" Chaiet inquired.

"Yes," Wambold answered. " 'Trigger pulls' vary greatly depending upon the make, manufacturer, whatever the case may be. However, as a rule of thumb, a standard that some factories use, if a 'trigger pull' is less than three pounds when they measure it at the factory they don't ship the gun."

Chaiet indicated the longer rifle. "So this would be, as far as 'trigger pull,' it would be at the bottom of the scale?"

"That's correct."

During these proceedings, Schottland raised another objection. Although he noted that the state had made most of its discovery available to him, he was unprepared for the areas Wambold was exploring. "I feel that, in a murder case, if I ask for expert opinions and reports ahead of trial, I should have them so that I am prepared to meet them in the event there is a dispute," he told Judge Arnone. "I am in a position now that I have no idea what this man is going to say."

"This trial was originally scheduled as a joint trial with Mr Franz on February 28th, if you will recall," Schottland continued. "Your Honour was in the process of hearing a motion to sever the case, brought by Mr Chaiet who wanted to try Mr Franz first. We were going to hold an evidentiary hearing with respect to a claim of a *Miranda* violation against Mr Franz before your Honour ruled on the motion to sever. The following day, March 1st, while all this was transpiring, Mr Franz decided to plead guilty. At that time I asked for a March 28th trial date and Mr Chaiet objected to that and insisted we go forward on the 14th.

"I received this" — Schottland waved Wambold's test reports — "on March 9th. I feel I'm being jacked in terms of the preparation of this case."

Judge Arnone decided to allow the testimony but said to Schottland: "During the luncheon period you can discuss it with whomever you have to discuss it with and advise me after lunch. Okay? I mean, it gives you more time to think about it and make whatever phone calls you have to make or whatever is necessary... If you need more time beyond Monday, let me know that."

Schottland, unsure whether to delay his cross-examination of Wambold or plunge ahead, made a quick decision. "Wambold was a relatively young guy, a conservative type with a crew cut," he recalls. "I decided to pretend I knew what I was doing, so he'd feel he was up against a real pro who knew as much about a Winchester .30-.30 as he did. At lunch-time, Dempsey, who knows a lot about guns, and Dennis Fahey, who's a retired cop, grabbed me and we went over to the Jersey Freeze, where you can get a nice hamburger. Those guys opened up my head and poured in everything they could about Winchester .30-.30s. And you're talking about a guy who don't know anything about guns."

In his cross-examination that afternoon, Schottland sought to establish that the rifle Curtis had been carrying could have had a "trigger pull" lower than industry standards. Responding to a question from Schottland, Wambold explained that "trigger pull" was measured by adding half-pound weights to a rod attached to the trigger until the gun discharged. It was the answer Schottland had wanted.

"Incidentally," he said casually, "how do we know they are half-pound increments?"

"My weights are half-pound increments."

"That is what I mean," continued Schottland. "How do we know whatever you are adding is really a half-pound and not an ounce more or less than half a pound?"

"I don't think they have been certified by the Division of Weights and Measures," admitted Wambold stiffly.

"Is it fair to say that a half-pound is eight ounces?"

"Yes."

"Seven or nine?"

"Well," Wambold said, "I don't know. Like I say, I haven't actually scaled those particular weights. However, they are marked as being one-half pound."

Schottland began circling closer. "How do you know that the .30-.30 — again, the longer one — wouldn't go off if you put two pounds and twelve ounces on it?"

"Because when we weight it, we start out with one pound and we gradually increase," offered Wambold.

"I understand that and I heard what you said," Schottland said firmly. The courtroom was silent. "But you go, one pound, then one pound and eight ounces, right?"

"That's correct."

"Then you go to two pounds. The gun didn't fire, right?"

"That's correct."

"You then went to two pounds and eight ounces, right?"

"That's correct."

"The gun did not fire, right?"

"Right."

"You then went to three pounds and the gun fired?"

"That's correct."

"My question to you is, how do you know that gun won't fire using the same weights at two pounds and twelve ounces, which is halfway between two pounds and eight ounces, where it didn't fire, and three pounds?"

"With the system that we are using," Wambold told him, "there would be no way of knowing that."

Having made his point that Curtis's rifle may have been below the safety specifications of the manufacturer, Schottland moved on to the test pattern firings. He knew that the absence of powder residue on Rosemary Podgis's clothing, according to Wambold's earlier testimony, suggested that the muzzle of the rifle had been at least thirty-six inches away from her. The further away Curtis was standing, the less credible it would seem that he had been startled as they came upon each other in the dining-room doorway.

"With respect to the longer gun," Schottland said, "it would be your opinion that at twenty-four inches there would be some residue that you could identify with your eye?"

"That's correct," replied Wambold warily.

"At thirty-six inches there was not?"

"That's correct."

"But there might not be at twenty-nine, twenty-eight, thirty, twenty-seven, twenty-six or, for that matter, twenty-five inches. Isn't that so?"

"That's correct."

"So that means that if an individual was, just on your test alone, twenty-five inches from the end of the muzzle of the long rifle, you would not necessarily find evidence of powder burns or particles or anything like that?"

"You may or may not," replied Wambold, "depending upon variables."

"Is it completely up in the air?" pressed Schottland.

"Yes."

The counsel for the defence nodded his head slowly. "That's all I have. Thank you very much."

Although his demeanour remained composed as he returned to the defence table, Schottland was triumphant. He knew that he had routed Chaiet's expert witness, and suspected that even the least technically minded of jurors understood that. He watched as Chaiet began an effort to repair the damage on his second, or "redirect," examination.

Chaiet ran over the act of arming the lever-action rifles again, concentrating on the operation of the safety mechanism. On the Winchester model 94 .30-.30, a spring-loaded pin positioned behind the trigger must be depressed by the lever before the rifle can be fired. Franz was going to testify that he had armed Curtis's rifle but had not prepared it for firing. Chaiet wanted the jury to realize that Curtis must have performed at least one action before firing his gun.

"In the position that this weapon is in now," said Chaiet, holding the rifle used to shoot Rosemary Podgis, "it is loaded. You have lever-actioned the weapon. It is armed, I think you used that term?"

Wambold nodded. "Okay."

"Okay. If you press the trigger now, will it go off?"

"Not until the lever safety has been pushed up into the tang."

"So what do you have to do in order to pull the trigger?"

"Well, you have to squeeze the lever up, as we illustrated before, getting the lever safety up into the tang which releases the block behind the trigger."

On re-cross-examination, Schottland walked to the witness stand. "If, in fact, the individual who is actually cocking the weapon...returns the lever flush at the time he is going through the cocking motion, you don't need another separate motion in order to fire the weapon do you? Other than pulling the trigger?"

"No."

"That's it?"

"That's it."

"That's all I have," Schottland concluded.

Chaiet rose. "And when you do that," he said to Wambold, handing him the long-barrelled .30-.30 again, "will it [the safety pin] automatically stay flush once you put it flush to the stock?"

Wambold told him the lever had to be held tight against the gunstock to prevent the safety pin from engaging. He demonstrated by squeezing the lever.

"So if I would let go now," Chaiet continued, directing Wambold to allow the lever to fall away from the gunstock, "the safety is on again?"

"Right," said Wambold, pulling the trigger. There was a loud click.

"You just fired it," cried Schottland, jumping to his feet. "He just fired it that way. Can the record reflect that, Judge?"

Chaiet frowned at his opponent. "You want to say it again?"

"Well, I think it's important, Mr Chaiet, that the record reflect what happened."

Schottland suppressed a grin. The state's own expert witness, under the direction of the prosecutor, had demonstrated that Curtis's rifle was faulty. The net effect of Wambold's testimony had weakened — or at best, confused — the state's case, although Chaiet completed his redirect examination in an effort to correct that impression.

(Sixteen months later, James Wambold's career as a law enforcement officer and expert witness would come to an abrupt halt. On July 25, 1984, he was indicted on one count of "committing official misconduct" involving the theft of ninety-one weapons between May 30, 1980 and January 12, 1984, plus eleven counts of failure to make the required dispositions of property. After his conviction in Superior Court in Mercer County, he was court-martialed by the New Jersey State Troopers. He was dismissed from the force on August 22, 1985.)

At that point, at the end of the third day of Curtis's trial, Schottland had every reason to feel confident. That Curtis's rifle had a malfunctioning safety mechanism reinforced the premise that the weapon had discharged accidentally. Also, Chaiet apparently did not plan to use a wild card he had included in the discovery on the opening day of the trial: traces of white powder in a plastic pill bottle found in Curtis's vinyl bag the previous July had initially been tested with negative results. Then, six days before the trial began, it had been resubmitted to the state police laboratory to check for the presence of an insecticide containing nicotine. The report instead found a trace of arsenic. Schottland didn't know what that meant, but he could imagine explanations that weren't necessarily sinister. Besides, how would Paul introduce *that* into evidence? How did it connect to the case? If anything, it further confirmed for Schottland that his opponent was getting desperate. (As Schottland guessed, Chaiet never tried to use this evidence in the trial.)

Much to Schottland's delight, the state would now have to rely almost entirely on testimony from a most disingenuous witness: Scott Franz.

That evening, Jim Curtis's sister, Lorraine Peever, and his mother, Jennie Curtis, arrived from Ontario and took a room near Jim and Alice in the Marlborough Motor Lodge in nearby Englishtown. Jennie Curtis, who came prepared to make "a proper cup of tea," boiled water in a tiny electric pot and poured the tea into four china cups brought from home. Then Jim and

Alice told them about Wambold's testimony and Schottland's devastating cross-examination. The family had so scrupulously obeyed Schottland's instructions not to discuss the case that this was the first time they had compared theories and exchanged details among themselves. Peever and her mother were also anxious to help Jim and Alice relax. They recalled folk-tales about country life outside Paris, Ontario, and commented on the forsythia that bloomed beside the highways in New Jersey while all vegetation remained snowbound in Canada. Jennie reported sighting a robin, and told Jim about the early break-up of the ice on the Nith River, where her son used to set his muskrat traps and still knew every bend where the ice was likely to jam. They passed around Jennie's home-baked cookies, muffins and poundcake and Alice's home-made jam, a ritual they would observe every night during the trial proceedings. At some point after everyone had retired, both Alice and Jennie spent some time reading their Bibles.

A few minutes before court convened on Thursday, March 17, St Patrick's Day, the seats in the spectator's gallery were nearly filled. The case was being reported in the local newspapers and on radio and television and there was particular interest today because Scott Franz was to testify. Among the reporters assigned to cover the trial were Sue Epstein, representing the *Newark Star-Ledger*, and Arlene Newman, of the *Asbury Park Press*. Epstein was intrigued by the case because "it contained all the elements necessary for good drama" and because "never, in ten years, have I ever covered anything that happened in Loch Arbour." When she and her fellow reporters gathered at lunch-hour — at the coffee-shop in the American Hotel, or one of two snack-bars in the County Courthouse: Mark's in the west wing or Joan's in the east wing — they discussed the unusual circumstances of the case and the personal styles of the opposing attorneys.

Chaiet was characterized as "smooth, level-headed and dynamic." Epstein compared his openings and summations to "watching a show on Broadway." Schottland was described as "very obnoxious," and "explosive and emotional." The reporters often debated whether Schottland's aggressive strategy would succeed untempered by a greater effort to make his client appear more likeable to the mainly middle-aged jury.

Of Curtis, Epstein observed: "He was almost like a mummy. He didn't move, even when Schottland talked to him, and he didn't acknowledge his parents when he was led into the courtroom." Newman noted that "he certainly didn't make a sympathetic figure. He never had any expression on his face, and even when I saw him greet his parents there was no emotion." But both women acknowledged that, having spent months in the Monmouth County jail — known locally as the "Gulag Archipelago" — he may have simply been in shock. (Curtis himself now says, "I was in shock at that time, yes. I could tell by the way I acted, and the things I wrote. For six months in Monmouth County I really wasn't myself. All my faculties weren't there...")

Newman and Epstein watched as Jim and Alice Curtis, joined by Lorraine and Jennie, took their customary seats in the front row of the spectator's gallery, directly behind the prosecutor's table. Sitting in the impersonal, high-ceilinged courtroom surrounded by strangers, their nervousness was heightened by coincidence. In front of Peever, on a bench reserved for the state's witnesses, sat Scott Franz. He was so close that Peever could have reached out and touched the back of his head.

Chaiet called the prosecution's key witness to the stand. Franz, sober and pale-faced, was wearing a beige sports jacket, white shirt and striped tie. Chaiet began by asking him to outline the terms of his plea agreement with the state. Although Franz told the court he had pleaded guilty to the murder of his stepfather and that four additional charges against him had been dropped, he carefully avoided admitting his actions.

"Could you please tell us why you entered your plea of guilty?" Chaiet asked.

"My lawyer advised it," Franz replied.

Chaiet asked Franz to describe his relationship with his stepfather.

"I tried to avoid him as much as possible."

"Were there any incidents of violence between the two of you?"

"Yes."

"Could you tell me about these?"

"They would be physical, whether it be punching or beating me for some reason."

The prosecutor then asked him about his mother. Franz said quietly, "I loved her very much, and cared for her."

Then Chaiet led his witness through a day-by-day account of that week, beginning with his stepfather's anger at the late arrival of Bruce's flight at the Newark airport. Franz told the court that on Thursday, July 1, he and Curtis spent part of the day at the warehouse where he worked before driving to the post office in Englishtown.

"Now when you got to the post office, did you have any conversation with your mother?"

"Yes. She asked me to go and get my stepfather some bullets and put some gas in the car."

"Did she mention the type of bullets you were to get?"

"Yes, .30-.30."

"Thirty-thirty," Chaiet repeated. "Let me ask you something; had you ever purchased ammunition for your stepfather before?"

"No."

"You had not?"

"By myself, yes."

"When you say, 'by yourself,' what do you mean?"

"I was with him when he had purchased ammunition before."

Franz described an argument over a misplaced Social Security cheque later that afternoon, and how the next morning his stepfather had not waited to give him a ride to work. That evening, another argument developed just as Franz, Curtis and Rosemary Podgis were leaving for dinner. "It was first verbal, and then my mother finally took my side and it made him out to look like a liar," the boy said. "So as we were leaving for the restaurant he punched me on the shoulder twice."

Franz then told the court that on the morning of Saturday, July 3, while he and Curtis were cutting the lawn, they saw Al Podgis locking six rifle boxes in the back of the International Scout.

"Was there any conversation between you and Bruce Curtis at that time?" Chaiet said.

"Yes. I said that he was in his hyper mood so we better leave."

"Did Bruce Curtis say anything to you?"

"When he first came out he said, 'he must have found them.'"

"I didn't hear that," Chaiet said.

Franz spoke louder. "He said, 'he must have found them.'"

"Did you question Bruce Curtis about what he meant by that?"

"No."

"And any reason?"

"I just wanted to get out of the area where my stepfather was before he got physical with anyone."

"You used the word 'hyper,'" Chaiet said. "How did you know he was 'hyper'?"

"By the way he walked, and his face was totally red."

"And can you tell us what that meant to you?"

"That he was very, very upset."

Franz said they spent the rest of the day in shopping malls and fast-food restaurants, afraid to go home. At about 10:00 P.M. they returned to 401 Euclid and hid in a camper in the garage.

"Do you recall what you were discussing at that time?" Chaiet asked.

"How angry we were that we were out walking in the rain, and how cold it was. That type of thing."

"Now after you spent time in the camper, what then happened?"

"We went out and walked around the house."

"Okay. And what observations did you make then?"

"That my mother was downstairs making a cheesecake and Al was floating from upstairs to downstairs, back and forth."

"Did you enter the house then?"

"No. I heard they were arguing, so we went underneath the back porch to see what it was about."

"Could you describe the argument for us?"

"He said, 'I should never have married you,' you know. 'All it is is trouble with you,' you know. 'Scott and his friends, and Mark and Dawn.'"

Chaiet asked what they did after the argument.

"We stayed there until Al eventually came out to bring my moped in out of the rain. That's when he said — that he made a threat on my life, type of thing."

"You are saying he made a threat on your life?"

"Yes. He was bringing the moped in and he was looking down because he was having trouble with the kickstand and — would you like me to quote what he said?"

Chaiet said that he would.

"'If I get my hands on that son-of-a-bitching kid, I'll kill him.'"

Later, Franz explained, after his stepfather had gone to bed, his mother unlocked the door so the boys could get inside. They slept on the couch rather than risk waking Al Podgis by going upstairs to their bedrooms. The next morning, Sunday, July 4, Independence Day, Franz went upstairs to retrieve Curtis's suitcase and traveller's cheques. He heard his stepfather's footsteps on the hardwood floor. "So I went into his den, which is located next to my bedroom, and I stood at the crook of the door to see where he was going. And that's when he fired at me." After fleeing from the house, Franz told the court, they spent the rest of the day at the boardwalk in Asbury Park, and watched the fireworks that evening.

"Did you have any conversations with Bruce Curtis at that time, or up until that time, about your situation?"

"Yes," Franz said. "It was basically, you know, what are we going to do and how are we going to get back into the house and get our stuff out of there so we can leave?"

"And where were you going to go?"

"I believe Nova Scotia."

"Okay. Did Bruce Curtis say anything to you at all about his feelings concerning what was happening?"

"Yes," Franz said. "He thought Al was a total pain and that we have to pay him back for making us stay outside."

Chaiet then asked the witness about a time, later that night, when Franz spoke to his mother outside the house.

"I told her that Al tried to kill me, that he fired a gun at me and that she shouldn't, you know, stay around with him."

"What did she say?"

"She said that he was only trying to scare me, and that he missed and that I should come back into the house and talk things over."

Chaiet asked Franz whether he had ever had a conversation with his mother about the rifles. Franz replied: "She said that I better not have fired one of his collectable rifles because they would lose their value if I did."

"Why did she say that to you?"

"Because there were two guns found underneath the mattress in the bedroom at the top of the stairs."

Chaiet turned towards the jury. "And who was staying in that room?"

"Bruce Curtis."

Chaiet paused to let Franz's statement settle into the minds of the jurors. Then he resumed by questioning Franz about breaking into the Scout to get his stepfather's rifles. "Was there any conversation leading up to you doing that?"

"Yes. That we had to get back into the house and that we would need protection after, you know, after he shot at me. And we knew that the guns were in the Scout so we broke into the Scout. I did."

"How did you do that?"

"With a piece of wire."

"Now, could you tell me whether or not you wanted to come back into the house on Sunday night at all?"

"I object to that," Schottland said loudly.

"Overruled," said Judge Arnone.

Franz looked at Chaiet. "No, I really didn't want to come back."

"And did you have a conversation with Bruce Curtis about that?"

"Yes."

"Could you tell me what the conversation was?"

Franz paused. "I don't remember the exact words."

"Okay. Do you recall the gist of the conversation?"

"That we had to go back into the house to get our personal things so we could leave."

Chaiet changed his tack. "Do you recall whether it was you or Bruce Curtis that suggested — strike that. Do you recall whether it was you, Bruce Curtis or the both of you jointly who suggested the bringing of guns into the house?"

Schottland half-rose out of his chair. "I object."

Judge Arnone turned to Chaiet. "Rephrase that question."

Chaiet began again. "In your conversations concerning the guns and bringing them into the house, could you tell us when one of you initiated the conversation? Do you understand the question?"

"Initiated," Franz mumbled. "Yeah."

"Began it," Chaiet offered.

"I don't remember."

Apparently Franz had not only forgotten who suggested getting the rifles out of the Scout in 1982 — he had implicated himself in his initial statement to New Jersey investigators — but also that he had told Chaiet three weeks earlier, on the day he signed his plea agreement with the prosecutor's office, that it had been Curtis's idea. Chaiet, unwilling to appear antagonistic towards his own witness, dropped the subject.

Franz went on to explain that he unloaded "either seven or eight" shells from the short rifle, divided them, and reloaded both weapons in Curtis's presence. Chaiet asked him to step down from the witness stand, handed him the rifle, and asked him to demonstrate. Then Chaiet asked whether Curtis had said anything about loading the weapons. "That he didn't know how," Franz told him, then added that when the rifles were taken into the house, neither was cocked, nor were there rounds in the chambers. The boys slept on the couch in the living-room with the rifles between them. At Chaiet's direction, Franz pointed out the location of the couch on a large diagram depicting a floor plan of 401 Euclid. Then Chaiet asked him to repeat his conversation with Curtis in the morning, moments before he took the short rifle upstairs with him.

"That I'm going upstairs to take a shower," Franz said in a monotone. "And if Al tries anything, like shooting at me, that I'm going to shoot at him. And if you have to go out of the house shooting, go ahead."

"You said, 'if you have to go out shooting, go ahead.' You said that to who?"

"Bruce."

Chaiet asked what his stepfather's position in bed had been. Franz described him as "sort of leaning up," and holding a .22 rifle "pointed...in my direction...and he took a shot at me." Franz, who admitted he had already lever-actioned the rifle, said he began to run out of the room, stopped, pointed the rifle, closed his eyes and fired. When he saw blood on the wall he ran into the bathroom and threw up. Then he heard a single shot downstairs. "Bruce was standing in the living-room," he said. "He was standing there and yelling, 'What are we going to do?'"

"And when he said, 'What are we going to do?' what did you say or do?" Chaiet asked.

"I said, 'What happened?'"

"And what did he say?"

"I shot your mother."

"I shot your mother," Chaiet repeated gravely. "And then what did you do?"

"I ran over to my mother," Franz said hoarsely, indicating the location on the diagram and marking an X in front of the door separating the kitchen from the bar room. "I took her pulse."

"And did you find any?"

"No."

Franz admitted he was crying at the time because "I was just very sad that my mother was dead."

"What did you do then?"

"I went to pick up the phone."

"Okay. Did you make a telephone call?"

"No."

"Why didn't you call?"

Schottland interjected. "I object."

"Overruled."

Then Franz said, "Because I looked at Bruce and he shook his head."

"He shook his head in what manner?"

Franz moved his head from side to side. "Like that. In a negative response."

When Chaiet began to question Franz on what the boys did next, Schottland objected and took up the issue with Chaiet at the side of the judge's bench.

"I'm not sure what his answer is going to be," began Schottland. "But based on his answer to the earlier question, it seems to me that Mr Chaiet is going to get into what happened after the event in a lot of detail . . . I think maybe that's material, assuming Your Honour believes that flight is an appropriate piece of the case, but not anything else in terms of gory details. If we are going to get into some gory details about cleaning up, that at most would be a separate crime of concealing a crime. My client has not been indicted for concealment. . . . In other words, he can prove they left the scene, but not the concealment."

Judge Arnone did not subscribe to Schottland's view. "I disagree with you. Objection overruled."

"After you went to make the phone call," Chaiet continued, "and by the way, was any force used by Bruce Curtis at that time?"

"No, no." Franz answered quickly.

"After that, can you tell us what conversation occurred?"

"I said, 'What are we going to do?'"

"Yes," Chaiet said. "And then what happened?"

"Bruce replied that we will have to get rid of the bodies."

At the defence table, Schottland scribbled a note to himself on a yellow legal tablet. Under Chaiet's patient questioning, Franz described Curtis's cleaning up of the walls and floor in the master bedroom and how, at approximately 9:30 A.M., the two boys had driven to Seaview Square Mall to buy rope at Sears. When they returned, Franz explained that the rope was used in a first unsuccessful attempt to pull Al Podgis off the bed and into a large steamer trunk.

At this point, Schottland objected again. After Judge Arnone sent the jury out of the courtroom, Schottland argued that the state was setting out to do precisely what he had warned it would do in his opening statement. He invoked Rule 4, which stated that the probative value of evidence must outweigh the risk that it would unduly prejudice or mislead a jury. He requested that the court should at least conduct a *voir dire* (a hearing, held outside the presence of the jury, to determine the admissability of evidence) because "once he [Franz] says it in front of the jury, Your Honour, you can say twenty times to them to disregard it, but you are not going to change the jury's impressions."

Judge Arnone overruled Schottland's objection.

Chaiet resumed his direct examination. "I believe we left off where you were attempting with the rope to get your stepfather off the bed. Did that work?"

"No," Franz replied.

"What was then done?"

"The room was cleaned some more and we tried leverage."

"Now when you say leverage, describe what you did."

"I went upstairs and got an axe handle and a paddle."

"What happened when you tried to use leverage?"

"The axe handle or the paddle broke."

"And what did you do?"

"Got some bed slats."

Franz's testimony continued in this vein. When Chaiet asked him to describe Curtis's appearance while he was cleaning up, Franz told him: "At one time I was in the hallway and he came out with a dustpan and there was a grey piece of gum on it. He thought it was my stepfather's pituitary gland. I told him it was a piece of gum."

Chaiet asked about other similar conversations and Franz said: "When the trunk was at the head of the stairs, some blood slipped out of it and was on a plastic bag. It was congealed blood, and Bruce sort of got it all in one spot and kind of cut the bag out around it and put it back into the trunk or into a garbage bag."

"What was his facial appearance when he was doing that?"

"A slight grin."

"A slight grin?" Chaiet repeated, emphasizing each word.

"Yes."

"Did he make any comments in reference to that?"

"It was sort of like Jello."

The courtroom was silent. Chaiet asked him, "Up until this point, did he cry at all?"

"No."

In the course of his testimony, Franz admitted that he and Curtis had loaded his parents' bodies into the van in order to "remove the bodies from the house...to hide them." He also told Chaiet that his mother's head hit the stairs while she was being carried to the van. After dumping the bodies in a ravine in Pennsylvania, they returned to 401 Euclid "to get the stuff that we left...to get rid of it." After seeing Chief Newman's car in front of the house, Franz said they drove to the Hilton Inn to throw the guns away because "neither one of us wanted it to be in the same spot that the bodies were." Franz added that Curtis threw the last of the ammunition out the van window.

"Could you tell us whether or not — before the weapons were disposed of, was anything done to them?" Chaiet inquired.

"They were wiped off."

"And could you tell us who did that?"

"Bruce."

Finally, Chaiet asked the witness whether he had ever told any members of his family that the shooting of his mother was an accident. Franz said he had told his sisters, Barbara, Noreen, Rosie and Dawn.

"When you advised them of that fact, had Bruce Curtis at any time stated to you that the shooting of your mother was an accident?"

"No," Franz told him. "I just assumed that it was."

After lunch that day, Schottland glanced at his notes before rising to begin his cross-examination of Franz. He was in a peculiar position with the state's witness. On the one hand, he wanted to show the jury what a perfidious liar Franz was, how he'd changed his story several times and had, since March 1, been acting as an agent of the prosecutor. There was no question of a moral imperative inspiring Franz to tell the truth, and it went beyond just a frightened teenager who'd made a deal to save his skin. By steadfastly taking the position that the only reason he'd pled guilty to murder was because his lawyer had advised him to do so, Franz was covering his ass, Schottland thought. If the defence were lucky enough to win an acquittal, Franz could turn around and withdraw his plea, claiming that his lawyer had talked him into it.

On the other hand, Schottland realized he had to be careful with Franz. Much of his testimony didn't harm Curtis. In fact, some of it helped. Here was a kid, Franz, who had just blown his stepfather's brains out. He came downstairs carrying a loaded rifle and saw his friend standing over the mother that he loved. But he resisted an impulse to shoot because he was convinced it had been an accident. Schottland wondered whether he could get Franz to say that in front of the jury. If he succeeded, did he also want to pound it into their heads that Franz was a manifestly unreliable witness who didn't know truth from fiction?

Schottland marvelled at the way Chaiet had turned the same dilemma into a strategy. Franz's 1982 statement and other independent evidence confirmed many of the details of the shootings. Franz's testimony, in sum, placed Curtis in the house that morning and placed a gun in his hands. Even though his star witness might be seen as a murderous liar, Chaiet knew the jury would still associate Curtis with the cleaning up and the flight and convince themselves it had been a joint slaying. Criminal trials were always complex affairs. Human lives were at stake and the concept of justice, so fundamental to western societies, was on trial alongside the defendant. If that was so, Schottland mused, this trial would never serve as a model. It was turning out to be particularly subtle, a trial of inferences and contradictions, a chess match played predominantly with knights.

Schottland began his cross-examination by reaffirming the details of Franz's plea agreement, although he highlighted different aspects of it. "Now let me ask you this," Schottland said. "Would you say your recollections and memory of the events of the weekend, July fourth weekend...is better now or was it better on July 11, 1982?"

"July 11," Franz admitted.

Schottland went on to emphasize for the jury's benefit the extent to which Franz had been coached and shown sensitive discovery materials in order to shape the case against Curtis. He began steering his questions towards Franz's state of mind at the moment he discovered his mother lying on the dining-room floor and saw his friend standing over her.

"At that time he had a rifle?" Schottland asked. Franz said that he had.

"And he said something?"

"He was screaming, 'What are we going to do?'"

"He was screaming?" Schottland said.

"Yes. It seemed to me."

"He was very upset, wasn't he?"

"At that point, yes."

"And at that point you knew Bruce Curtis had shot your mother, didn't you?"

"I knew something had happened to her," Franz allowed.

"Now, at that point you also became angry with Bruce, didn't you?"

"Sort of, yes."

"Isn't it a fact that you toyed with the idea of shooting Bruce at that point?"

"I thought about it myself."

"That's what I just asked you," Schottland snapped.

"Yes," Franz said. "But I didn't."

"Just answer the question, please."

"Yes."

"You thought about shooting Bruce Curtis when you saw him downstairs and you saw your mother on the floor, isn't that so?"

"Yes."

"But you decided not to."

"Right."

"Isn't it a fact that the reason you decided not to shoot Bruce Curtis right there that afternoon, or that morning, was that he convinced you that he had accidentally shot your mother while trying to run out of the house? Isn't that what happened?"

"No," Franz replied. "I just couldn't kill a person for no reason."

"Well, isn't killing your mother a reason?"

"Yes."

Schottland stepped back from the witness box. "Let me ask the question again. Isn't it a fact that the reason you didn't shoot Bruce Curtis right there when the thought popped up in your mind was that you satisfied yourself from his attitude, from his mental condition, from his emotional condition, and from the physical facts that you saw and from what he said that he had accidentally shot your mother?" Schottland stared at him. "Isn't that the case, sir?"

"I believe so."

Schottland confirmed the location of Rosemary Podgis's body inside the bar room near the entranceway to the kitchen. Referring to Franz's original statement dated July 11, 1982, Schottland then asked him about his directions to Curtis before the shootings occurred. "You said something to Bruce to the effect that if he had to shoot, to go ahead and shoot. But you weren't sure. You told Officer Lucia you were not sure of everything you said to him. Isn't that in the statement?"

"Yes."

"Now, when you said that to Bruce, when you were going upstairs, you weren't suggesting to him or telling him that he should shoot your mother, were you?"

"No."

"What you were talking about was that in case you didn't get downstairs alive and Alfred Podgis came downstairs, he should do whatever had to be done to Alfred Podgis. Isn't that what you told him?"

"Yes."

Schottland then elicited from Franz countless examples of physical abuse inflicted by Al Podgis on various members of the family. "In fact," he said, "you thought Mr Podgis struck your mother that very night before you went to the Scout to get the guns. Isn't that true?" Franz said that it was.

"How many times would you say your stepfather hit your mother that evening?"

Franz, who had shrunk into his chair, said quietly, "Two or three times."

"Could it have been four or five?"

"If when I wasn't there, yes it could have."

Schottland asked Franz about his mother's statement to him that guns had been discovered under Curtis's mattress. He read the portion of Dennis Fahey's interview with Franz on March 3, 1983, that dealt with this allegation. "You didn't tell Mr Fahey in that interview anything about Bruce being the reason why he was putting the guns out in the Scout, did you?"

"No."

"Did you intentionally mislead Mr Fahey?"

"Intentionally, yes."

"You were saving that?" Schottland asked him.

"I wasn't saving it. I just didn't tell him."

Schottland continued to quiz Franz on the inconsistencies between his original statement to Lucia and Duerr and information he provided to the prosecutor's office following his plea agreement.

"You indicated in your July 11 statement that it was your idea to get rid of the bodies and not Bruce's. Isn't that true, sir?"

"May I explain..." Franz began.

"Just first answer that and I will give you a chance, promise."

"I suggested it, yes."

"Okay. In other words you testified here on direct examination this morning and said to Mr Chaiet and this jury that Bruce said, 'Let's get rid of the bodies,' and the fact is that you first suggested you would have to get rid of the bodies."

"After I put down the phone I said, 'Well, what are we going to do then, hide the bodies? Get rid of the bodies?' And he said, 'Yes, we'll have to get rid of the bodies.'"

Schottland picked up a copy of Franz's statement from the defence table. Brandishing it, he said: "Let me read this to you and you tell me if this was accurate, what you said: 'At first I said, I don't know, and then I said, we got to get rid of the bodies.' You said that to the officer, didn't you?"

"He interpreted that and he typed it and I signed it," responded Franz defensively.

"Well now," said Schottland. "Wait a minute. You are not suggesting that the officer misstated what you said here, are you?"

"It is very possible. Yes."

Schottland asked Franz why, if there may have been incorrect information included in his statement, he signed it. Franz replied: "Because I was tired."

Schottland paused. "Are there other things in the statement that you signed just because you were tired, or you agreed with or agreed to just because you were tired?"

"There might be."

In conclusion, Schottland addressed the other piece of damaging information Franz had provided. "You mentioned something, a comment you said Bruce said about 'we are going to have to pay them back,' or something like that. Do you remember that?"

"Yes."

"Isn't it a fact you didn't take that to mean that Bruce wanted to kill him?"

"No," Franz answered, although he seemed to be agreeing with Schottland.

Schottland persisted: "That was just the way Bruce is sometimes when he speaks, isn't that the case?"

"Yes."

When Chaiet began his redirect examination, he asked Franz about a discrepancy between the location of his mother as indicated by the X he had marked on a photograph of the bar room area, and the X he had placed on the diagram. Franz placed a second X closer to the doorway between the bar room and the dining room. Schottland, realizing that the second X suggested that his client might not have encountered the woman as unexpectedly as he had been trying to establish, raised an objection. It was overruled.

Chaiet then asked Franz why he had misled Dennis Fahey over the matter of the guns under Curtis's mattress. "Did you have a particular reason? What was your thought process in not telling him?"

Franz looked at the prosecutor. "Well, when Bruce's investigator asked him the reason why he [Al Podgis] put the guns in the Scout, Bruce said there wasn't any. And [Bruce] came back and told me not to say anything about them. So I never said anything to him or my lawyer."

"Why, then," Chaiet asked, "did you ultimately decide to tell what you say is the truth?"

"Because I was asked to."

"By whom?"

"You."

Finally, Chaiet asked the witness to explain what his attorney, Mr Smith, had advised him regarding a possible self-defence plea prior to his decision to sign a plea agreement with the state. "He told me that technically, if I was going to trial just for being up in the room at that time, that I wouldn't be found guilty," Franz informed the court. "Legally I wouldn't. And he said if we look at the overall case, such as flight afterwards, me passing the stairs twice, that I would be found guilty."

After Chaiet resumed his seat, Schottland rose and walked into the centre of the courtroom. Then he repeated one earlier question.

"Did you plead guilty to murder because your lawyer told you or because you are guilty?"

"No," Franz answered.

"None? Neither one of those two reasons?" Schottland said incredulously.

"He advised me to."

The trial resumed the next afternoon, Friday, March 18, at 1:30. Before the jurors were brought into the courtroom, Schottland informed Judge Arnone that the state's next witness, Dr Halbert Fillinger, would be testifying that Al Podgis died of a contact wound to the head. "Certainly if this was the trial of Scott Franz...and the issue was, is it murder, manslaughter or not guilty or self-defence or whatever, Dr Fillinger's opinion on what the autopsy revealed might be material and relevant," he argued. "But he is testifying directly contrary to two other state's key witnesses: Trooper Wambold and Scott Franz. And I do not believe that it is proper in a trial of this sort to allow the prosecutor to do that."

Chaiet countered that the jury should be permitted to understand "an entire mosaic, an entire criminal event that involves two murders."

In his ruling, Judge Arnone said: "The court is satisfied that the killing of Mr Podgis forms an integral part of this case with regard to this defendant, and it becomes an issue for the jury's determination on credibility [of Scott Franz] and the circumstances that existed at the time."

Fillinger, who for twenty-three years had served as assistant medical examiner of the city of Philadelphia, provided testimony that confirmed Schottland's worst fears. The jury heard graphic details about the wounds to both Al and Rosemary Podgis, and viewed gruesome colour photographs. At one point, in describing Al Podgis, Fillinger said: "There is an area of dark black superficial skin scraping, or erosion, on the back, which is characteristic with what I often see produced by either fly larvae or ants...there is a blackish discoloration, there are a number of fly larvae embedded in the skin" — he paused, then added helpfully, "Fly larvae are maggots — embedded in the skin at the side." Lorraine Peever, who was seated in her usual spot behind the prosecutor's table, would later swear that before court was called to order, she overheard Chaiet instruct Fillinger: "Don't forget the maggots."

After describing his autopsy procedure, Fillinger was asked to classify the gunshot wound that killed Al Podgis. He replied: "Contact gunshot wound."

"You've given an opinion just now," said Chaiet. "You say this is a contact wound?"

"That's correct."

"Muzzle touching skin?"

"That's correct."

"Muzzle touching skin?"

"That's correct."

Fillinger told the court that he had based his opinion on his observations of the entrance and exit wounds. The fact that the muzzle was touching Al Podgis's head would explain the absence of partially burned gunpowder around the entrance wound. Although exit wounds are usually larger and cause more destruction, Fillinger continued, a shot fired from a distance "wouldn't empty the skull of most of its brain contents. That is what happened in this case." The advanced state of decomposition further hampered his efforts to find gunpowder residue, he explained. "Besides that, the granular material blown into the skull is dispersed along the brain as the bullet and the pressure move throughout. But the brain is blown out of the head, and I don't have much to look at."

In describing the wound to Rosemary Podgis's abdomen, Fillinger stood up and indicated that the bullet had passed "from front to back, from right to left, and from above downward," and was recovered near her left hip. He concluded that the range had been "greater than two to three feet, based on the fact that there is no residue around the wound." Chaiet asked him to explain how, despite an absence of residue in both cases, he could determine that one was a contact wound and the other a shot of intermediate range or greater.

"We have two different kinds of target material," the pathologist replied. "We have a rather obese, fat — I hate to use that term, I'm a little overweight — but we have someone who is a little heavy with no bony structure behind it except deep in the pelvis. We have a projectile that produces only holes in the bowel and supporting tissue. When it hits the bone, it makes a perforation. It doesn't shatter the pelvis; it winds up in the muscle of the left hip ... If the wound in the abdomen of the lady had been a contact wound, we would see a great deal more destruction inside caused by the piston of compressed air blowing inside the abdomen. We don't have that."

Chaiet concluded by asking Fillinger to repeat his findings about "extensive bruising" to the victim's scalp. After the pathologist had indicated the areas by pointing to his own head, Chaiet took his seat.

Schottland was enraged. He knew that even though Franz had said his mother's head hit a basement step while being transported to the van, Chaiet was dangling references to the bruising like bait. If the prosecutor managed to plant in the minds of the jurors the idea that the bruises could have been caused by blunt blows to the head, it would suggest that after shooting Rosemary Podgis, her assailant had struck her repeatedly to ensure she was dead. It created a sensational impression, like reading a supermarket tabloid headline. Schottland knew he had to dispel this notion and attempt to discredit Fillinger, a venture he would undertake himself and with the aid of an expert witness later. Meanwhile, Schottland fumed, Chaiet was trotting out the blood and gore and raising themes of evil and revenge that had to be affecting the jurors. And through it all he enjoyed the favour of the judge's rulings. Schottland's defence, depending as it did on highly technical evidence about bullet trajectories and forensic pathology and subtle inconsistencies in Franz's testimony, did not carry the same emotional impact. Schottland was beginning to feel like a man trying to climb backwards up a waterfall.

This, and the fact that it was the fifth day of the trial and well into Friday afternoon, may partly explain what followed. In a series of increasingly testy exchanges, Schottland questioned Fillinger's memory, methods and conclusions.

"Now, do you know how many autopsies you did the week of July 11, 1982?"

"No counsellor. I have four scheduled for tonight when I leave here. I couldn't keep track of what I did last week, much less last month or year."

"My next question is do you know how many autopsies you have done since July 10 or 11, 1982?"

"Not off the top of my head. I could check back through the computer and it would take several days. We could find it if it is germane to the case."

"I'm testing your recollection, Doctor."

"I don't know how many, no."

"Do you remember each and every autopsy that you do?"

"No, not each and every one. I sometimes remember the more spectacular, the interesting or the unique ones, or the complex ones, but not each and every one."

Schottland then asked the pathologist about Dennis Fahey's efforts to contact him. "Do you recall telling an individual in connection with this case...that you could not speak to him about this particular matter because you needed your reports in front of you to do that. Do you remember that?"

"No."

Schottland moved on to Al Podgis. "Now incidentally, with respect to the two reports you prepared, you would agree with me...that there is not one word that says Mr Podgis received a contact wound in that report, is there?"

"Of course not."

"And I also understand that there is no approximation or estimate of the distance that the weapon had to be with respect to Mr Podgis in that report either, is that correct?"

"Of course not. That is absolutely right."

Schottland then queried Fillinger on the accuracy of his examination of the body of Rosemary Podgis. He pointed out that Fillinger had not measured the victim, nor could he provide a precise angle of entry for the bullet. Schottland wanted to establish the steep downward path of the bullet to support his contention that Curtis's rifle had accidentally discharged while pointing at a clumsy angle. But the sparks between the two men frequently overshadowed the point being made.

"No, no, Doctor. I want you to please answer my question. I want you to get this..."

"I can't answer that question, counsellor."

"I want you to tell us what the angle was you showed the jury, and then I'm going to ask you about the angle of the body. We know that there is a difference, but if you let me take this cross-examination step by step it is going to go a lot faster."

Fillinger frowned. "I'm not frightened, counsellor."

"I'm not trying to frighten you, Doctor. I want you to answer my question."

"Approximately thirty degrees, but with a variation of five to ten degrees or more on either side."

Later, in a truly bizarre exchange, Schottland returned to Al Podgis's wound. "Are you saying that you can't have a distant gunshot wound which blows someone's brain out of their head?"

"That's correct. That did not occur with this degree of velocity, with this much emptying of the skull."

"Where were you November 22, 1963?"

Chaiet quickly objected. Schottland then said: "That was the day John F. Kennedy was killed. Do you remember that?"

"Very well, counsellor. I can tell you where I was."

"Did you ever view the Zapruder films of that assassination?"

"I have."

"Isn't it a fact that the President's brain came blowing out of his head? Isn't that a fact?"

"No, that is not a fact, counsellor," Fillinger replied icily. "Some brain matter came out, I believe, but if you looked at the amount, not on the Zapruder film but on the autopsy report, you would see it was not blown out of his skull."

Schottland, who shared the obsession of many Americans with Kennedy's shooting and had read countless books on the subject, including the Senate Investigation Report, wisely retreated before his cross-examination became hopelessly sidetracked. "Doctor, you would agree that the wound to John Kennedy was not a contact wound, wouldn't you?"

"That's correct."

Schottland turned away. "No further questions."

Unable to resist a final jab, Fillinger said: "*Wounds.* That's plural."

Chaiet then asked Fillinger if, as a matter of practice, he did not measure the heights of bodies in order to accurately determine the location of a wound.

"I used to years ago, but no longer," Fillinger told him. "They have led to so many misleading interpretations that I found they had no value."

While that may have been true, it must have seemed odd to at least some members of the jury that a professional like Fillinger could so casually dismiss a universally accepted procedure such as measurement. Chaiet then asked why an opinion as to range was not included in his autopsy reports.

"My autopsy report consists of a series of observations of what I saw," Fillinger said. "They do not include my conclusions, except to indicate something that is very specific about the wound itself. Now, as to determination of range, because there are so many variables that can enter into it, I do not speculate except when asked specifically and given more information."

It had been an inelegant example of courtroom theatre. A gracelessly aggressive Schottland had made several blunders during his assault on Fillinger. The savagery with which he conducted part of his cross-examination may have generated sympathy for the witness and obscured genuine issues being raised. Fillinger, in turn, appeared defensive and unable to satisfactorily account for certain inconsistencies in his findings and methodology. It was difficult to imagine, however, that the net effect on the jury could have been anything but confusing.

Before Judge Arnone dismissed the court for the weekend, Chaiet rested his case. He did not intend to call more witnesses. Schottland was, for the most part, pleased. The state had displayed many bloody photographs and implicated his client in murder through the use of innuendo and circumstantial evidence. But its case, Schottland thought, was based almost entirely on the testimony of Franz — a manifestly unreliable witness — and Fillinger's opinion that Al Podgis had been killed by a contact wound, an opinion that should never have been introduced, but if accepted only emphasized Franz's deceitfulness. Schottland closed his briefcase. For all its messiness, he reflected, the evidence presented in this trial was a law-school test on the degrees of culpability assigned to an individual who walks into a house with a loaded weapon. It was a case of negligence, reckless stupidity. It was probably manslaughter, but it was not murder. If the gods were kind next week, Schottland mused, he might even win an acquittal.

For Bruce Curtis's family, the inactivity of the weekend proved even more arduous than the stressful days spent in the court-room. On Saturday morning, they arrived at the Monmouth County jail two hours early in order to secure a place at the beginning of the line-up of visitors that would, by the 11:30 A.M. opening, stretch down the long driveway. When it began to rain, they took turns sitting in the car, sipping tea from Jennie's ther-mos and eating cookies. In the scramble for a place in the visiting room, a chair was claimed for Jennie but the rest of the family stood. They told Bruce they felt the case was going very well, and pointed out that the gun misfiring in court surely sym-bolized the paucity of the state's case. He, in turn, said he was so exhausted after court each day that he returned to his cell and fell immediately to sleep.

On Sunday morning they were permitted an extended visit prior to visiting hours, a concession granted because of the distance they had travelled and the infrequency of their visits. Later, they drove past the airfield at Lakewood where the Ger-man airship, *Hindenburg*, had exploded into flames in 1937. They strolled along the boardwalk near Seaside Heights. Since it was still the off-season, there were no crowds, and the ocean had a calming effect. None of them had any interest in driving into Loch Arbour to look at 401 Euclid Avenue.

In the evenings, they stayed in their motel rooms and read the dozens of local country newspapers Jennie had brought from home. "It was very relaxing, in its own way," explains Lorraine Peever. "They're chatty, or perhaps I should say 'gossipy.' The kinds of papers Jim would read through and say, 'Oh, so-and-so's home visiting his parents,' and we would reminisce about that family.

"We seemed to take a lot of naps, too," Peever recalls. "We just felt like someone had pulled the plug on our energy reservoirs."

In one restaurant Peever noticed a tapestry hanging on the wall across from their table. It depicted an eagle, its wings outspread, clutching in its claws a banner that read: "We owe allegiance to no crown." Peever was so upset she insisted that they move to a table out of view of the tapestry. "The banner seemed to embody all the rejection of this society which we had already felt in the court and in the newspapers," she recalls. "It seemed to me that this nation that had once rejected our British heritage was now rejecting Bruce's humanity and right to justice."

Schottland spent most of his weekend preparing for the coming week. On Sunday afternoon, as he sat jotting notes onto a legal pad, he finally resolved a question he had deliberately left open until the last possible moment. He knew that some jurors might expect that a teenager claiming that the shooting of his friend's mother was an accident would get up on the stand and say so. But Schottland suspected his client would not fare well on the witness stand. He had discussed it with Dennis Fahey, who had interviewed the boy at length, and he had talked to Curtis himself. Although Curtis was not keen on testifying, a more significant influence on Schottland's decision was the boy's habit of carrying his book with him into the courtroom. Once, when Schottland had observed him reading on the sly during a break in the proceedings, he had had to tell him to stop. "That told me a lot about him," Schottland says. "He was doing that as a defence mechanism, obviously, but I felt he was very detached."

Moreover, if Curtis did testify, Chaiet could cross-examine him on the contents of his journal. Even though Schottland believed Curtis's morbid writings amounted to no more than the fantasies of a kid who intellectualized too much and lived his life through books, he didn't especially want to explain that to a jury. "I always got my best results when I left my defendant sitting. Defendants in criminal cases are generally not good witnesses. In fact, it's only an extraordinary person who is a good witness, and I felt Bruce was anything but that. Dennis and I spent hours with him in jail, and we just felt he was a space cadet, you know what I'm saying? We felt he was going to botch it."

Schottland continued scribbling notes on his pad while he

reviewed the previous week. Although the state had introduced testimony about Curtis's allegedly ghoulish behaviour after the shootings, and the fact that the two boys had left the scene could not be disputed, Schottland had established two critical points in his client's favour: if the rifle Curtis had used could go off in the courtroom, it could have fired accidentally on the morning of July 5. And doubts about the nature of Al Podgis's wound had been raised and would be strengthened after Schottland called an expert witness the next week. As he had told Fahey after court on Friday: "Paul hasn't proven diddly in this case."

Schottland ended his notations by writing: "In summary, what has the state proven — very little: suspicion, speculation, uneasiness about what happened. Bruce not testifying."

Over the weekend, Paul Chaiet also gave the case much thought. It had not been what anyone would describe as a triumphant week. Schottland, whom Chaiet described as "a good lawyer and a good advocate," had exploited the vulnerable spots in the state's case. Fillinger's testimony had proven more confusing than enlightening, and the rifle going off in the courtroom was an embarrassment best forgotten. ("My stomach did a flip-flop," Chaiet would later recall. "It was one of those things you never want to happen in a courtroom.") All of this bothered Chaiet because his guts told him Curtis was "more active in what happened afterward than we know." James Newman, the Allenhurst police chief, was still calling it "a Leopold and Loeb case." Chaiet, a pragmatist, doubted that theory. ("Nah. I suppose anything was possible, but you gotta prove it to me. I didn't have proof of that.") But that didn't mean Chaiet doubted Curtis's complicity. He ran a checklist through his mind: going to Sears to buy rope; removing the rings from Rosemary Podgis's hand; playing with blood; disposing of the bodies; scrubbing the walls and stuffing bloody evidence into garbage bags; hiding the rifles. These were considered, deliberate actions. Chaiet simply could not accept that shock accounted for Curtis's acquiescence and participation.

When he discovered, on Monday morning, March 21, that Schottland did not intend to put his client on the stand — a move, quite frankly, that Chaiet agreed was prudent — the prosecutor moved to reopen his case, a decision that was up to the discretion of the trial judge. He wanted to recall Scott Franz, Chaiet explained to Judge Arnone, in order to present Franz's interpretations of Curtis's journal entries based on conversations the boys had had in Monmouth County jail last fall. Schottland complained to the judge that he had never received any such interpretations in the state's discovery. In order to test the admissability of the evidence, Judge Arnone agreed to hold a *voir dire* hearing, from which the jury was excluded.

After establishing that Franz had discussed the excerpts with Curtis "one afternoon in October or November," Chaiet referred the witness to the first entry, dated May 28, 1982. "Can you go through there, and any particular passage that he explained to you, can you read the passage and also give us his explanation?"

" 'Today I found out about the death of Patricia Hirtle,' " Franz read. " 'She shot herself. Very memorable occasion. On Monday, 17 May. I do hope it was not an attempt at a very old cliche. Was not like that. Sunset rather nice. I am afraid Rory goes tonight.' "

Franz stopped reading. "The first part is that he found out about the death of a friend of his. And 'I'm afraid Rory goes tonight,' I guess he was going to do something to Rory tonight."

"When you say 'guess,' " Chaiet said, "this is not guessing here. We are talking about what Bruce Curtis said or didn't say to you."

"Well, he said he was going to do something to Rory tonight," Franz said, visibly uncomfortable.

"Who is Rory?"

"His room-mate."

Later Franz read: " 'Did not live up to her quote or other discussions.' The quote would be, 'Better to reign in hell than serve in heaven.' "

"Better to reign in hell?" Chaiet asked.

"Than serve in heaven."

"And when you say reign, *R-E-I-G-N*, as opposed to *R-A-I-N*?"

"Yes."

"And this is something Bruce said to you?"

"Yes." Franz continued to read. "'Very disappointed. I have no mouth and I must scream. But that is not true, correct. Wonderful outlets present themselves. We shall see. Very pink. I really wished I had been there, could have saved her.'"

Franz looked up. "He wishes that he was there before Patricia committed suicide."

"Did he say anything about the 'very pink' part?" Chaiet inquired.

"It referred to blood." Franz paused, then read: "'Too late everybody got to go, got to leave behind the slow.' Okay, that's you have to get rid of all the unintelligent people."

"All the what?" the prosecutor asked.

"Unintelligent people," Franz replied. The next few lines were part of the lyrics of a pop song. Then he read: "'Revenge is very necessary.' He wants to get back at somebody or something for the death of Patricia."

Franz described the stanza from the Edgar Allan Poe's poem, *Alone*, as "just a quote from an artist. I forget who it was."

Franz continued. "'Not true Patricia, I loved too. But you are gone. I still here ready for my destiny. Why you did not come bothers me.'

"All right," Franz said, "he is saying he wanted Patricia to go to him before she committed suicide and that he probably could have helped. And the fact that she did not bothered him."

He then read: "'I shall reign supreme, not for you but I shall devote some to your mind and memory. Memory is all we ever really have, perverted and twisted to our own desires.'"

Franz stopped and looked at Chaiet. "He wants control over everything."

"'All that we see or seem is but a dream within a dream. I hate the world, we both did, but the idea is to have fun, sweet red revenge over the earth. Get back and take as much and more, much more from the earth as it has taken from you. Nothing should stop you, certainly not your own hand. Was it pleasant as the bone cracked, flesh flying. Enjoyable! God I hope so. Hope you got something, to make it worthwhile.'"

"And what did he say about that last passage you just read?" Chaiet asked.

"That she shouldn't have shot herself, nothing should make a person commit suicide. And that he hated the world and she did also, but the idea was to enjoy everything you could enjoy. And 'sweet red revenge over the earth' would be to kill everybody on earth. The 'red revenge' would relate to blood."

Turning to the diary entry dated only "Sunday, June," and the time "1:00 A.M.," Chaiet asked Franz to tell the court what Curtis had said about these passages.

Franz read aloud: "'A choice, the simple, the kind, the tedious, the complex, hard, adventurous. Have you chosen. I believe so. Mother got sick and went to the hospital yesterday. I had to make and bake the bread. Went through Ann's memory books 12, 13 a few interesting selections. She is very conceited as are you.'

"Okay," Franz said. "That's Sunday. His father or mother were not home, and he went into the house, well, looking through different things in the house. His mother had to go to the hospital, and before she went there there was some dough, and he finished making the bread. And he looked through his sister's old diaries."

Chaiet nodded patiently. "And did he talk to you about what he meant by 'a choice, the simple...' That first sentence there?"

"Yes," Franz answered quietly.

"And what, if anything, did he say about that?"

"It relates to someone's death."

"Someone's death?"

"Yes."

"And whose death?"

Franz, his head lowered, peered up through his eyebrows at the prosecutor. "His mother and father's."

Franz read on: "'Are you normal, I do not think so. I am mad, insane as I always wanted to be. I have achieved it. A difference however. I am fully aware of my madness and thoughts, my intellect still reigns supreme, obsessions do not become fixed for I know them as such. My insane qualities are controllable. I want power, or more specifically I wish to occupy a large chapter in future world history texts. That way I achieve immortality, something I shall also strive for in a physical sense. I do not want to die. I want to do it but the thought grows more frightening by the hour. However, it makes sense, freedom, money a start on my life. I must carry it through.'"

"Okay," Chaiet said to the witness. "Now, what was he talking about in that passage you just read to us?"

"At first that his ideas were very strange and not normal compared to society," Franz said, "But he could make it himself, be presented whereas people would not know that he had these ideas about reigning supreme and becoming very power hungry. And then, 'I want to do it, but the thought grows more frightening by the hour. However, it makes sense, freedom, a start on my life. I must carry it through.' That's in relation to killing his parents..."

In the first row of the spectator's gallery, Lorraine Peever gasped and became agitated. Alice Curtis placed a hand firmly on her knee and whispered, "If you cause a fuss, they'll only throw you out."

"...whereas, it was getting more frightening as he was coming closer to do it, but it makes sense because it gave him freedom," Franz continued. "He would get money and he would get a start on his new life, and he must carry it through."

"Did you also have a conversation with him in regard to his feelings toward his parents as a result of his mother's illness?"

"He was" — Franz paused thoughtfully — "how would you describe it? He was demeaned by the fact that when his mother went to the hospital he had to phone a taxicab for her, and before he did, his mother asked him to tie her shoes. He thought that was very demeaning, so he was quite angry at that."

Chaiet began his argument supporting inclusion of the diary by citing Rule 7(f), "all relevant evidence is admissable." He told Judge Arnone that since the issue of whether the shooting of Rosemary Podgis was before the jury, the state was entitled to present evidence indicating the defendant's state of mind. "We have heard from the testimony of Scott Franz and the explanation of the diary that he [Curtis] had a general feeling that the world was bad, a general seeking of red revenge, violence, as a result of the death of Patricia Hirtle."

Finally, Chaiet made the tenuous connection between Curtis's diary entries and the Podgis murder case: the suggestion that Curtis had transferred an alleged intention to kill his parents in Nova Scotia to the mother of his friend in New Jersey. "When we talk about the death of someone else's parent, albeit a different parent, within a week and a day of these thoughts running through Bruce Curtis's mind, I submit that has to have some relevance towards his state of mind on the first floor of that house."

Schottland began his counter-argument by reiterating his earlier objection to the state's overall strategy: it was the state's witness, Schottland complained, who testified that he believed the killing of Rosemary Podgis had been an accident; it was the state that had introduced evidence about Al Podgis's shooting and the subsequent autopsy; and it was the state that produced an expert to undermine the state's own key witness by testifying that Al Podgis died of a contact wound. "This was all done after the state, on its own motion before we empanelled the jury, moved to dismiss the conspiracy charges and the aiding and abetting charge of the killing upstairs."

"My mind has been boggled," Schottland said in exasperation, "by some of the directions we have taken in this trial."

Schottland pointed out that Franz, a convicted murderer who neither contributed to nor was present when the diary entries were written, should not be interpreting ambiguous passages based on a jailhouse conversation to which he could not fix even a month, let alone a date. Schottland also noted that the final entry was made at Curtis's Canadian home eight days before the shootings occurred, and was so vague that Franz's interpretation had to be taken at face value. After citing appropriate rules of evidence and precedents, he concluded: "Isn't there something missing here, Judge, and isn't there a total lack of continuity... Maybe Mr Chaiet should have gotten a psychiatrist to testify that if on Sunday he said this, the following Monday what he did couldn't be an accident."

After the lunch recess, Judge Arnone made his ruling. "Okay, with regard to the prosecutor's argument and motion in connection with the diary of the defendant, Bruce Curtis, the court is satisfied that after reading all of these cases and rules that have been cited to the court, that this should not be admitted under Rule 4. It has more prejudicial value than probative value."

Chaiet again rested his case. Schottland seized the opportunity to request a judgement of acquittal, arguing that the state had not proven beyond a reasonable doubt that Curtis had purposefully intended to kill Rosemary Podgis. In describing the state's evidence, he said: "It is speculation, it is surmise, it is suspicion . . . it is just not in the record and the inferences are not there to be drawn."

Chaiet responded quickly. He reminded the judge that Franz, in his testimony, had said he had loaded, but not armed, Curtis's rifle. That suggested Curtis had first lever-actioned the weapon, then pulled the trigger. In addition, Chaiet continued, the flight indicated guilty knowledge.

"The court is satisfied," Judge Arnone told the attorneys, "with regard to the third count which charges this defendant with murder, that the state has not only established a *prima facie* case, but has established a case upon which the jury can make a finding of guilt of murder or one of the other related homicides."

In light of the media attention the case was receiving, Judge Arnone again gave the jury his daily reminder of their duty before dismissing them. "Remember my admonitions. Don't discuss the case with anyone. If anyone attempts to discuss it with you, let me know about it. Don't discuss it among yourselves. Don't read the newspaper accounts or listen to any radio accounts or make any independent investigations."

That evening, Jim, Alice and Jennie Curtis and Lorraine Peever waited nervously in Peever's room. Before the afternoon session had begun, Dennis Fahey had told them that when he had visited Bruce in the holding cell at lunch, the boy had been distraught. He was concerned about how his mother and father had reacted to Franz's testimony that morning, especially the references to "killing his parents." Through Fahey, they had instructed Bruce to telephone them at the motel. The family doubted the call would come. It was difficult to use a telephone in the Monmouth County jail, and their motel did not usually accept collect calls. Lorraine Peever recalls: "By some miracle, Bruce's call was put through to our room. We were able to speak to him and each of us reassured him that we didn't believe a word Franz said, least of all that Bruce would ever have thought of killing his parents. We told him we loved him."

Although his voice sounded "flat and lifeless" to Peever, she felt he had taken strength from their encouragement and support. After ten minutes, the line was abruptly disconnected. Alice stood holding the dead receiver to her ear as snow flurries swept past the motel room window.

The next morning, Tuesday, March 22, sensational coverage of Franz's testimony appeared on local radio and television outlets and in newspapers. "Killer's diary: 'I shall reign supreme'" screamed the headline on the front page of Red Bank's *Daily Register*. The story, which quoted extensively from Franz's interpretations, began: "Accused murderer Bruce Curtis labelled himself 'insane,' mused about killing his parents, and advocated mass murder, according to Scott Franz, Curtis's friend and alleged partner in the killing of a Loch Arbour couple." Arlene Newman's story in the *Asbury Park Press* began: "Accused murderer Bruce Curtis thought of killing his own parents a week before the slaying of Rosemary F. Podgis, the mother of his preparatory school classmate, according to an interpretation of his diary." The headline read: "Diary tells of accused slayer thinking of killing his parents." Only later in both stories was it reported that the evidence had been given outside the presence of the jury and was ruled inadmissable by Judge Arnone. Only

Sue Epstein's account in the *Newark Star-Ledger* demonstrated restraint. Under the headline, "Judge rules out slay dismissal," Epstein began her story with the judge's refusal to dismiss Curtis's murder charges, and referred to the diary, using only two brief phrases.

The Curtis trial symbolized the traditional conflict in the United States between the public's First Amendment "right to know" and a defendant's Sixth Amendment right to a fair trial. The purpose of open trials was to make judges and juries accountable for the outcome; since any citizen has a right to attend a trial but most do not, the media act as surrogate eyes and ears. In 1953, the New Jersey Supreme Court established a state-wide policy advocating open proceedings that was re-affirmed and strengthened thirteen years later. Hoping to strike a balance between a fair trial and freedom of the press, a joint committee of Supreme Court justices and members of the New Jersey Press Association adopted voluntary guidelines in 1972 that dealt with coverage of criminal trials. The guidelines are frequently ignored. In an article being prepared for the magazine, *New Jersey Reporter*, at the time of Curtis's trial, a *Newark Star-Ledger* journalist observed: "In short, the press demands open courts in most cases and the opportunity to report freely any facts they are able to gather — regardless of the harm it might cause to a defendant's chances of receiving a fair trial."

In Canada and other Commonwealth countries, laws governing the publication of trial materials are much tougher. The publication of *voir dire* evidence, for example, is prohibited in Canadian legal procedure. American tradition, however, considers *voir dire* hearings to be part of open court proceedings since only the jury, not the public, is excluded. Michael Schottland was angry at himself. He could have requested that the press leave the courtroom but was so preoccupied with Franz's testimony that he forgot. "You get tied up in a thing and you can't think of everything," he would confess later. "I was busy, and who the hell notices who's listening so long as the jury is out of the room?"

Shortly after 9:00 A.M. on March 22, the day the newspaper articles about the diary appeared, the defence called the last witness, a forensic pathologist Schottland hoped would demolish what was left of the state's case. Dr Dominick Di Maio, sixty-nine, the former Chief Medical Examiner for the City of New York, was considered one of the most eminent figures in forensic pathology in the country. His credentials were impeccable — his curriculum vitae ran to three full single-spaced pages — and he had appeared as an expert witness — "on both sides of the fence," he informed the court — in a dozen different states. He was spending his semi-retirement acting as a lecturer and consultant and trying to find time to write an autobiographical book that, he explained, would be quite unlike celebrity coroner Thomas Noguchi's "dirty stories."

Schottland began by establishing through Di Maio that the accepted practice of describing autopsies employed such precise nomenclature that a reviewer "should be able to see through my eyes . . . what I actually saw on the autopsy table." After asking Di Maio to read the first part of the autopsy report on Al Podgis, Schottland asked him whether, in his opinion, it described the entrance of a contact gunshot wound. Di Maio said it did not. "This sounds like a wound that is long on one side, narrowed on the other. You could almost say it is a rectangular type of wound. There is no burning, there is no powder deposit, there is nothing."

Schottland handed Di Maio an 8″ x 11″ colour photograph of Al Podgis, his head sewn together following Halbert Fillinger's autopsy, and asked him to offer his expert opinion as to whether the wound to the victim's head looked like a contact wound. Di Maio studied the photo carefully.

"It is not a contact wound," he announced, noting the absence of soot, powder and burning, as well as the shape of the wound which he described as "more typical of a distant shot."

Schottland took a few steps towards the jury box, observed the jurors staring spellbound at the distinguished doctor, and turned back to Di Maio. "Dr Fillinger opined, in answer to questions by the prosecutor and myself, that the reason he concluded this was a contact wound was because there was an extrusion of a large amount of brain matter and very heavy destruction of skull fragments and tissue. If you assume that is correct, have you seen cases of a distant shot which produced a similar type of brain injury involving a high-velocity hunting-type rifle?"

"Yes," Di Maio said, and commenced a technical explanation of that phenomenon, interspersed with folksy anecdotes to help the jury understand his points. ("Those are pressure waves. My youngster likes to speak about it as a good motor boat going down the river. If you watch one, you see these big, heavy waves, and if you are in a rowboat, as I have been, you can topple over.") He concluded with a personal touch. "I have seen it in several cases. One of which I can't forget was a police officer friend of mine who was shot with a .30-.30 rifle at about one hundred feet or more during a shoot-out. He had no head left."

Turning to the autopsy performed on Rosemary Podgis, Schottland said: "When a forensic pathologist does an autopsy where there is a gunshot wound, as part of the autopsy should he measure the victim?"

"Yes," Di Maio replied, explaining how the conventional method of measuring from the heel up helps pinpoint the entrance wound and establish the angle of the shot.

"And when you look at this autopsy report, did Dr Fillinger measure the distance from the heel to the entrance wound, and from the heel to the exit spot, or the place where he found the bullet?"

"No."

Schottland also asked Di Maio to comment on the bumps to Rosemary Podgis's head. Di Maio pointed out that the bumps could have been produced when the woman fell after being shot.

When he was asked about the case three years later, Di Maio still remembered it. "There were things lacking [in Al Podgis's autopsy report] that I think should have been included, or more specifically stated. I know it wasn't a close shot. Period. That was my big contention, that if he had summarized it as a contact wound you could have said he knew about it but he didn't describe it, or it may have been omitted during the typing. But there was no mention of it anywhere.

"That sort of disturbed the other fellow," Di Maio speculated, "because there was no reason for him to have taken a plea. And when he took a plea, he made it more difficult for the poor second fellow."

After a short recess, Schottland began his summation.

"The case involves the deaths of two human beings," he said. "Even though my client is not charged in any way with respect to the death of Alfred Podgis, it somehow found its way into the case. You can realize the stakes are very high. A case like this is a real tester as to whether or not you people, as a group representing the community, supposedly a cross-section of society, can adhere to the rules and the law and decide the case solely on the evidence that has been presented and not on the basis of suspicion, not on the basis of speculation, and not on the basis of any type of anger, bias, any type of feeling sorry for someone or not feeling sorry for someone."

Schottland walked slowly towards the jury box and made eye contact with first one, then another, juror. Although his courtroom strength lay in intense displays of righteous indignation and an aggressive scrappy attack, he had elected to adopt "the cool mask of reason" in the face of the prosecutor's "mudslinging match."

"You are supposed to decide this case, as I said in my opening, as scientists. You are supposed to look at what has been submitted to you and say to yourselves: has the state proven *beyond a reasonable doubt*" — Schottland placed emphasis on each word — "what they charged? In other words, have they submitted to you enough evidence, and of such a quality, that you can walk out of the jury room without an uneasy feeling, feeling that you are doing the right thing based on whatever conclusions you reach?"

Schottland then focused the attention of the jurors on Scott Franz, and the inconsistencies inherent in the state's case. He pointed out that the prosecutor had undermined his own witness's credibility regarding the shooting of his stepfather with the testimony of Fillinger, which in turn was undermined by Di Maio. "You might say to yourselves," he said, spreading his arms in a gesture of bewilderment, "what the heck does that have to do with the defence of Bruce Curtis?"

Noting a reaction on several faces that he interpreted as agreement, he continued: "I am sure some of the things Scott Franz had to say to you were true. But I am also sure that some of the things he said to you were edged a little bit where they had to be edged."

Schottland outlined to the jury what he called the six "gimmies" Franz provided for the state:

After seeing his stepfather loading the rifles into the Scout, Franz quoted Curtis as saying "He must have found them." Later, he added that his mother had told him Al Podgis had found guns under Curtis's bed. Both of these damaging admissions emerged only after the plea agreement.

Franz said his friend wanted to go back into the house with the guns, although he had not mentioned it in his original statement on July 11, 1982.

Franz said that he had loaded Curtis's rifle, *but did not arm it.*

In his original statement, Franz took responsibility for the decision to get rid of the bodies. After plea bargaining, he implicated Curtis by saying his friend shook his head "in a negative response" when he picked up the telephone to call the police.

After the plea agreement, Franz quoted Curtis as saying: "We will have to get rid of the bodies."

The stories of Curtis describing gum as a pituitary gland and playing with congealed blood, designed to "turn Bruce into a ghoul," also emerged after the plea agreement.

In a summation, it is important for a defence attorney to give sympathetic jurors the words to help them argue their support once deliberations begin. Schottland offered the jury an explanation for why Franz may have wanted Curtis with him. "Maybe he needed help getting rid of the bodies. Maybe he needed somebody to talk to. Interestingly enough about that, do you realize that when Bruce came to visit, for the five days or six days these two boys were together, not once did Scott have friends over, not once was there any intermingling with other people.... This kid, Scott, was isolated, and he isolated Bruce with him after this happened."

Reminding the jury that by assisting the state, Franz expected to receive a reduced sentence for the murder of his stepfather, Schottland pointed out that Franz had never admitted to committing the crime on the witness stand and could still withdraw his plea if Curtis was acquitted. "He is playing a game with you," the defence counsel insisted. "He is playing a game with the judge, and he is playing a game with the prosecutor. He is a crap-shooter, a gambler."

Shifting the direction of his remarks, Schottland addressed the concept of flight. "The inference is that he who runs from something, you can imply or infer that he must have felt guilty.... Basically that's the guts of the thing. However, a defendant in a case has the right to argue to you, just from the facts that were produced, an explanation for that. A human explanation such as in this case, where Scott wanted to go see his sisters to find out what to do."

Recapping Trooper Wambold's testimony, Schottland reminded the jury that Curtis's rifle was so unsafe that it had misfired in the hands of the state's own expert witness. And Wambold's testimony about the distance at which a gunshot still leaves powder burns on clothing or skin further reinforced Di Maio's opinion that Al Podgis's death had not been caused by a contact wound. "And you say to yourselves, well, why does the prosecutor put it in that it is a contact wound upstairs? Very simple. He wants you to believe that it is an assassination upstairs, therefore it is an assassination downstairs. And I can't say it more clearly than that. And he wants you to say: 'Those two you-know-whats, one guy put a gun [to Al Podgis's head] while he was asleep and shot him, and one, God only knows what the kid did downstairs' — the conspiracy of life theory."

The eyes of several jurors turned to Curtis, who stared miserably down at the defence table. Schottland decided to pursue the point. "We do not subscribe to something called guilt-by-association in our society. We are not supposed to. What happened upstairs is a separate thing for which Scott Franz has to pay. Because he committed murder gives you a very good explanation as to why what happened after happened. Bruce Curtis did not have a driver's licence, was not familiar with where he was, was in a strange country...Scott said, 'We have to get rid of the bodies,' and Bruce, being in the state you might find him in after five days, went along with his friend. Because he went along with his friend doesn't mean he subscribed to everything his friend was doing, that he subscribed to the intent with which his friend shot and killed Mr Podgis."

Schottland defined the various levels of culpability that could be ascribed to his client, beginning with an intentional shooting — murder — and touching on classifications of manslaughter. The heart of his argument was a subtler distinction. "Reckless conduct requires something more than negligence. It requires a consciousness of an unreasonable act in the face of a known danger.... I suggest to you, keeping in mind the circumstances Bruce found himself in as alluded to by Scott, that that wasn't reckless conduct. It might have been negligent conduct, it might have been stupid, poor judgement, but I submit to you, if you conclude Bruce acted negligently you should acquit him."

Then Schottland made his final appeal. "And let me say this in closing. It is a momentous decision you have to make in this case. Is it murder, is it aggravated manslaughter, is it manslaughter? There are three ways, in my view, you can acquit the defendant. One, he was stupid and used poor judgement. He was negligent. He was culpable to that level, and that is not guilty.

"The gun went off by accident, completely through no fault of his own. And that's not guilty.

"And thirdly, when you sit down and you analyze this case and you say to yourselves, what has the state proven here?" Here he paused, then added: "Not what has the defence proven or not proven. Not that the kid didn't testify... what do you infer by that? You are not allowed to infer anything from that. And if you do, that's wrong.

"What has the state proven? They haven't proven anything. They have proven that Mrs Podgis died from a rifle wound inflicted under circumstances that you don't know about, and that a couple of stupid kids — or at least one stupid kid and one kid who says he committed murder — put the bodies in the van, left the scene. They made a bad judgement there. Left the bodies somewhere in Pennsylvania and went to scooting around the country, ending up in Texas, hoping to get to the sisters. That's what they proved in this case. If that amounts to murder, you convict him. I respectfully submit they haven't proven anything. It does not amount to anything culpable under our law. I respectfully request that you should acquit Bruce Curtis and send him back to Canada, from whence he came.

"The prosecutor, in his opening, alluded to Shakespeare, *The Merchant of Venice*. I suggest to you that when he was talking about murder in *The Merchant of Venice*, that was not what *The Merchant of Venice* was about. The thrust of *The Merchant of Venice* is good sense and mercy. Acquit this boy and send him back to Canada. Thank you very much."

Before dismissing the court for lunch recess, Judge Arnone spoke to the jury about the publicity the case was receiving, and gave them his usual warning: "Sometimes newspaper articles get the front pages because of the arguments of the attorneys, or the summations or whatever it is. I am going to ask you, since we are almost at the end of this case... that you not even pick up a local newspaper, including the *Star-Ledger* if you have it. If you want it, buy it, fold it, and read it tomorrow or when the case is over, just in case there might be something in there that might get your attention and you might be inclined to read it. Even if it is a headline, you might read it. I don't know what is in today's papers, I haven't read them. But I'm just suggesting that since we have reached this point, thank God, uneventfully, we don't want anything to happen between now and the time you reach a verdict."

After lunch, Chaiet rose to make his closing remarks. Not unexpectedly, he addressed himself to the state's most important — and most vulnerable — witness first. On the subject of Scott Franz, Chaiet was sanguine: "He was necessary to the state's case to give you a picture of what happened at 401 Euclid Avenue. So the state entered into a plea agreement with him and you have heard the terms of imprisonment that he faces. But in doing that, the credibility, the believability of Scott Franz is not for Paul Chaiet, the prosecutor. It is for you. You have to look at him and you have to make those value judgements as to whether he is telling the truth or not. And you know, he was not an eyewitness to what happened downstairs. So how do you use his testimony, whether you accept it or not? If you believe Scott Franz, what you do is take that version you believe and apply it as circumstantial evidence to determine what happened downstairs. Was it a purposeful, knowing act on the part of Bruce Curtis? That's how you use the testimony of Scott Franz."

Chaiet then began picking apart the defence's case. He asked the jury to consider why Al Podgis would have locked his rifle in the Scout. ("Is it so illogical that he was concerned about having those weapons in the house?") And why Rosemary Podgis would coincidentally dispatch her son to buy .30-calibre ammunition a few days prior to the shooting. ("... and this defendant somehow, because he thinks it's cute or peculiar or something, ends up with the Woolco receipt in his Samsonite bag.") As for a motive, Chaiet pointed out that Franz had been abused and Curtis apparently "expressed some outrage" at the treatment they were receiving.

"And what do we do with that den, that bullet in the den? Now, as I recall the testimony, on Saturday Mr Podgis takes the .30-calibre weapons out to the van. On Sunday morning, Scott tells us he is shot at with a .30-calibre weapon, and on Sunday night he breaks into the van . . . and he somehow gets that same .30-calibre weapon. Because we know that .30-calibre weapon is the one that killed his stepfather and put the bullet in the den. So how did that happen? Or could somebody else have put that shot in there?"

Even if the jurors doubted Franz's story, Chaiet reasoned, Curtis "had said 'We have got to pay Al back.' How do you pay Al back? And what you can't remove, and what you can't talk about in this case, is you have got to operate that firearm. You have got to lever that weapon and you have got to pull that trigger. Whether it takes a hair or what, you have to go through those steps."

Referring to the defence's contention that Franz accepted the shooting of his mother as an accident, Chaiet asked: "And what about Scott Franz and his inclination to accept that. His mother is dead and he has just killed his stepfather. He tells his sisters, you know what happened to Mom, gee, that was an accident. And do you think maybe he has a little guilt feeling about that? When he sees his mother lying dead, what does he do? Call for the last rites? No, they end up dumping her in some ravine in Pennsylvania. So when he faces the family, what's he going to say?"

Chaiet stood in the centre of the hushed courtroom, directing a sober gaze at each juror. Sometimes his closing arguments were meticulously crafted, fired with the precision of a marksman. This time he was using a shotgun approach, relying more on intensity and the accumulation of damning detail. Chaiet tried to project an image that he hoped mirrored the view most of the jurors held of themselves — that of a decent, upright citizen disturbed by the evil in society yet fair, reasonable and, above all, just. He expressed outrage at the savage way Al and Rosemary Podgis had met their deaths, and the motives of the teenaged boys responsible for it. Chaiet was confident that although the technical aspects of the state's case had been weakened by his worthy opponent, the jurors would respond to the enormity of the crime and the apparent ruthlessness of the boys' actions afterwards.

"And you can talk about eighteen-year-olds however you want. This was no panic. You have to look at their attitudes. What did they do? This wasn't, 'Oh my God, what have we done here?' and fleeing the house. You have heard testimony from Scott Franz that his reaction was to pick up the phone. And Bruce Curtis, Bruce Curtis who, if we listen to the defence, was just going along for the ride in all this, says 'oh no,' and they don't. And then what do they do in that house? The trunk, going out and getting rope, the scrubbing of walls, the putting of bags down in the basement. Was that some manic reaction or was that a plan to cover up the crime they both had committed? How can you ignore it when it's so deliberate and so calculating?

"And they go to Pennsylvania and dump these bodies. And where do they go next? They come back to New Jersey. For what? To finish cleaning up the job they started. And when they see the police, what do they do? They keep running. And to give you an illustration of what we are talking about, they were thinking all the way, what about the guns? Why don't we just dump the guns out in Pennsylvania? We didn't want to dump the guns with the bodies. We wanted to make it a little more difficult for anybody trying to put this case together. So don't think that you are talking about panic reaction and flight. You are talking about cold and calculated actions in a situation where you would think it would be almost unbelievable to be so."

Chaiet concluded by referring to his opening statement, made seven days earlier. "When I started this case, I said it wasn't a Shakespeare play, and I didn't mean to refer to any meaning or lack of meaning in *The Merchant of Venice*. What I said was: 'Truth will come to light; murder cannot be hid.' Well, you know, hindsight being twenty-twenty, maybe that saying wasn't appropriate. Inappropriate in the sense that maybe all the facts" — Chaiet's voice rose — "*all the true facts* in this case have not come out."

According to Peever: "As he bellowed these words he leaned forward and waved his long bony finger inches from Bruce's face."

"But it was not inappropriate," Chaiet roared, "when I said

that murder cannot be hid. On March first of 1983, Scott Franz pleaded guilty to the murder of Alfred Podgis. On July fifth of 1982, Bruce Curtis took that .30-calibre Winchester and he lever-actioned that gun and he pulled the trigger. And that's murder. And yes, if you have to look someplace for what was in his mind, what he was thinking about, you judge it by what they did afterward, their actions, their callous disregard.

"Do you accept Scott Franz when he tells you about his actions, about the playing with the blood, about the pituitary? If you do, fine. If you don't, fine. But you can't escape from those bodies in that ravine...the blood wiped off the walls, the pillows in the basement. And when you use that to arrive at a state of mind, Bruce Curtis should be found guilty of murder. Because on the evidence in this case, Bruce Curtis *is* guilty of murder. Thank you."

After the jury had been dismissed, Schottland approached the bench and called for a mistrial on the grounds that Chaiet's comment that "all the true facts in this case have not come out" inferred that Curtis, by not testifying, was hiding something.

"I never, for one minute, thought the remark was directed toward the defendant, Bruce Curtis, not taking the stand," said Judge Arnone. "I interpreted the statement to mean that maybe Scott Franz didn't tell the whole truth about what happened."

Schottland pressed the point. "I mean, at one time he was pointing at Bruce. In other words, during the time he was making this comment, maybe not at the precise second, but immediately before and after. Mr Chaiet was very dramatic and he was pointing at Mr Curtis... That adds some strength to the inference."

"I can appreciate what you are saying," Judge Arnone said, "but my interpretation was otherwise. Even I can't tell you exactly when he was pointing at the defendant, Bruce Curtis. As you say, probably it wasn't at the precise moment. I don't think it was because then there would have been no question about interpreting it that way. But that is the way I felt about it, and I am going to deny your motion for a mistrial."

The following morning, Wednesday, March 23, Judge Arnone delivered his charge to the jury. No longer an arbiter ruling on procedural matters, it was the judge's turn to take centre stage and explain to a jury of laypersons the law as it applied to the facts in evidence. It was his duty to establish guidelined even-handedly, so that his personal convictions did not influence the jury. Although Judge Arnone had received suggested instructions from the attorneys representing both sides, he was free to accept or reject them.

He began by reminding the jurors that the indictment against Curtis was not evidence of his guilt but merely an accusation. "Basic to your determination as to what the facts were in this case is your evaluation of the credibility and reliability of the various witnesses.... Does what the witness said accord with your own knowledge, common sense and experience? If there were inconsistencies, were they of a substantial nature or a trivial nature?"

Then he commented on the state's key witness. "Scott Franz, one of the defendants in this case, has testified on behalf of the state. The law requires that the testimony of such a witness be given careful scrutiny. Therefore, you may consider whether he has a special interest in the outcome of the case and whether his testimony was influenced by the hope or expectation of any favourable treatment or reward or by any feelings of revenge or reprisal. If you believe Scott Franz to be credible and worthy of belief, you have a right to convict this defendant on his testimony alone provided, of course, that upon consideration of the whole case you are satisfied beyond a reasonable doubt of the guilt of this defendant."

Judge Arnone went on to say: "It should be pointed out here that there is nothing unholy in honest plea negotiating between the prosecutor and the defendant and his attorney in criminal cases." Then he added: "At times, it is decidedly in the public interest."

It took Judge Arnone one hour to complete his charge. He reminded the jurors that the defendant, Curtis, was presumed to be innocent until proven guilty beyond a reasonable doubt. He made an effort to translate complex principles of law into language the jurors could easily understand. Occasionally he turned to metaphor: "Let's assume the problem is proving that it snowed during the night. You would prove it by direct evidence with testimony indicating the witness observed snow falling during the night, and you would prove it by circumstantial evidence with testimony indicating there was no snow on the ground before the witness went to sleep, and when the witness arose in the morning, it was not snowing but the ground was snow-covered."

In explaining the legal meaning of flight, the judge said: "If you find that the defendant, fearing that an accusation would be made against him or that he would be arrested, took refuge in flight for the purpose of evading the accusation or arrest, then you might consider such flight in connection with all the other evidence in the case as an indication or proof of consciousness of guilt."

Murder, the jury was told, had to involve one person *purposely* and *knowingly* causing the death of another. When a person kills *purposely*, their conscious goal is to cause death or serious bodily harm resulting in death. A person who kills *knowingly* is aware — "or practically certain" — that their actions will cause death or serious bodily harm resulting in death. "In order for you to find Bruce Curtis guilty of murder," Judge Arnone said, "the state must establish beyond a reasonable doubt, one, that the killing of Rosemary Podgis was committed by Bruce Curtis, and two, that the killing of Rosemary Podgis was done purposely and knowingly as I have defined those terms for you."

Then Judge Arnone told the jurors they had a right to consider the lesser offence of manslaughter. He cited two alternatives: aggravated and reckless manslaughter. Both crimes required that the defendant "recklessly caused the death of Rosemary Podgis." The judge defined reckless as meaning the defendant "consciously disregards a significant and justifiable risk that death will result from his conduct," and that his disregard involved "a gross deviation from the standards of conduct that a reasonable person would observe in the defendant's situation."

The distinction between the crimes was one of degree. Judge Arnone explained to the jury that in order to find Curtis guilty of aggravated manslaughter there had to be an additional element present: not only must the defendant have recklessly caused the death of Rosemary Podgis, but he must have done so under circumstances manifesting extreme indifference to human life. That meant the jury must believe that Curtis was "aware that the risk of death or serious injury is very great and he conducts himself with no regard for that risk."

After outlining the second count in the indictment — that Curtis was Franz's accomplice in the theft of the van — Judge Arnone ended his charge by reminding the jurors that they should not consider the fact that the defendant exercised his right to remain silent when arriving at their verdict.

When Schottland indicated he wished to present exceptions to the charge, Judge Arnone excused the jury. Schottland then told the judge he felt that the charge dealing with Franz's plea agreement — especially the reference to being "in the public interest" — undermined the message that careful scrutiny was required by jurors when faced with the testimony of a co-defendant. The judge had also indicated that flight inferred a consciousness of guilt, Schottland argued, without explaining to the jury that they could disregard the inference if other evidence provided an explanation for the defendant's actions. Furthermore, Schottland continued, when Judge Arnone referred to Curtis as an accomplice in the theft of the van, the jury might not have understood that he was not charged with being an accomplice to murder.

Most importantly, Schottland argued that the judge had not defined an accidental shooting. "A jury in this case could find that the defendant, Bruce Curtis, negligently killed Mrs Podgis. The [New Jersey Criminal] Code has a definition of negligence when it describes culpability. Your Honour did not indicate this to the jury, that if, in fact, the jury finds Bruce Curtis was negligent, and negligently inflicted the death of Mrs Podgis, they should acquit him.... A jury, or someone not astute or trained in criminal law and making these fine distinctions, might feel that in order to conclude that someone is blameless for the death of another under circumstances of an accidental shooting, the accident must be without fault or must be without traditional notions of misconduct in that sense...by doing that, you may be forcing a reckless manslaughter conviction."

Judge Arnone overruled all but one of Schottland's objections. At 10:40 A.M., after informing the jury that Curtis was not charged as an accomplice to murder, the judge sent them out to begin their deliberations. An hour later, the jury requested a written document redefining murder, aggravated manslaughter and reckless manslaughter. At 2:20 P.M., they requested Franz's testimony from the time the rifles were removed from the Scout until the shootings. At 6:05 P.M., the jury sent a note to the judge that read: "Please further define 'extreme indifference to human life.' " Because of the time, Judge Arnone told them he would do so the following morning.

Jim and Alice Curtis were alone in court that day. Jim's mother, Jennie, and sister, Lorraine, had driven back to Ontario after the summations the previous afternoon because Lorraine had to return to work. During the jury's deliberations, the Curtises sat outside the courtroom watching people milling about the corridor, apparently waiting for the verdict. Some of them were court officials and some were reporters. Jim and Alice wondered who the others were. Carrion, maybe, Jim thought. At least there wasn't a repeat of the incident last week when an earnest young student-reporter had approached Alice and explained she was doing a story on why people came to trials. Lorraine had nearly exploded. Alice told the girl they didn't want to speak to her. Later, Lorraine was furious that a case like this that was screaming out on so many issues could be reduced to a fluffy feature on trial-watchers.

That evening, alone in their motel room, Jim and Alice realized how much they missed Jennie and Lorraine's support and optimism, their absolute faith in the integrity of the justice system. Before they left Nova Scotia, a neighbour's relative who worked in corrections had said: "If it's the States, he'll be convicted." Neither of them had believed it, although the remark disturbed them. Then they had watched in dismay as the prosecutor, Chaiet, had ravaged their son's reputation, misinterpreting his actions and entirely misunderstanding his gentle nature. Now Jim and Alice's hopes intermingled with something else, like the smell in the air that precedes an Atlantic storm.

The next morning, Thursday March 24, Judge Arnone responded to the jury's request to define "extreme indifference to human life." He said: "A person acts with extreme indifference to human life when in the face of a clear and apparent risk that death or serious bodily injury will probably result from his conduct, he proceeds to act with a total disregard for the consequences of the act.

"I will give you an example of conduct which manifests an extreme indifference to human life. If a man were on the tenth floor of an apartment building in Times Square with crowds of people passing in the street below and he pushed a piano out of the window simply to see how high it would bounce when it hit the ground.... Whether recklessness is so extreme that it demonstrates an indifference to the value of a human life is a question of fact for you to decide after a consideration of all the evidence leading up to and including the actual shooting of Rosemary Podgis."

After the jury withdrew, Schottland approached the bench. "I think when you read that charge in the context of the deliberations, you should have reminded the jury that his conduct could be looked at in such a fashion that while it might be a gross deviation from what they would consider appropriate under the circumstances, if he did not perceive the high risk, they could acquit him. Your Honour has not furnished them with a definition of accidental killing. Your Honour has not indicated to the jury that accidental killing can include a level of culpability which the Code recognizes as negligence, which is more than civil negligence, but still the legislature elected not to make that criminal homicide. I just feel that jury may be in there wrestling with three concepts. They may be wrestling with a concept of accidental in the pure sense without any culpability or any fault as the same as an acquittal. They may be arguing whether it is reckless, and they may be arguing whether it is extreme recklessness, which is the aggravated manslaughter. But you only gave them two of the three.... And you didn't give them the alternative to acquit him. That's my position, Judge."

Judge Arnone looked down at Schottland impassively. "I didn't give it to them because they didn't ask for it."

"But Judge," Schottland protested. "They don't know that the legislature of New Jersey made that decision when they adopted the Code. They don't know the alternative is open to them. And I am saying they can't read anyone's mind."

"Okay," Judge Arnone said. "I am not going to comment on your exceptions. They are noted on the record, and your request to charge has been filed with the court." As Schottland would later complain bitterly: "Sure, I protested. But I could have stood on my head and spit nickels for all the good it did."

At 2:20 P.M., after eleven hours and forty minutes of deliberations over two days, the jury filed back into the courtroom. Some of the jurors glanced at the defendant, but Curtis sat frozen, as he had for most of the trial, staring down. The clerk asked: "Madam Forelady, had the jury reached a verdict?"

"Yes, we have," said Elizabeth Miller, a widow with two children who worked as a telephone operator for New Jersey Bell.

"On the first charge, how do you find the defendant on the charge that he committed the murder of Rosemary Podgis?"

"Not guilty," the forelady announced.

Jim and Alice Curtis, who were leaning forward on the bench in the first row of the spectator's gallery, felt a great surge of exhilaration. Schottland, who hadn't eaten breakfast once over the nine trial days in order to acquire the edge that hunger brings, felt his stomach churn.

The clerk asked: "How do you find the defendant on the charge that he committed aggravated manslaughter?"

"Guilty."

The Curtises sagged.

"On the second count," asked the clerk, "how do you find the defendant on the charge of theft?"

"Not guilty."

When Judge Arnone asked Schottland if he wanted the jury polled, Schottland said he did. The clerk faced each juror individually and asked if they agreed with the forelady's verdict. Each indicated in the affirmative. After thanking them, Judge Arnone excused the jurors and waited as they filed out of the courtroom. Then he set sentencing for April 22, almost a month later.

When Jim and Alice met with Schottland later, they thanked him for his efforts and told him they wanted to launch an appeal. That night, they phoned Lorraine Peever, who expressed shock, despair and anger in that order. Since they were not permitted to visit Bruce on a Friday, nor even leave a letter for him at the jail, they checked out of the Marlborough Motor Lodge the next morning and left. "We couldn't get out of that state fast enough," recalls Alice. In the back of their station wagon lay a sleeping bag in which their son was to have recuperated during the long drive back to Nova Scotia. It remained unused.

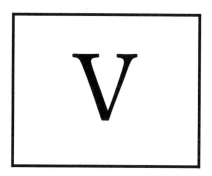

Robert W. Eisler, Esq.
Court Administrator
Office of the Court Administrator
Monmouth County Court House

Dear Mr Eisler:

I am enclosing, herewith, the excerpts of *The Daily Register* and *The Asbury Park Press*, which newspapers covered the entire trial....

This was a trial of a murder case with an unsequestered jury. The material which formed the basis of the stories came out during *voir dire*. The jury never heard this testimony based on Judge Arnone's ruling. In fact, Judge Arnone felt it was so privileged under Rule 4 it was improper. Notwithstanding this ruling, and notwithstanding the existing guidelines to the contrary, both of these newspapers carried these stories in this fashion.

When I confronted the reporters who had written

the stories, both told me the guidelines were only per-missive and their attorneys had advised them they could print the stories. Needless to say, I feel that both stories represent a shocking disregard of the existing understanding between the Supreme Court and the media pertaining to the coverage of a criminal trial.

As you know, the jury in this case convicted my client of aggravated manslaughter. Frankly, we will never know whether any of the jurors either saw the articles, heard the radio commentary, or had someone mention to them something about them.

I, for one, would like to go on record as strongly opposed to an expansion of media coverage [the use of still or television cameras] of significant trials. The newspaper articles contained herein are evidence in support of my opinion.

> very truly yours
> Michael D. Schottland

April 5, 1983

Dear Grandma:

I really don't know what to say. Everything really didn't turn out the way it should. But I am not depressed actually. Much of my anxiety and worry lifted when the trial was over. The trial was a time of relief compared to the period of uncertainty and indecision that preceded it. Waiting is always worse than knowing, not that I was conjuring up disasters of trial while waiting, but it was not knowing when one's fate will be decided. They keep you drifting from one date to another, April 22 is the big one now. It was good to see you and talk to you, but the trial must have been very distressing for you, with truth and lies intermingled until they can not be told apart. But I really do not want to discuss it anymore, the whole process disgusted me and it is over at least for a few months. The most bitter taste was left by Scott. I could not believe the things he said and did. He has totally destroyed his life and any friendships that existed. I have not seen him or talked to him, nor do I wish to. Anyway....

Have also been having long discussions with a person very much interested in Christian Science. This person has been in jail four times for drugs or deception and desperately wishes to break away from his cycle of crime, so we discuss the methods to achieve this and the many pitfalls encountered. Having been to various institutions he has taught me and told me what to expect, what things are offered, how to handle oneself. I will, in all certainty, be going to Yardville, the Centre for Young Offenders. It is infinitely better than this place. M.C.C.I. is the lowest you can go in New Jersey. Yardville, near Trenton, has many programs. You have your own room with your own key and allowed to have personal radios and stereos. They give you milk every day and the selection and quality of food is quite good. They have contact visiting every Sunday for four hours, can have food, personal books and clothes sent in or left there, have a real law library and reading library, recreation every day, HBO (Home Box Office, the pay-television movie channel) and a theatre. They offer many vocational courses and college courses I think in either literature or sociology. A professor comes in to teach them and after awhile after showing your ability and knowledge, you are allowed to go to Trenton State University for the day for courses and return to the Centre at night. They also have a chapel and religious services every day and a resident priest. I noticed on the church service that they had one of my favourite hymns, *Ride On, Ride On.* I really love that hymn and wish it was sung more often than at Palm Sunday. It is very similar to another favourite, *Come, O Come, Emmanuel....*

I know now that I will be spending two or three years in institutions. I have resolved to use that time constructively and learn a number of things. I don't intend to waste the opportunity, that would be very foolish, setting my career back further than it is now. I will need support though and I am sure you will help. Thank you for all the support you have given already. It means alot especially in a place like this.

Love Bruce

Ten days later, on Friday, April 15, Scott Franz appeared with his attorney, Thomas Smith Jr., before Judge Arnone. Paul Chaiet stood to address the bench first.

"In light of this defendant's co-operation with the state and in light of the fact that in assessing the actors in the crime it is my opinion, and it is just my opinion, that the worst of the two individuals was Bruce Curtis. With that in mind, Your Honour, I would ask the court not to impose the minimum parole of fifteen years, but to impose a minimum parole period not to exceed ten years."

Tom Smith rose to place his client's circumstances in the best possible light. "Universally, all of the members of this family, whether they be blood children or stepchildren, stand behind Scott Franz. They were advised, and the court should know this at the outset, that Scott Franz could not, were he to plead guilty or be convicted, take in any of the estate if somebody had objected because a person under our law cannot profit by his own wrongdoing.

"These children have decided that Scott Franz should not be placed in that category.... They felt that this was not a cold-blooded, calculated, premeditated event. That it was a killing that was unlawful, a killing they wish had never happened, but that perhaps could have happened many, many years ago as these other kids were growing up....

"With what this boy went through, he has never had a life. Perhaps the only life he may have had was when he was up in

Nova Scotia, when he came under the influence of who Mr Chaiet has just described as 'the far worse of the two.'

"And I agree with Mr Chaiet that if Bruce Curtis faces a maximum of twenty years with a minimum parole eligibility of ten, then certainly the less influential of the two, the less evil of the two, the one who came under the spell of Bruce Curtis, the one who saved the state the time and expense of a trial, the one who co-operated in the presentation of the case against the co-defendant shouldn't get the same numbers. It would be unfair to treat them as equals based on the factual situation of the event and the background of this boy as opposed to the background of the Curtis boy."

Judge Arnone asked Franz if there was anything he wished to say before sentence was imposed.

"That I'm very sorry that the whole thing happened," Franz said. "I would like to thank my family for supporting me and for Mr Smith's representation."

Judge Arnone, noting the aggravating circumstances, the nature and seriousness of the offence, and the need for deterrence, sentenced Franz to twenty years — the minimum for his crime — with a parole eligibility of ten years, to be served at the Yardville Youth Reception Center.

On April 22, Curtis appeared with Michael Schottland before Judge Arnone. After outlining a number of mitigating factors that favoured his client and making an unsuccessful motion for a new trial, Schottland protested an inclusion in the pre-sentence report of remarks by Chief James Newman of the Allenhurst police department. That section of the report read: "He compared Scott Franz and Bruce Curtis to the Leopold and Loeb murders of 1930.* Chief Newman believed that these two young men played a premeditated game and never exhibited any remorse or emotion over the acts that they perpetrated. The chief stated that he believed Bruce Curtis to be the mastermind of the

*The Leopold-Loeb case actually occurred in 1924.

whole scheme . . . . The chief stated that 'I would like to see both defendants get the maximum sentence as I feel they will kill again.'"

After Judge Arnone told Schottland that he would not be influenced by Newman's remarks, Schottland continued: "Frankly, I was shocked by some of the comments made by the assistant prosecutor and Mr Smith regarding who's worse and who is not worse, and who is the evil guy and who is not the evil guy. I am practising law now for, it is a long time, going on eighteen years, Your Honour. That is the first time I ever saw somebody stepping on someone else's shoulder to get out of trouble. You know what I mean by that. They were stepping on Bruce Curtis's shoulders here to try and help Scott Franz. What for? I don't understand this.

"I don't understand why the person who pled guilty to murder is entitled to be considered the good guy and the person who the jury said is only guilty of aggravated manslaughter, he is the bad guy. That is what they said to Your Honour last week. As I have said, I have never heard that technique used in the past eighteen years. I object very vociferously and strongly. It is almost like they are going to have a legal lynching here. I hope Your Honour is not persuaded by that kind of talk."

Curtis was asked to stand before the court. "I appreciate the arguments made by Mr Schottland," said Judge Arnone. "I don't know, when you consider the type of offence, as to who is the bad guy and who is the good guy. I don't think that evaluation could properly be made. In any event, notwithstanding the arguments of counsel, I find that the aggravating circumstances outweigh the mitigating circumstances . . . .

"I am going to sentence you to the custody of the Commissioner of the Department of Corrections for a period of twenty years. You are not going to be eligible for parole until you have served a minimum of ten years. I am going to direct that you serve this sentence at the Youth Reception and Correction Center at Yardville."

When Jim Curtis telephoned Schottland that evening and learned of the sentence he was devastated. He and Alice called their daughter, Anne, who relayed the news to Lorraine Peever. Two hours later, Peever, her husband, Bob, and her brother, Don Curtis, and his wife arrived at Jennie Curtis's home to break the news. That evening, they called Jim and Alice to express their outrage. They recommended that the Curtises appeal the sentence and offered them a financial contribution. Three days later, Schottland sent a letter to the Curtises confirming his willingness to appeal. He wrote: "I can assure you I will make every effort to set aside what I consider to be an unjust conviction and manifestly ridiculous punishment."

In a letter to Lorraine Peever, dated April 22, Curtis wrote: "Perhaps you in Canada have been wondering about my emotional health with the trial, conviction and sentencing. Actually I have been quite fine and not affected to deeply. About a week before the trial I was overwrought, but one night while I was sleeping in the isolation cell I resolved several things. I resolved that no matter what happened I would not fall apart. That if I got time I would use it to advance my mind and not waste away or feel excessively depressed or do nothing, that when I emerged I would have gained something.

"I set several potential goals among them to pick up another language, at the time I was thinking of either french or german. Among other things I resolved I could do was make a study of the people around me and try and understand the environment. I also thought of all the literary classics I wanted to read, all the authors I wanted to study. That is one thing missing from contemporary education, a firm basis in the classics. When reading biographies of people who lived or grew up around or before the turn of the century they all seemed to have read the 'great works.' Perhaps reading Goethe or Dickens or Dante on a Saturday afternoon was replaced by movie matinees. I also thought of attempting writing fiction...

"Anyway I came to terms with the possibility of being convicted of something and receiving a sentence. When the verdict was read it was not earth shattering or very dramatic. I was very bored and relieved that I would not have to spend another day waiting around, not because the waiting was a time of nervousness but because it was boring and very tiresome. This whole experience and especially the time of trial has seemed unreal, has had the quality of a play. Only once during the trial, when Scott testified, did it feel like I was personally involved and not simply an observer. I still have not accepted the reality and probably never will, though I continue to function within the context of the unreality. It is an extended dream that will one day end and my life so incredibly different from that of the dream will resume."

Bruce Curtis's experience with the New Jersey criminal justice system coincided with a trend in the state towards a stricter rule of law and order. Revisions to the Criminal Code in 1978 allowed judges to send more criminals to prison for longer terms. The 1981 Graves Act imposed minimum sentences of eighteen months to three years for any crime involving the use of a firearm. The result, by 1983, was a 70 percent increase in the number of people sent to prison and a 61 percent increase in the average duration of prison terms.

One justification for tougher sentencing was a commonly held belief that too few offenders were jailed. In fact, the rate of imprisonment in the United States was twice that of Canada and three times that of Great Britain, and its per capita prison population was the third largest in the world, behind the Soviet Union and South Africa. A second justification was a belief that tougher sentencing reduced crime. Aside from a lack of consensus among academics, politicians and members of the judiciary as to the relationship between incarceration and deterrence, the financial and social costs were enormous: according to a study published by the U.S. Justice Department's National Institute of Justice, "for every person who goes to prison, two people don't go to college." And because the New Jersey Department of Corrections, like most state agencies, was affected by budget restraints, the prison system was not expanding quickly enough to accommodate the additional prisoners. Since Monmouth ranked fourth among the twenty-one counties in New Jersey for sending offenders into the prison system, the backlog at the Monmouth County jail was particularly acute. At one point, Curtis lived in a wing designed for six that was being used to hold between seventeen and twenty-three, some of whom slept in shower stalls. Although overcrowding meant that many prisoners experienced delays in being transferred to state institutions, Scott Franz, the state's star witness, left the Monmouth County jail on August 4, while Curtis lingered in isolation through September, five months after his sentencing.

After an inquiry from the Canadian Consulate in New York, prompted by letters Jim and Alice Curtis and Lorraine Peever had sent to government officials in Ottawa, Curtis was finally transferred. He and five other inmates — handcuffed together in threes — boarded a minibus on Thursday, September 29. It was a splendid Indian Summer afternoon: warm, the countryside a verdant green under a wash of blue sky. After more than a year behind bars, Curtis found every sight worthy of attention: passing cars, children on bicycles, pedestrians walking dogs.

Their destination was the Yardville Youth Reception and Correction Center, located twelve miles east of Trenton, not far from the New Jersey Turnpike. A modern institution that could be mistaken for a college campus, Yardville received and classified all male offenders in its reception unit before assigning them to one of the institutions in the state prison system. When Franz arrived in August, he was assigned to stay at Yardville in its medium-security reformatory for inmates between the ages of eighteen and twenty-six. It was known throughout New Jersey as a progressive, relatively desirable place to serve time. He was given a key to a room in R-1-B, a housing unit designed to slowly integrate an inmate into the general prison population "when he has overcome his apprehension and improved his ability to be appropriately assertive." Franz was given a clerical job in an administrative department, and eventually enrolled in college courses, music classes and a graphic arts program.

A week after Curtis arrived for processing at Yardville's reception unit, he discovered he was being assigned to Bordentown, a gloomy brick structure adjacent to Yardville that had opened

as a prison farm fifty years earlier and become a medium security reformatory in 1948. (It was a policy, Curtis learned, never to
house co-defendants in the same institution when one turned
state's evidence against the other.) On October 6, Curtis and a
dozen other prisoners dressed in ill-fitting orange jumpsuits
were driven from Yardville to a basement receiving entrance at
the back of Bordentown where they stood amidst puddles of oil
waiting to be issued regulation clothing, boots and a cup. Then
Curtis was taken to a fourth-floor tier and placed in a cell.

His first glimpse of Bordentown had reminded him of the
workhouses in the novels of Charles Dickens. At sunset, he stared
out a barred window at the institution's rooftops outlined in a
russet glow. He noted the stonework and castle-like formations.
A mass of pigeons suddenly filled the air with a great flapping
confusion. Although he had initially been disappointed that he
was not going to serve his sentence at Yardville, now he told
himself that Bordentown might be preferable to "some modern
institution of no character." His new designation was 93852.

In the weeks that followed, Curtis improvised a clothesline by
stringing a cord from a grill over the open toilet in his cell to one
of the bars on the window. He was given plastic hangers in
fluorescent shades of yellow, blue, green and pink. At the front
of the tier were showers and a large mirror for shaving. When his
parents brought him a portable AM-FM radio and cassette
player, he was able to tune in Philadelphia stations, and in the
evening, when the weather conditions were right, public radio
from New York. Eventually he resumed his correspondence
courses from Queen's University and also enrolled in courses offered in the prison by a local community college. Although the
standards were below Curtis's level, he knew the parole board
viewed these studies favourably when reviewing cases.

Curtis was assigned to work in the prison's school area. Every
weekday morning he walked down the long tunnel — known as
"the turnpike" — that was the main artery connecting all areas
of the prison. If anyone taunted him — as a frail-looking,
bookish newcomer, he was a natural target — he ignored them.
The school consisted of one corridor with classrooms on either

side and two offices in the back. As an aide to a teacher named Joseph Alcorn, Curtis assisted with paperwork and tutored inmates in grammar, reading and mathematics. Sometimes Alcorn brought in a movie on videocassette for him and Curtis to watch. "At first he was very, very quiet," Alcorn recalls. "He didn't bother with many people because he didn't have much in common with them. But he was especially good with poor readers because he would go over and over things with them patiently.

"Then I realized he was very intelligent. He's like a camera, seeing everything and taking it all in."

October 22, 1983

Dear Grandma:

I have been here two weeks now, in Bordentown. The name, Bordentown, is appropriate for in the institution they have a dairy and dairy cattle and the name Borden I associate with milk products. Perhaps the Borden company comes from around here, probably. They finally turned the heat on, so I am not so cold, though I do have a cold. Outside still lingers warmth, but these old stone walls capture the cold night air and refuse to give it up. My window looks toward the dining area and kitchen, the sky half hidden by the tallness of the building. The sun sets quite abit to my left among the mass of building, and all that I see of the sunset is its darker, deeper outermost reaches, turning purple to black. The many cats outside my window seem a lazy lot, providing little diversion. When I first came here I was in another wing, on the fourth floor, looking out over a stone quad and across to a tiled roof. From my window I could watch the flights of pigeons, many and varied, in particular a lone white, as they landed, often akward. Or see great masses of smaller birds, as they flew, as a flock, across the sky, and then wait for the one or two stragglers, beating fast to catch up. Better too were the sunsets, the rich golden of the middle stage seeping into the roof. A few days ago I glimpsed a star, my first in many months.

I thoroughly enjoyed the food you sent down for me. Thank you. When eating it this strange thought appeared. I was eating part of Canada, that to me had been delivered, particles Canadianized, distinct from all that was around me. And each kind of food consumed resulted in separate memories. The apples had a glorious fragrance which made me think of Paris [Ontario]. Each bite, each flood of juice and firm flesh conjured up in vivid emotion and hazy sight Banfield Street...walking along under the massive maple trees eating an apple, jacket on, the warm flush of Indian summer and the constant soothing rustle of the countless leaves. Just walking and eating, nothing more, but very vivid. Apples that retain their fragrance always remind me of Paris in the fall or a summer field in N.S. [Nova Scotia]. The remembrance with the walnuts was your driveway, the hard black surface bordered by a pipe and lush greenery leading down into the hollow where the gold fish pond is, while overhead the tall, tall walnut trees sway, their strange leaves twitching and producing odd shades and plays of shadow again on the black surface of the driveway. With 20 Banfield, I always associate greeness, lush ferns and evergreens and huge overspreading walnut trees. Though I have seen your house many times in the grip of winter, its memory does not exist, overpowered and nulled by visions of greeness in a summer afternoon.

The oranges did nothing except provided the gorgeous taste they possess. The plums were rather a cheat, reminding one of nothing but the taste of tomatoes. The carrot cakes were so incredibly good that I had little time to enjoy the memories produced, as all my time was involved with the contemplation of gastronomic delight. I liked the addition of walnuts. It was a fantastic mixing of flavours, walnuts, coconut, carrots and whatever else they contain. I am a nut for coconut. The food here is reasonable. Salad at least once, usually twice a day, though their idea of salad is rather limited. A Bordentown salad consists of lettuce with Thousand Island dressing and an occasional bit of onion.... We had pizza today for lunch. A poor attempt, but still pizza is pizza. One gets milk once, sometimes twice a day. I thought with a dairy right next door we would be overpowered with milk, but no, lots and lots and lots of hot tea, which I just cannot stand. Coffee and tea both turn me off. I really can not see how people drink them. Perhaps it is an acquired taste, one which I never shall acquire. Usually one or two vegetables for lunch and supper, peas, corn or beans. Sometimes for breakfast, hardboiled eggs (2), pancakes (2), sausages, fryed eggs (2), coffee cake. Oatmeal most days plus an individualized box of cereal. An occasional orange or banana or canned pears or apple sauce. I will survive.

Bought a bottle of multivitamins. I went to see about getting on a vegetarian diet but the nurse said they did not have them. I know this to be false since several people on my wing are on the vegetarian diet and eat after the regular meal, but I would get nowhere calling her a liar. I shall have to go about it another way, through the social worker. Each section has a social worker who helps with problems and gives counselling. On the wing one has permanent guards unlike Monmouth where they changed every day. Having permanent guards assigned to each wing is so much better since they get to know everyone and what exactly happens on the wing and how it operates. The guards here are so much nicer than Monmouth, much older. Here they think of their job as a career, in Monmouth most were young and staying on for only a few years until they found something better. These guards also respect you more and want to see you get paroled and make a decent job of it on the streets. A very different atmosphere.

I went to see the library last night. I was surprised, expecting a dismal, dimly lit cavern with a few books stuck forlornly on dusty shelves. Instead it was quite large with reading tables, a fair number of books, recent magazines, an extensive up to date law library, even card catalogues. The fiction section, several hundred books mostly paperbacks and not really my kind of reading. Their nonfiction, several thousand volumes, heavy on sociology, business and surprisingly, literature. I was astounded at all the gems I found in the literature section. Dickens, Faulkner, Joyce, Burgess and quite a few Greek dramas. Then they had one or two novels from a great many good novelists. It was quite enjoyable going through the books because the order they have is hopeless and I suspect the librarians are incompetent, so going through the physics section one would come across Dickens' *Bleak House* or find *A Clock Work Orange* among books on techniques employed in metal shops. It was like Christmas discovering by chance longed for books in the wildest of places....

Reading right now James Joyce's *Ulysses*, this massive horribly difficult novel and Ayn Rand's *The Fountainhead* similar in style and purpose to *1984* and *Brave New World*. I go to Bible Study classes on Tuesday night and Thursday night. Someone comes in from a local church to lead the classes. Church services are Sunday about eight o'clock. I go to the catholic service but it is very different from a traditional mass. They sing a great many songs, not hymns but modern songs that one might sing around a campfire. Several ladies from the area come in to help with the service, one lady brings her guitar to provide the music. Every second Sunday the ladies also bring in coffee and squares they made themselves, which is nice. For such an old place I was surprised to find that there is no real chapel. The services are held at one end of the auditorium where they have set up permanent pews. At the other end of the auditorium is the prayer mat, where the Muslims meet after we finish. They also show movies there. I must end this here, so I can send it off today.

Love Bruce

A pall of gloom settled over the Curtis farmhouse. Spring 1983 turned to summer followed by a melancholy autumn. Jim and Alice comforted themselves with the belief that their son's conviction would be overturned on appeal, but inwardly they were devastated. They found many expressions for their frustration and rage: Jim described Paul Chaiet as having "the scruples of an alley cat"; of Dr Halbert Fillinger, he said: "He was lying through his teeth, the bastard." Alice, who continued to rue the decision to send Bruce to New Jersey, also blamed King's-Edgehill School. "To a certain extent, I think we were wrong to send him down there when we didn't know these parents. But that was our faith in the school, in the kind of people who went there and in their screening system, in the fact that we believed we would have been told if anything had been wrong." They also wrote letters to their local provincial and federal representatives.

Jim Curtis, in a letter to his Member of Parliament, wrote: "Bruce is an excellent student who has the potential to make a large contribution to his country. This potential will be lost if we cannot obtain justice for him. We still find it hard to believe that it is Bruce who is involved in this disaster. Bruce is the most sensitive, non-aggressive boy we know, too much so for his own good in dealing with the world we have always thought. He should have abandoned his friend to sort out his family problems himself..."

Although they complained bitterly about the justice system in New Jersey, their obsession with legal issues inevitably led them to their own province of Nova Scotia, and to Donald Marshall. In 1971, Marshall, a seventeen-year-old Micmac Indian, was convicted of the murder of a friend in a Sydney, N.S. park. In March 1982, he was released on parole after serving eleven years of a life sentence because an RCMP report calling for an inquiry into allegations of police intimidation of witnesses, fabrication of evidence and official cover-ups cast doubt on the validity of the original trial. Then in May 1983, three weeks after their son was sentenced, Jim and Alice Curtis heard the news that the Nova Scotia Supreme Court had acquitted Marshall. Although Marshall's troubled background and tough character hardly matched Jim and Alice's view of Bruce, the Marshall case had a profound effect on them: if error and deceit could permeate the law enforcement and judicial systems in Nova Scotia, it could certainly have happened in New Jersey.

Sometimes Alice stood at the door of Bruce's bedroom staring at a museum that remained frozen to the day he had left for his vacation. He had not unpacked all of his belongings, and the room was cluttered with details of the boy's life: the twenty-volume *Great Ages of Man* series from Time-Life Inc., Carl Sagan's *Cosmos*, a biography of Peter the Great, and the four-volume *The Mind Alive* encyclopaedia. There were two chessboards, a Rubik's Cube and several board-games, including one based on *The War of the Rings* in J.R.R. Tolkien's *The Lord of the Rings* trilogy. A kite stood against one wall, and Bruce's Skillcraft junior chemistry lab was packed away in its box. A huge map — "Rise and Fall of People and Nations for Four Thousand Years" — and several other posters adorned the walls. There was also a Tolkien calendar that had hung in his room at King's-Edgehill. It was opened to the month of June 1982.

In Brantford, Lorraine Peever had been "stumbling around in a daze" ever since the sentencing. There were many questions that kept her awake nights: why had Bruce been given the same sentence as Scott Franz, who had pleaded guilty to murder? Since it seemed senseless to incarcerate for twenty years a bright boy with a supportive family and an unquestionable potential for rehabilitation, why had it happened? Would this experience in prison destroy the boy?

The more Peever thought about it, the more convinced she became that, despite the family's mistrust of the media following the trial coverage in New Jersey, it might be necessary to create a public issue out of their private tragedy. One day she read an article in *The Brantford Expositor* written by the general manager of Southam News, an Ottawa-based wire service. He was angry because a Southam correspondent in Washington, D.C. had been singled out from a large group of mainly American journalists who had been writing stories about information contained in semi-classified documents. It occurred to Peever that Southam News might be sympathetic towards her nephew's treatment in New Jersey. After sending a brief outline of the case, a political reporter, Dave Todd, called to inform her that he had been assigned to the story and wanted to visit Bruce.

On October 19, five weeks after Michael Schottland filed an appeal to the Appellate Division of the New Jersey Superior Court, Todd's account of the case was published in more than a dozen newspapers across Canada. In *The Vancouver Sun*, beneath the headline, "U.S. justice: A liar, his pal and 2 killings," it began:

> LOCH ARBOUR, N.J. — It takes about five hours to drive from this village of 300 people on New Jersey's southern shore to the lonely forests of Clinton County, Pennsylvania.
>
> It will take forever for two young men to forget why they took that journey July 5, 1982....
>
> An extensive, three-month investigation in Canada and New Jersey has determined that:
>
> — Curtis, now serving 20 years for "aggravated manslaughter," was convicted solely on testimony

from Franz, who has admitted to lying repeatedly in the months after his arrest, and who offered his services as chief prosecution witness in return for a 10-year reduction in his own sentence.

— Police, for reasons unknown, prevented Curtis from contacting Canadian consular officials after his arrest.

— New Jersey authorities, lacking any material evidence to link Curtis to the killings and forced to rely on Franz's word alone, undertook a behind-the-scenes campaign to portray him as the "evil" mastermind of a so-called "Leopold and Loeb-style" thrill killing... This is an element in an appeal of Curtis' conviction currently in progress.

The Curtis case offers fuel for a new debate over the justice meted out to Canadians in trouble in the U.S. External Affairs Minister Allan MacEachen has been informed of the matter (he became involved in the case of Toronto businessman Sidney Jaffe who was abducted to Florida by bounty hunters) and the Canadian consulate in New York is acting to ensure Curtis is well-treated....

During their last year of high school, they became best friends. Curtis, the girl-shy, socially awkward A-student, Franz, bright but lazy, the fast-talker and aspiring lady's man. Vastly different in character, they grew to know each other through mutual interests in computers and backgammon....

July 5, 1982, 8 a.m. on an Independence Day holiday Monday: Different versions of what happens over the next few hours make it impossible to determine whether Curtis is a clever psychopath or a naive, easily-led teenager whose long suit is bad luck.

The essential problem is that Franz switched his story radically from the one he told police after his arrest, when he virtually took full responsibility for events leading up to the killings....

Oct. 5, 1983: Curtis is transferred to the Bordentown, N.J. youth detention centre, where he will likely spend the next nine years of his 20-year sentence if his appeal fails.

After 14 months in the Monmouth County Correctional Institution, an overcrowded, racially-tense pressure cooker, Curtis, tall and gaunt, seems as numbly disoriented as he is said to have been the day of his arrest.

Throughout a lengthy interview, his right arm quivers uncontrollably: he is not the picture of health.

Asked to discuss the day of the killings, he says that after he shot Rosemary Podgis, he felt as if he had entered a state of suspended reality, where he stays. It's a way of coping.

"It was happening to somebody else. It wasn't happening to me... My mind is set on a course now where, the day I get out, this will cease to be reality and it will become a dream."

His favourite authors are Joyce, Dickens and Dostoevsky. He wants to be an astrophysicist. During the trial last summer, he wanted to bring along a book to pass the time. He was advised it wouldn't look good.

"He's bright, maybe too bright,' says (Allenhurst police) Chief (James) Newman.

"I consider this a Leopold and Loeb killing... I'm not happy with what they got." Despite the 20-year sentences, Newman feels Curtis and Franz got off lightly.

Two days later, Todd wrote a letter to Jim and Alice Curtis on Southam News stationery:

Dear Mr and Mrs Curtis,

By now you may have learned that I have written a story concerning your son's difficulties. I don't know that you will entirely agree with my assessment of his plight, but it's at least what I regard as an honest rendering, from my perspective.

I do believe he has been foully maligned.

I will continue to do whatever I can to make the truth ring out.

My best regards and good wishes for you and Bruce,

Dave Todd

The same day, the first of many letters in response to Todd's article was mailed to the Curtises:

Dear Mr and Mrs Curtis:

I have just read with deep concern the article regarding your son which was printed in the Vancouver Sun of the 19 October 1983 by Southam Press correspondent, Dave Todd.

I am horrified to hear of the harsh treatment metered [sic] out to your son on the sketchy evidence available. Also I have written to our M.P. [Member of Parliament] Tom Siddon to ask him to try to bring to the attention of Allan MacEachern [sic] the problems of Canadian citizens being tried in the States.

I have written to Bruce directly and can only hope my letter reaches him. I just wanted him to know personally that he has friends out here in western Canada and we think of him every day.

If there is anything I can do, as a parent to help your son's case, please let me know. I feel helpless but I am willing to assist in any way that may be possible. I can only pray that the Appeal is a fair one and effective.

I have visited Middleton twice during summer holidays and know what a beautiful part of Canada you live in. Please accept my sincere sympathy and please write and let me know if there may be anything at all that I can do to help your son.

Yours very truly,
Sally Murgatroyd (mrs.)

Surprised by the volume of mail they were receiving, the Curtises asked Lorraine Peever to help with replies. They suggested that each person write letters of protest to local politicians. Alice and Lorraine travelled to Ottawa to meet with legal advisers from the federal department of External Affairs, who proved unhelpful, and speak to a group of concerned office workers who wanted to hear more about the case, an experience that proved inspirational. In Paris, Ontario, a few miles outside Brantford, Peever's cousin Norma Labron invited a dozen friends and acquaintances to her home to meet Peever. As a result of that meeting, the Paris Bruce Curtis Defence Committee was formed to organize letter-writing campaigns and look into fund-raising to help the Curtises underwrite the expense of an appeal.

In Halifax, a few weeks before Christmas, Jim Curtis contacted Roxanna Spicer, executive producer of the Canadian Broadcasting Corporation (CBC) local current affairs program, *Inquiry*. Over lunch, he discussed the case with Spicer and the show's reporter-host, Joan Melanson, and gave them copies of the sentencing transcripts and Schottland's appeal brief.

"Jim Curtis, desperate to find a sympathetic ear, was making the rounds of media people," recalls Spicer. "When we finished reading the documents we were convinced we were sitting on a hot story." Spicer tried unsuccessfully to interest national CBC documentary shows in a co-production. "There was a fantastic degree of skepticism, a hard-nosed kind of thing found in journalistic circles: where there's smoke, there's fire. No one else wanted to touch it. No one could get past the fact that the Curtis kid had packed up the bodies. Why go to bat for a kid who admitted he'd shot the mother? We didn't go in with that attitude."

While the family's persistence and Todd's article were beginning to stir curiosity and sympathy in Canada, in the United States the incident was forgotten. Almost. When the October issue of *Official Detective Stories*, a pulp magazine published in New York, appeared on the news-stands, the cover featured a man, stripped to the waist, menacing a partially undressed girl with a butcher's knife. "Decapitated for 14 sexy centerfolds!" ran a headline above the logo. A large blurb heralding the lead story read: "Maryland sleuths found a pin stuck in the girl's chest but the real shocker was the HIDEOUS PHRASE SCRAWLED ON SHIRLEY'S BACK!" And in small type at the bottom of the cover: "The New Jersey killer screamed: 'I shot your mother! What do we do now?' "

The article, written by a "special investigator" for *Official Detective Stories* named L.J. Roie, was a hastily researched account of the Podgis murder investigation and Curtis's trial taken from police reports, court transcripts and newspaper coverage. Apart from some imaginative liberties taken with the facts of the case, the article was also riddled with typographical errors that had Al and Rosemary Podgis employed at the "police" office, described William Lucia as an "inventor" and identified the first assistant prosecutor as Paul "Chalet."

In the hierarchy of the news media, *Official Detective Stories* was a seedy peep show: it boasted cheap thrills and neither promised nor provided any insights into the tragedies it presented. But along with Todd's article, it foreshadowed the major role the media were soon to play in the lives of Bruce Curtis and his family.

In mid-January 1984, Roxanna Spicer and Joan Melanson were in New Jersey with an *Inquiry* film crew gathering research and conducting interviews. During a session with Scott Franz at Yardville Youth Correction Center, in a small room painted in institutional pastel, the subject responded to questions with monosyllables and appeared tense.

FRANZ: He [Curtis] was quiet.
INQUIRY: And what were the rest of them [the boys'
fellow students] like?
FRANZ: Outgoing a little bit. And always hell-raising
or something.
INQUIRY: What did you see in Bruce?
FRANZ: Try to get him to be the same way.
INQUIRY: Why?
FRANZ: He's a deadbeat.
INQUIRY: So why bother with him?
FRANZ: Don't know. Just don't like seeing deadbeats.

The interview also touched on the moment when Franz had
gone downstairs after shooting his stepfather and found Curtis
holding a gun and Franz's mother lying on the floor.

FRANZ: Well, he said that he shot my mother.
INQUIRY: Did you think it was an accident at that
time? He said it was.
FRANZ: Yeah, I did at the time.

When asked about his plea bargain and his subsequent
testimony against Curtis, Franz replied, "I went by the advice of
my lawyers."

INQUIRY: He [Curtis] thinks that you lied. What
would you say to him?
FRANZ: I could show him that I didn't.
INQUIRY: So who's lying?
FRANZ: I don't know.

Later, while assembling the show in Halifax, Spicer and
Melanson were excited. Melanson's interview with Franz had,
on several occasions, cut close to the bone with a difficult subject. In fact all of the footage — which included interviews with
Curtis, Michael Schottland, Dr Harry Brunt, who provided the

defence with its psychological profile of Curtis, and Paul Chaiet — was strong. The only surprise came when they were unable to interview any members of the King's-Edgehill School faculty, and the headmaster, Tom Menzies, was tight-lipped. The school's presence in the item would be purely architectural.

On February 22, *Inquiry* ran "The Curtis File." The headline above a five-column story in a local paper, *The Daily News*, summarized its theme: "WAS N.S. YOUTH RAILROADED IN U.S.?" A subhead replied: "A CBC probe says yes." "The Curtis File" gave viewers in Canada's eastern provinces their first opportunity to watch Curtis, who appeared quiet and articulate and was shown working with inmates at Bordentown's school, and Franz, who spoke tersely and kept his head lowered, peering up at the camera from under a pair of eyebrows that arched like the Devil's. On a medium in which appearance is at least as important as content, and both fact and fiction become drama, Curtis and Franz were cast as Good and Evil.

The show inspired further outpourings of letters to Jim and Alice Curtis, some of them from parents of children who had attended King's-Edgehill. Virtually all of them expressed sympathy and support. One dissenting view, however, appeared on Spicer's desk a few days after the show was aired. It was written on King's-Edgehill stationery by Colleen Smith, the mathematics and computer science teacher:

Feb. 22, 1984

Madam:

This letter is, I believe, long overdue. I have been hesitant to communicate with CBC previous to this because of recommendations by the headmaster and the Governing Board of King's-Edgehill School.

I watched with great interest the *Inquiry* program this evening on CBC. I feel that there are further questions to be answered when considering the innocence of Bruce Curtis or Scott Franz. Upon reflecting on events that took place at K.E.S. one is led to question the characters of the two youths.

The boys are suspected of having been involved in two poisonings. There is a lack of concrete evidence but the circumstances surrounding these incidents are very suspicious. Let me recount some of these circumstances.

I was approached by Bruce and Scott to take them out to supper of a Saturday evening. This is not an unusual event but is peculiar in that it was initiated by the students. I was reluctant but after much persuasion finally agreed. The boys insisted on a restaurant in New Minas, several miles away, and insisted on their choice of location of desserts as well. They insisted on the Dairy Queen and Scott went into the D.Q. to purchase the desserts. He returned with a chocolate milkshake for me that definitely contained a foreign substance that had a very nicotine-like taste and produced most unpleasant side-effects — dizziness and vomiting. I returned the milkshake and it was disposed of at the Dairy Queen. At this time I presumed that a foreign object — perhaps a cigarette butt — had found its way into my drink (but none was found when dumped out) and did not pursue the possibility of deliberate poisoning.

However, on graduation day,* two graduating students experienced a remarkably similar sickness and this was traced to an open container of pop which, after lab tests, was shown to contain nicotine — a harmful, possibly deadly pesticide. Most of the students had left the dorm at this time but Bruce Curtis and Scott Franz had returned to the dorm that same evening.** One of the poisoned boys was a prize winner in closing ceremonies — winning prizes that

*Antonio Maher and Steven Ho became ill on the evening after Graduation Day.
**Curtis and Franz were reportedly in the dorm on the morning following Graduation Day.

Bruce was runner up for.*

None of this is conclusive evidence but if considering background information on Scott and Bruce's
earlier lives, such incidents at the school should warrant further investigation.

I know you tried to talk to me and possibly other
staff members when on campus. What you may not
understand is that we were told at a staff meeting that
our official position was "no comment" and to refer
any questions to the headmaster. . . .

> yours truly,
> Colleen Smith

Most of this information was not new to Spicer. Paul Chaiet
had made a passing reference to an alleged poisoning incident
at the school that may have involved Curtis and Franz. Spicer
and Melanson had discussed this issue while assembling the
show, but satisfied themselves that since Chaiet had not used
the information in presenting the state's case, it fell outside their
purview.

"We felt it was tangential to the story," explains Spicer. "It
wasn't really about Bruce Curtis's background, it was about
whether Bruce Curtis got a fair trial. We needed to focus on one
point, and we didn't want to introduce gossip or innuendo.

"I never took the story at face value though. If I were asked to
give an assessment of Bruce Curtis, I would be at a loss. He was
highly intelligent but the young man expressed no emotion. It was
like he wasn't dealing with the world. Both Joan and I vacillated
between feeling sorry for Curtis because he was in over his head,
and feeling unqualified sympathy for his parents, the real victims."

On the evening of Wednesday, January 25, 1984, with Halifax in
the grip of the worst blizzard of the winter, Jennifer Wade

---

*That Curtis was a runner-up for prizes that Antonio Maher won was a
common misconception.

ushered Jim Curtis into her living-room. Wade, a professor of
English literature at Mount Saint Vincent University and St
Mary's University, had read about the Curtis case. It struck her
as a tragic story of lost innocence and the poor judgement of a
teenager the same age as her eldest son. It was also a chilling
reminder of the effects of domestic unrest on children. But most
of all it was the role of the state in Curtis's trial that incensed her.

Wade, who would turn forty-seven in March, was chairman of
the Halifax chapter of Amnesty International. She had been involved with the human rights organization for twenty-two years,
ever since attending an inaugural meeting in 1961 when she was
a student in London, England. She had lived for a period of time
in the American south, where she took part in the civil rights
movement, and in Pakistan during the late 1960s, when that
country was in upheaval. She later moved to Vancouver, in 1971,
and was a founding member of that city's Amnesty group before
coming to Nova Scotia in 1979, where her family's roots were
sunk generations deep.

Although New Jersey was not Chile or Turkey, and the Curtis
case did not fall under Amnesty's mandate, that did not, in
Wade's view, make a breakdown in North America's sacred
adversarial justice system any more acceptable. She had, for example, made a donation to help offset Donald Marshall's legal
costs as a personal gesture of support long before his case
became a *cause célèbre*. But that did not mean she had any intention of getting involved in the Curtises' plight. When Jim
Curtis had called and explained that a sympathizer in Ontario
familiar with her reputation had recommended the family seek
her help, Wade had reluctantly agreed to see him, only out of
kindness. Along with her classes and Amnesty duties, she was
also editing a book and was a little irritated by this additional
demand on her time. She agreed to review the court documents
and other materials that Jim had brought her, but warned that it
was unlikely she could be of any service. She watched out her
front window as he trudged through the snow towards his car.
"He struck me as very, very shy and a perfect gentleman," Wade
recalls. "I remember, as he walked away into that terrible storm,

he touched his cloth cap and I felt terribly sorry for him."

Late that night, as she read the documents, Wade grew more and more outraged. The twenty-year-old Curtis, she realized, was "a native son, a country boy from the Annapolis Valley." Wade had a deep conviction that she had been given life to use in the service of others. For Wade, that had meant resisting forces that sought to limit justice and fairness. She had also learned that such efforts were often most effectively handled not by statesmen and public servants but by ordinary people armed with a simple weapon: persistence. She decided to call Jim Curtis the next day.

"I wasn't concerned whether the boy was innocent or guilty," she says. "It was the trial that bothered me, the use of plea bargaining, the perjury, the shenanigans of lawyers. I told the Curtises that I wasn't formally trained in law but I could guarantee that every second or third Canadian would hear about the case."

The first part of Wade's strategy consisted of getting something into print. After gathering information from the family, Wade wrote an article that was published in the March issue of *New Maritimes*, a monthly magazine. After summarizing the case, Wade concluded: "The account of Bruce Curtis's trial given by his father is shattering. The story is one of officials seemingly perjuring themselves, of a judge issuing prejudicial rulings, and a prosecution lawyer concerned less with justice and two boys caught in a tragic situation than with his own career...

"The whole terrifying tale prompts several questions. Why, when the police had approximately 200 reports on the Podgis household, was this family allowed to harbour approximately a dozen guns? With so many warning signs, why could the law not have intervened long before this tragedy occurred? And the main question: how could what is legal be so far removed from what is just?"

The second stage of Wade's strategy was distributing the article across Canada and putting it on the desks of politicians, religious and community leaders, and the media. Friends in Vancouver handed photocopies of the article to drivers whose cars were stalled in rush-hour traffic on Lions Gate Bridge. Wade soon found herself devoting most of her spare time to reporters who needed to assemble background information for their stories.

The efficiency of Wade's efforts became apparent within a few weeks. On April 14, *The Toronto Star*, Canada's largest circulation daily newspaper, ran an article on the front page of its Saturday Magazine section. The headline read: "Downfall of a shy scholar." Curtis, described as a "sensitive nature-lover from a close-knit, caring family," was quoted as saying: "I made the biggest mistake of my life. I got in over my head in that weird, violent house. And when it got as bad as it did, I should have come home immediately." Lorraine Peever asked: "How is it that a Canadian youth can be invited into an American home where he is terrorized half out of his mind, and then gets slapped with a twenty-year sentence?"

Two days later, *Maclean's*, Canada's weekly national newsmagazine, published a story called: "A disputed killing in New Jersey." It noted that among the points Michael Schottland would be raising on appeal was the judge's failure to adequately explain negligence and accident to the jury. The article also reported that External Affairs Minister Allan MacEachen had informed the family Canada could not interfere in a foreign trial. The article concluded: "Still, the persistent efforts of the Curtis family to focus attention on the plight of their son has clearly succeeded in raising new questions about the aftermath of events on that grim New Jersey morning."

On April 21, Alan Ferguson, *The Toronto Star*'s Saturday Magazine editor, wrote in his column: "The response to our story in Saturday Magazine last week on Bruce Curtis has been phenomenal. Michael Hanlon, who wrote the piece, says he cannot recall any story in recent years that produced such a flood of concern.

"Hanlon's phone this week was ringing almost constantly. Readers all ask the same thing: what can they do to help? All feel a terrible injustice has been done..."

Then on April 27, a story appeared on the front page of the

national *Globe and Mail* newspaper under the headline: "Slayings by 2 school chums spark bitterness, questions." Although the chronology was fundamentally the same as the others, it contained two small but important additional details. The prosecutor had tried to establish an inconsistency in Franz's contention that the bullet recovered from a second-floor hallway doorframe was the one his stepfather fired in his direction on the morning of Sunday, July 4, 1982. (Chaiet pointed out that the bullet was traced to the rifle locked inside the Scout on the previous afternoon, and was the one Franz took from the locked vehicle on Sunday night and used to shoot his stepfather on the following morning, Monday, July 5.)

Since Curtis had stated that he was outside the house waiting for Franz at the time, he presumably had not heard the shot but had accepted his friend's story. In earlier news reports, the alleged Sunday morning shooting had been presented as fact. In the *Globe and Mail* article, Curtis was quoted as saying: "I heard a shot and Scott came running out of the house...," providing corroboration for Franz's story. (In other interviews then and since, Curtis has stated that he did not hear a shot, and knew of the incident only from Franz.)

But the second detail raised different questions. In the article, Curtis reiterated that Franz consistently lied after negotiating his plea bargain. But the *Globe and Mail* succeeded in talking to Franz, who elaborated on his courtroom testimony that his friend wanted to return to the house. He told reporter Victor Malarek: "My natural instinct was to run. He coaxed me back into that house. I don't know what Bruce was thinking."

Finally, on Tuesday, May 2, the CBC's respected newsmagazine program, *the fifth estate*, aired a report on the Curtis case entitled "Convicted." Host Eric Malling began by telling viewers: "At some time or another, every mom in the world, it seems, has warned her kids about keeping bad company. It's every parent's nightmare to have an impressionable child get in over his head with a crowd he doesn't understand and circumstances he can't control. That seems to be what happened to Bruce Curtis, a teenager from rural Nova Scotia. His first trip away from home ended in violence and death. And now he could spend twenty years behind bars thinking about the company he was keeping."

Viewers across Canada watched a clip from Joan Melanson's *Inquiry* interview with Franz — Franz was, by then, refusing most interviews — and saw Malling sitting with Curtis in his tiny cell. (When asked why he didn't leave the house earlier, Curtis replied: "Because at that time Scott was my friend. I felt that he would need my help, you know. That maybe I could support him with his family turmoil, that maybe, you know, I could do something.") They also saw the shaky, hand-held videotape made by the Monmouth County Prosecutor's Office during its investigation and shown to the jurors at Curtis's trial. The camera moved slowly and eerily through the first and second floors of 401 Euclid Avenue while an officer read from Franz's original statement in a flat monotone. Only a horror movie's sound-track was missing.

When asked to explain his feelings on the case, Paul Chaiet described to Malling the elaborate cleaning-up of the house and disposal of the bodies. "If this was a complete mistake, then you call the police. You reach out for someone to tell them what happened. They didn't do that. Now, on the other side, you could say, well, they were eighteen or nineteen years old, and they were afraid. But really, we're not dealing with two stupid individuals."

The fifth estate gave Jim and Alice Curtis the final word. "He made a mistake," acknowledged Jim, "and I certainly expect him to pay something for the mistake..."

"He has paid," his wife interjected.

"But we don't think that you pay for a mistake by ruining a person's life," Jim continued. "And if he has to serve the sentence that he's now stuck with, it will be the waste of a life because he won't be any good when he gets out."

Lorraine Peever had been compiling a master list of names and addresses of supporters from across the country. A few weeks later, she undertook to mail each of them a copy of the first newsletter prepared by the Paris Bruce Curtis Defence Committee.

NEWSLETTER OF THE BRUCE CURTIS CASE

May, 1984

APPEAL DATE:

The appeal date has finally been set. Oral arguments will be heard in the Justice Complex, Trenton, New Jersey, June 6, 1984. There will be, undoubtedly, extensive Canadian media coverage.

GROUP ACTIVITIES:

PARIS: This group of interested citizens has undertaken to put out a periodic newsletter to keep those people who have expressed an interest in this case, aware of developments.

VANCOUVER: These people are impressively well organized. They hold regular meetings and have sent minutes of these meetings to other parties. Such a sharing of ideas is very helpful. The Vancouver people are doing a great job of raising public awareness of this case, in the West.

HALIFAX: People in Halifax have been instrumental in helping Bruce and his parents locate an excellent legal adviser.

OTTAWA: Members of the Ottawa group spent hours on the phone before the FIFTH ESTATE presentation of the Bruce Curtis case, alerting our Ottawa M.P.'s to the program.

NIAGARA FALLS: A bulletin board has been set up in a church in Niagara Falls with press clippings of this case, also with addresses of various government officials for letter-writing purposes.

LETTER-WRITING: The members of the Outreach Committee of St. Paul's United Church, Paris, Ontario, composed letters to both the Hon. Allen MacEachen and to [New Jersey] Governor Thomas Kean. Copies of the letters were available after Sunday service, May 6, for any interested persons to sign and send. There have been inquiries, also, from other churches in the Paris, Halifax and Vancouver areas.

Many individual citizens have written letters to both American and Canadian government officials. It is hoped that such sincere public concern will be recognized.

LETTERS TO BRUCE - At last count, Bruce has received 55 letters from caring and concerned Canadians. These must surely have bolstered his spirits. He is planning to answer all that have return addresses, which is most of them.

What does the future hold? Maybe an acquittal, maybe a new trial, maybe 18 more years in prison. Bruce will continue to need your loving support.

Jennifer Wade was pleased at the media reaction to the Curtis case and the public support it engendered. A great flame follows from a tiny spark, she thought.

Of the scores of letters Wade had dispatched to politicians, she received only one immediate and personal reply. Alexa McDonough, leader of Nova Scotia's New Democratic Party

(NDP), telephoned her with an invitation to meet in her office. The Curtis case had left McDonough, a former social worker, with two impressions. She was, like Wade, the mother of two teenaged sons. They had been raised in a protective, supportive family environment far removed from domestic strife, and they were often billeted in homes in Canada and the United States while attending tennis tournaments. Her heart had stopped, she told Wade, when she considered how easily either of her sons could have found themselves in a similar predicament.

McDonough's second impression was pragmatic. Although she was eager to help, the Curtis case struck her as a federal issue. With Donald Marshall, for example, it had not been difficult to inspire public outrage and a sense of personal collective responsibility over a miscarriage of justice within Nova Scotia's own legal system. McDonough recognized that the Progressive Conservative government of John Buchanan — and specifically Attorney-General Ron Giffin — could easily blunt a frontal assault by asking, correctly, what on earth a provincial government could do about a foreign-affairs dilemma. In fact, McDonough knew there were letters that could be written and subtle pressure applied in Ottawa to convince federal officials that Curtis's home province advocated action of some kind. But that was incumbent on the Buchanan administration to commit itself to the cause.

McDonough's view was understandable. She was not just the leader of the province's third-place opposition party; the NDP she had inherited in 1980 had been, in her words, "on a slippery slope, in total chaos and disarray." Its meagre pair of seats in the Legislature had both been from the party's traditional power base, the industrial heartland of Cape Breton Island. In 1981, McDonough won a seat in the metropolitan Halifax area — an impressive inroad into urban Nova Scotia — but in the process the party lost its two other seats. McDonough found herself the leader of a party of one, an experience that made her, by necessity as well as inclination, a shrewd and aggressive opposition critic, a political terrier.

Wade asked McDonough to do two things: write a letter to Jim and Alice Curtis to let them know that one of the province's political leaders cared about their son, and raise the issue in the Legislature. McDonough agreed to do both, then made an initiative right there in her office that impressed Wade. In response to Wade's observation that Michael Schottland's performance on the *Inquiry* program had convinced her that the attorney was "a nice guy, but a wimpy guy," McDonough called her cousin, a corporate lawyer in New York, for advice. Her cousin offered to approach Michael Shaw, a close friend and classmate from Harvard Law School, who was a top criminal lawyer. A few weeks later, McDonough notified Wade that Shaw was interested in the case.

Wade mailed Shaw a package containing information on the Curtis case. (It was typical of Wade that she also contacted Harvard to verify Shaw's credentials.) Her biggest concern, however, was that a high-powered New York lawyer like Shaw would charge exorbitant fees. To her surprise, Shaw agreed to match Schottland's price. An exuberant Wade immediately contacted Jim and Alice, who elected to decline Shaw's offer. "I felt very frustrated," admits Wade. "But you have to understand the conservative, Annapolis Valley mentality. It was four or five weeks away from the appeal and the Curtises were frightened. They'd already paid Schottland, and this just seemed like changing horses in midstream."

Another initiative of Wade's had finally succeeded, but she would come to regret it. She had long been campaigning for an "official observer" representing Canada to attend the appeal hearing. Her first choice was Ken Taylor, former Canadian ambassador to Iran who, in 1980, had helped six American fugitives flee that country and had become an American folk hero. Taylor, Wade felt, would attract a great deal of media attention and lend credibility to the case. Although Taylor was unavailable, the Canadian government eventually agreed to send an observer, but the effect his presence would create would lead Wade to admit sadly: "The original idea was good, but not what became of it."

Wednesday, June 6. A courtroom in the Richard J. Hughes Justice Complex in the state capital of Trenton, New Jersey.

Due to the backlog in the courts, New Jersey's twenty-one appellate judges were accustomed to hearing between ten and fifteen appeals at a sitting, and the number had been known to approach twenty. Although there were eight other cases scheduled for that court's three-man panel — made up of Judges Robert Matthews, James Coleman Jr. and Geoffrey Gaulkin — most of the spectators had come for the Bruce Curtis hearing. Along with the boy's parents, Jennie Curtis, and Lorraine Peever, there was a host of American reporters who seemed to be less interested in the judicial proceedings than in quizzing their Canadian counterparts — Dave Todd of *Southam News*, Merle MacIsaac of the *Halifax Chronicle-Herald*, and Alan Story representing *The Toronto Star* — on the reasons for a nationwide uproar over a young killer nobody had heard of. Their curiosity was piqued in part by the unusual presence of an "official observer" — who turned out to be a thirty-six-year-old lawyer in a junior position at the Canadian Consulate in New York — who told a reporter from the *Asbury Park Press* that his function was only to observe the hearing for a Canadian government that intended to offer no input following the decision.

The appellant, Bruce Curtis, did not attend the hearing; neither Canadian nor New Jersey jurisprudence guaranteed that right.

The oral argument lasted less than an hour. "Isn't the prosecutor under an obligation to deal consistently with the truth?" Schottland began, dramatically accusing Chaiet of accepting Scott Franz's perjured testimony. Although he was unable to present any new evidence, Schottland's appeal brief was built around eight arguments ranging from procedural errors (the admission of detailed evidence concerning the shooting of Al Podgis; the charge to the jury) and fundamental improprieties on the part of the prosecutor (the nature of Franz's plea agreement and contradictory testimony; Chaiet's inflammatory remarks during his summation) to scholarly abstractions (the constitutional integrity of the offence of aggravated manslaughter).

As strong as many of Schottland's arguments had appeared on paper, he did not fare well before the judges. A courtroom adage concerning appeal hearings was that a defence attorney should welcome even the toughest interrogation because that indicated the judges were awake and interested. But Schottland encountered impatience and hostility as well. At one point, during a complicated explanation, Judge Matthews snapped: "Get on with the sentencing argument." When Schottland proposed that Judge Arnone had confused the jury with his definition of aggravated manslaughter, Judge Matthews countered: "This jury was on top of the case, there's no doubt about that."

"But they were only human," pointed out Schottland, referring to the capacity of jurors for misunderstanding.

"Thank God," said Judge Matthews.

During a debate over the fuzzy distinction between manslaughter and aggravated manslaughter, Schottland emphasized that Judge Arnone had spent a great deal of time trying to establish the difference between a reckless killing and aggravated manslaughter, which was a reckless killing *under circumstances manifesting extreme indifference to human life.* The jury plainly wrestled with this question as well, Schottland added, noting its repeated requests for clarification. After presenting his case precedents, he drew the court's attention to a 1981 amendment to the Criminal Code. At that time, Schottland said, aggravated manslaughter was created as a first-degree crime, and reckless manslaughter was retained as a second-degree crime. A month later, the "death-by-auto" section of the Code was changed to "recklessly causing the death of another human being by operating a motor vehicle," a crime of the fourth degree. The implication was that Curtis's level of culpability most closely fit the kind of negligent behaviour implicit in the latter charge.

Arlene Weiss, a deputy Attorney General who appeared at the hearing with Paul Chaiet, responded. "Curtis fired a loaded rifle at his friend's unarmed mother from a distance of three feet," she told the court. "Even if we accept this was unintentional, this was not an accident."

During Schottland's rebuttal, one of the judges interrupted him: "I don't think you understood the Attorney General's argument. I don't understand your argument at all." (The debate was even more difficult for the Canadians to follow. Under the Criminal Code of Canada, there is no offence called aggravated manslaughter, and the Canadian charge of manslaughter is a broad category that is generally interpreted as an unintentional killing resulting from an unlawful act.)

Schottland argued that the court's failure to define accidental killing, and to explain to the jury that death resulting from negligence required an acquittal, rendered the conviction invalid. " . . . the level of culpability was a fundamental issue for the Curtis jury . . . it is also obvious that the court's charge was tailor-made to the state's theory of the case . . .

"When the jurors were arguing about the pre-shooting conduct and the stupidity of bringing the weapons into the house, none of them could take the position that they should acquit Curtis of homicide if they found his conduct to have grossly deviated from a reasonable person's actions, if Curtis failed to perceive the risk involved."

He supported this contention by quoting a recommendation from the final report of the New Jersey Criminal Law Revision Committee that advocated adopting a third-degree offence of negligent homicide. Chaiet quickly pointed out that the negligent homicide provisions were not adopted when the new Criminal Code was drafted in 1979, so the judge could not be expected to charge the jury with an offence that did not exist.

On the issue of the upstairs shooting, Schottland argued that when the state dropped its conspiracy charge against Curtis, it no longer had a right to raise and develop details concerning the murder of Al Podgis, a crime for which Curtis was not charged. "Simply put, Franz's testimony is blank as to any motive or intent on Curtis's part to cause bodily harm to either Mr Podgis or Mrs Podgis. . . .

"In effect, what the prosecutor did, since he had zero proof as to what occurred downstairs, was to place Scott Franz in the worst possible light in hope that this presentation of proofs would so poison the well for the defendant Curtis that the jury could not help but equate Curtis with Franz.... This portrait-making by the state was for one sole purpose: if one of the youths committed murder, *ipso facto*, they both did."

Schottland also directed harsh criticism towards the use of Franz's contradictory evidence. "The prosecutor allowed Scott Franz to take the stand and falsely testify that he stood across the room when he fired the fatal shot that killed his stepfather. In fact, and known to the prosecutor, the fatal shot was fired from a gun that was held to the victim's head, thus causing a 'contact wound.' Alternatively, the prosecutor, knowing that Dr Fillinger's conclusions were untruthful, on direct examination elicited that testimony anyway. An individual cannot obtain a fair trial when the prosecutor elicits testimony that is known by him to be false."

Chaiet disagreed. The reliability of witnesses had been an issue in legal circles since Cicero. No one, defence attorney and prosecutor alike, could vouch for the credibility of all of their witnesses. Chaiet told the court that the state had a responsibility to gather all the evidence and present it to the jurors so they could make their determination. "The prosecutor has no idea which witness is telling the truth and which is not," he said. It was the role of the jury, not the state, to determine the truth. " 'To hold that a party must accept a witness's testimony fails to recognize that a witness may be mistaken, may change his position, or may have forgotten,' " argued Chaiet, quoting from a 1979 case, *State v Ross*. " 'A party does not warrant or assume that each and every part of a witness's testimony will be credible.' "

Chaiet concluded: "The prosecutor, in the case at the bar, accumulated all the evidence and disclosed it to the jury in an attempt to seek the truth."

At the end of the hearing, the judges reserved decision. The Curtises and Lorraine Peever left the courtroom dejectedly, aware that they would have to wait weeks for the appellate court to tell them what they already knew in their hearts. They had been stunned at the behaviour of the judges. One of them had even spun his chair around and sat with his back to Schottland

during one of the attorney's arguments. And they were stunned
at what they remembered as Chaiet's admission that he did not
necessarily believe his chief witness had been telling the truth.
Peever asked angrily: "How can you seek the truth when you
don't believe your only witness is telling the truth?"

Six weeks later, on Wednesday, July 18, the appellate court ruled
against Curtis. In its decision, the court described the difference
between aggravated manslaughter and reckless manslaughter as
the degree of risk that death will result from the defendant's conduct. "We envision that the Legislature intended that the degree
of risk in reckless manslaughter be a mere possibility of death.
In aggravated manslaughter, however, the additional element that
death be caused 'under circumstances manifesting extreme indifference to human life' elevates the risk level from a mere possibility to a probability." Although the court acknowledged that Judge
Arnone's charge "was not a paragon of clarity," it ruled that his
explanations made it clear that the degree of recklessness necessary to elevate the crime to aggravated manslaughter was significantly greater than for reckless manslaughter.

The appellate court went on to dismantle Schottland's arguments point by point. It agreed with the prosecutor that negligent homicide was a non-existent crime, and it concluded that
Judge Arnone's charge had adequately defined accidental killing: "The jury was told that if the killing of Mrs Podgis did not
come within the court's instructions on murder, aggravated
manslaughter or reckless manslaughter, defendant must then be
acquitted. The jury was further instructed that if the killing of
Mrs Podgis was accidental...then defendant must be acquitted.
Furthermore, the jury was told that if the contention that the
shooting was accidental caused the jury to have any reasonable
doubt then the only verdict would be not guilty."

The court rejected Schottland's contention that Chaiet had
improperly alluded to Curtis during his summation, and that
"the prosecutor had to vouch for the credibility of witnesses
called." On the subject of the excessiveness of the sentence and

parole ineligibility, the court argued that the aggravating factors — the seriousness of the crime, the cleaning up, disposing of bodies, and flight — greatly outweighed any mitigating factors.

The final indignity: the court dismissed, without even bothering to write an opinion, what was arguably the most important point in Schottland's brief: that Curtis was denied a fair trial when the gory evidence concerning Al Podgis's death was admitted, a crime for which Curtis was not being tried.

One tradition of appellate procedure was that the trial judge had been in a position to personally hear and observe all of the evidence and witnesses, to become familiar with the nuances of the case. That means that when a question of inadmissable evidence or possible procedural error cannot be easily resolved, the benefit of doubt goes to the trial judge. This principle was reflected in Curtis's appeal judgement when the court, rejecting Schottland's claim that the prosecutor had referred to the defendant's failure to testify during his summation, wrote: "We agree with the trial judge's perception since he had a real feel for the case."

Examined in total, the judgement suggested that the appellate judges concurred with the prosecutor's view of the case. A reference to the contact wound that killed Al Podgis indicated that it was Dr Fillinger's expert testimony, not Dominick Di Maio's conflicting opinion, that had been accepted by the appellate court. A reference to bumps on Rosemary Podgis's head "caused by three blunt impacts" hinted that the judges were not convinced Curtis hadn't struck the woman after shooting her, despite Di Maio's and Franz's alternative explanations for the bumps. It was probably significant that the jury, after considering the evidence for eight days and deliberating for a dozen hours, chose to convict Curtis of aggravated manslaughter. Despite Schottland's insistence that the jury needed only to be instructed on negligence to have acquitted his client, three experienced appellate court judges must have wondered why a jury so uncertain of a defendant's guilt would convict him of the more serious of two manslaughter charges available to them.

Two years later, Schottland remained bitter. "Arnone knew he was in trouble with this case, with the gun going off, with all the nonsense that went on. So he lined up his ducks. He systematically took away all of my arguments. There's a book of model charges, suggestions to trial judges put out by a committee of judges. In some very subtle ways, Arnone departed from the suggested model charges in ways that favoured the state, yet you can't get a reversal on that. The juror who wanted to argue that Bruce had done something wrong but was still not guilty of a crime couldn't without knowing about the concept of negligence. If you ask nine out of ten people on the street what accident means, they'd say blameless conduct. But under New Jersey law, if you act in a careless, grossly negligent fashion, like you don't give a shit, but you fail to perceive the risk, that's not guilty. Arnone just wouldn't give me what I wanted because he knew what would happen if he did. He didn't dare tell those people that if they thought Curtis was guilty of gross negligence, but that he hadn't perceived how serious the situation was, then they could acquit him. And that, to me, was the guts of the whole thing.

"Don't be so naïve as to think that the court applied prim and proper decisions. Courts are very result-oriented, especially our appellate division when it comes to criminal cases. Once this kid was sentenced to his ten years with a twenty, the appellate division knew that if they reversed the conviction, they would never get Franz to testify again. If we got a new trial, he would move to set aside his plea. The appellate division was in a very, very delicate position. The case was only going to get weaker with time. So they made a gut decision. They felt that since there wasn't any question that the kid took the lady out, that he killed her, then he'll do ten years. That's really what it came down to, but how do you print that? How can you prove it?"

Two years later, Chaiet was satisfied that justice had been done. He dismissed his colleague's complaints, noting, "I think lawyers tend to give themselves too much credit. Factually, there were two murders there. The jury ultimately decided that it was reckless to bring a loaded gun into that house under the circumstances they heard, and they decided the firing of the gun was reckless. It's his job, as a defence attorney, to throw an additional element in there that he feels will help his client, and perhaps make the charge a little more confusing to the jury. The jury found him [Curtis] guilty of aggravated manslaughter. There was not guilty, reckless manslaughter and aggravated manslaughter, so the jury had to be convinced that it was something more than an accident before they could even get to the other charges. I believe a murder conviction would have been appropriate. He was convicted of aggravated manslaughter because there was a lack of motive. Without the diary for whatever evidence of state of mind that would have shown — mad at the world, wanting to kill — there was a problem for the jury to understand why he would do what no reasonable person would do.

"You know, everybody's saying Franz was a liar. But if you look at his original statement and how he testified in court, the material aspects weren't really different. He told me his story, and I'd say, 'Well, I don't believe that,' and he'd say, 'Well, that's the truth.' I don't know whether he was telling the truth or not. I don't vouch for the honesty and truthfulness of my witnesses. If I know someone is lying, it's my obligation not to present him, but ultimately I often don't know.

"I don't think [Dr Fillinger] was critical to the case, except in the sense that part of his testimony raised a question about Franz's testimony. You know, I'm not the expert. When I try a case and talk to somebody who did the autopsies and he tells me his opinion, I have an obligation to bring everything out that he says about it... even when the evidence kind of hurts me more than it helps me.

"In my own mind, I didn't accept that it was a contact wound. I kind of felt Di Maio was right about that. As far as I'm concerned, he [Al Podgis] couldn't have been sitting up in bed firing at Franz because of the physical location of the wound and the track of the bullet into the pillows. But that doesn't mean I believe it was self-defence. So if Franz wasn't telling us the truth about self-defence, if he went up there that morning to deliberately kill his stepfather while he was sleeping, what does that say about the rest of their story, and the involvement of Bruce Curtis? It changes the situation. Whether it changes the situation for the better or for the worse, it changes the situation."

Throughout the summer of 1984, friends and neighbours of Jim and Alice Curtis had been volunteering to write letters, place phone calls and put up posters informing the public about the Curtis case. There had been talk of fund-raising, although the Curtises had been unwilling to take that step before the appellate court decision. When the appeal — which had cost the family $15,000 — was struck down and a decision was made to hire Michael Shaw to handle a further appeal to the New Jersey Supreme Court, the Curtises knew they would need financial assistance. One day, Alice met her friend Barbara Mimms in front of the SaveEasy supermarket in Middleton. She explained that Barb MacInnis, the wife of the teacher at Lawrencetown's high school who ran the hunter safety courses, and Jim's air force buddy, Barry Dragan, were involved in setting up a defence fund. Another active supporter was their neighbour, Muriel Armstrong. The chairman was Shae Griffith, a local mother whose husband was a navigator with the Armed Forces. Mimms agreed to act as treasurer, and later that week opened a bank account. She also decided to contact Dr Gerald Sheehy, the provincial minister of health who owned a home in Middleton, and Tom Menzies, the headmaster of King's-Edgehill School whom she had met through mutual friends. (Mimms did receive a cheque from King's-Edgehill made out to The Bruce Curtis Fund in the amount of $250.)

At about the same time, rumours concerning the poisoning incidents at King's-Edgehill surfaced again. The Curtises had first learned that Bruce and Scott Franz were suspected of putting a substance in Colleen Smith's milkshake in the summer of 1982, after Bruce's arrest. The story had been related to their daughter Carol by a former student. Jim had gone directly to the school where Menzies and Smith had explained the details of

Smith's illness and the similar symptoms experienced by Antonio Maher and Steven Ho. He was also assured that Bruce was not a suspect. But now, in the summer of 1984, Barbara Mimms, Shae Griffith and other supporters were hearing references to Bruce "having been in trouble at King's-Edgehill." Roxanne Spicer and Joan Melanson of CBC Halifax, as well as Alan Story, *The Toronto Star's* correspondent in the maritime provinces, had heard about the allegations from Paul Chaiet. Alexa McDonough reported that during a discussion with Gerald Sheehy over possible actions the government could take, he had mentioned poisonings. When Jim visited the RCMP detachment in Windsor, he was told that he should make a request under the Privacy Act to obtain the information he was seeking. Then Jim and Alice heard rumours that government officials favoured a "hands-off" approach towards the case because the RCMP's file remained open.

The Honourable John Buchanan
Premier of Nova Scotia   29 August, 1984
                                          REGISTERED MAIL
The Honourable Ronald Giffin
Attorney General of Nova Scotia

The Honourable Gerald Sheehy
Minister of Health for Nova Scotia

Gentlemen:

Earlier this year I requested Dr Sheehy's help on behalf of my son, Bruce, imprisoned in New Jersey. He was convicted of aggravated manslaughter in one of the most blatantly unfair trials which I have ever had the misfortune to witness.

Recently it has come to my attention that Bruce has also been tried, convicted, and sentenced in absentia by the Nova Scotia government for one or more poisonings which took place in June 1982 either at or connected with King's-Edgehill School. (The sentence being the refusal of any help from the Nova Scotia government.) When I first heard a rumour of these events in July or August of 1982, I went immediately to King's-Edgehill to find out what had gone on....

It was my understanding from Mr Menzies (Headmaster) that both poisonings were thought to have been committed by Scott Franz, since he was the only one who could have committed the first poisoning and anyone in the school, 19 June 82 with access to the poison could have committed the second. It was also my understanding that since he [Franz] had left the country the matter had been dropped.

To what other government officials has your false or misleading information been passed? Could this be the reason that the federal government has been so reluctant to act on Bruce's behalf?

I was very disturbed this week to find that the Nova Scotia government was unable to work on Bruce's behalf because "there are charges pending against him if he ever returns to Nova Scotia." <u>BULLSHIT</u>! Scott Franz is the obvious culprit. You would be laughed out of court if you were ever stupid enough to lay charges against Bruce.

Consider the following points:
(1) Miss Smith poisoning;
    (a) Bruce was in the car with her all the time and <u>could not possibly</u> have doped her milkshake;
    (b) Scott had the motive (She had caught him with his name on her stolen calculator);
    (c) Bruce states that he knew nothing about either poisoning, and the RCMP have never questioned him (or even tried to contact him).
(2) Poisoning of Scott's Chinese room-mate;

(a) Scott still had the poison;

(b) It was Scott's room-mate who was poisoned in Scott's room;

(c) Bruce's room-mate wasn't poisoned; and

(d) Since the open soft drink can was left in the room <u>anyone</u> could have poisoned it, but <u>Scott</u> had the poison in the first place.

As far as we, Bruce's parents are concerned he is being held responsible simply because he was Scott's friend at the time even though he states that he knew nothing of these events at the time and to my knowledge no one has said otherwise. The only thing of which Bruce is guilty is incredibly bad judgement in choosing a friend. If Scott has made some statement (of which I am not aware) claiming that Bruce was involved in these poisonings with him I will give you a list of six or eight police, lawyers, and journalists who will testify as to what a diabolical liar Scott is...

Many things about these poisonings bother me:

(1) Why didn't King's-Edgehill inform us;

(2) Why didn't King's-Edgehill inform the RCMP;

(3) Why didn't the hospital inform the RCMP;

(4) Why didn't the RCMP attempt to question Bruce (neither King's-Edgehill nor the RCMP knew that he had left for New Jersey until July 6, 1982;

(5) Why were the RCMP unable to question Bruce and Scott after they were picked up; and

(6) Why have these incidents been resurrected now to smear Bruce's character when they have been allowed to lie dormant for 2 years?

It would appear to me that the answer to some of these questions could provide fertile ground for a lawsuit.

Monmouth County, New Jersey assistant prosecutor Paul Chaiet did not use either of these poisonings at Bruce's trial because there was nothing to use. Instead he spent 3/4 of the trial on the gory details of Mr Podgis' shooting for which Bruce was not on trial, nor was it ever stated or inferred that he was even on that floor before the killing. However, while Canadian journalists were in New Jersey for Bruce's appeal hearing in June 1984, Chaiet continued his character assassination by inferring that Bruce had been in trouble at King's-Edgehill. I have learned to expect such abuse from New Jersey officials, but it was with feelings of disbelief, outrage and betrayal that I learned of the same behaviour by officials of my own government. This insidious spread of misinformation must be stopped.

Sincerely,
J.E. Curtis

Shae Griffith and the other members of the Middleton support group had, by September, prepared one thousand letters urging Canada's Department of External Affairs to register its support for the Supreme Court appeal, to be filed that month. These were distributed around Middleton and surrounding area. The defence fund had collected nearly $5,000 in less than a month.

Griffith was an energetic woman in her late thirties with a take-charge manner. She and her husband lived in a two-storey, red-brick home they had built themselves just west of the graveyard on the outskirts of Middleton. They operated a small, part-time car and truck leasing business on their property, and in the summer sold fruits and vegetables from a roadside stand or supplied baskets to those customers who wished to pick their own. Griffith was inspired to get involved in the Curtis effort because she believed "Bruce was a fish out of water, totally out of his element on his first time away from home." She also remembered "being eighteen and stupid. If something had gone wrong, the last thing I would have done would have been to call my parents."

Although Griffith was delighted by the response of most people, she knew the entire community was not involved. Barbara Mimms had told her of some local citizens who had agreed to donate money to the fund but later crossed Middleton's main street to avoid meeting her.

"Most people are very sorry. They think it's a shame. They say he was a nice, quiet kid and what a rotten thing to have happened in New Jersey. And to the Curtis family. But I've also heard people say, 'Oh, you know those people up there on Mount Hanley are always fooling around with guns.' And once someone was in my car with me driving back from Lawrencetown. Her kids had gone to school with Bruce before he went to King's-Edgehill. She said, 'There, you see what happens. They never let their kids go anywhere.'

"The Valley is a very funny place. You have to be here three or four generations before you're accepted. The Curtises are outsiders and they're military. When you're military in a civilian community it makes a difference as well. I've heard resentment expressed because their daughter Anne went to the University of Toronto. What's wrong with Dalhousie, they'd say, not good enough? There was probably a resentment that Bruce was going to King's-Edgehill instead of a local school. It's jealousy, envy, whatever.

"One of our supporters said that if his name had been Bent or Bishop, a real Valley name, the whole community would have been behind it from the beginning."

Bookmakers would not have placed favourable odds on the chances that Bruce Curtis's appeal to the New Jersey Supreme Court would be a success. That was why Jim and Alice Curtis were anxious to improve their odds, if only slightly. Michael Schottland had even said to them once that in the event the case had to be taken to the Supreme Court, they should consider a

high-profile lawyer. It was that advice, and the urging of Jennifer
Wade, that brought them to New York, to the Fifth Avenue offices
of Edward Michael Shaw.

Shaw was a forty-seven-year-old native of Massachusetts,
assured and charming, a Harvard graduate who looked and
talked like one. At six feet five inches, his weight almost un-
changed since college days, he also had the appearance of an
All-American basketball star-turned-politician — New Jersey
Senator and former New York Knickerbocker Bill Bradley comes
to mind — except that Shaw's vocation was criminal law. On two
separate occasions he had worked as an assistant U.S. attorney
in the Attorney's Office for the Southern District of New York,
sometimes referred to as "the jewel of the federal system"
because of the distinguished young legal talent it attracted. In
1971, Shaw co-ordinated an operation involving a New York nar-
cotics detective named Robert Leuci who agreed to reveal information about widespread department corruption. (That story
became a best-selling book, and later a movie, entitled *Prince of
the City*.) He ran the New York Joint Strike Force Against Organized Crime from 1972 to 1974, and a year later was appointed
Special Assistant Attorney General assigned to investigate the
riots at Attica State Prison. It was an impressive career, and Jim
and Alice had felt their confidence renewed in his presence.

Shaw, in turn, found the Curtises extremely knowledgeable
about the case and its relevant principles, and "about as rational
and dispassionate as you could expect parents to be whose son's
whole life has been ruined." Although Shaw agreed that Curtis's
plight was an injustice, he was also keen on the personal
challenge it presented. In nine years of private practice — five on
his own and four with the firm of Stillman, Friedman & Shaw —
he had specialized in white-collar criminal defence work: tax
evasion, securities and mail fraud, bribery and related offences.
He had handled exactly three homicides.

The Curtis case was not an appeal "as of right." The New
Jersey Supreme Court was not obliged to hear it since it did not
raise substantial constitutional questions, nor had any of the
three intermediate appellate court judges cast a dissenting vote.

The only other "as of right" qualification was in the case of a death sentence. That meant Shaw had to petition for certification, and the New Jersey Supreme Court could use its discretion in choosing which appeals it would hear. There were several justifications for granting an appeal: if the case involved a matter of public importance that should be settled, if a similar case was already under appeal or if the interests of justice required it. The Curtis case fell under the latter.

"It was our job to sift through the record and choose something," Shaw explains. "It was easy because of the egregious nature of what I saw as the main issue: the introduction of all the upstairs evidence. There was no indication that Bruce Curtis had ever been in league with Scott Franz to harm the stepfather, and no indication Bruce Curtis knew the stepfather had been shot by his stepson rather than vice versa.

"This prosecutor seemed to have totally lost sight of the fact that the shot ringing out upstairs was relevant, and could easily have been introduced, but anything beyond that had nothing to do with Bruce Curtis. It had no conceivable relevance to his guilt or innocence. The defendant's trial lawyer had done a good job of squawking at the right times about it, so he'd made a record on that. But I think he made a really serious mistake on his appeal because, you know, if you make eight arguments all at the same decibel level, and the best one's buried in there, it's likely to get lost. And whenever the intermediate appellate court takes the time to sift through a case and make what appears to be rational judgements, it decreases your chances of getting a high court to even look at it. If you could get a judge to sit down and think about it [the admission of the upstairs evidence] though, he'd have to agree there is no rational argument in defence of it. None."

Shaw's petition to the Supreme Court, filed September 13, 1984, focused solely on two issues: the evidence concerning the killing of Al Podgis, and the harshness of Curtis's sentence.

"Always over objection," the brief read, "the trial court received a parade of eyewitness, expert, documentary, videotaped and photographic evidence describing the grisly blood and brain splattered circumstances of another killing which was absolutely irrelevant to Bruce Curtis's guilt or innocence in the death of Rosemary Podgis — that of her husband Al Podgis by his step-son Scott Franz.

"There was no excuse whatsoever for the admission of this massively prejudicial evidence in Bruce Curtis's trial: Scott Franz was not on trial in Curtis's case; Curtis was so obviously uninvolved in Al Podgis's death that the prosecution did not attempt to try Curtis as a conspirator or accomplice in that homicide; and the circumstances of the Al Podgis killing itself had <u>absolutely</u> <u>no legal relevance</u> to Curtis's state of mind, which was acknowledged by all to be the only issue in Curtis's trial.

"The trial error was all the worse because the admissable evidence was marginal that Curtis had acted with the recklessness necessary to establish that the death of Rosemary Podgis was manslaughter rather than merely a tragic accident.

"Albeit with insufficient emphasis, Curtis's trial counsel squarely presented this issue to the Appellate Division. The court did not even mention the issue in its opinion."

On the severity of Curtis's sentence, Shaw's summary was succinct: "The trial court, in addition, sentenced Bruce Curtis on the basis of aggravating factors totally unsupported by the record, and failed even to consider directly relevant mitigating factors. The result was a maximum sentence so shockingly excessive that even if reversal were not required, a very substantial modification of the sentence would be."

Shaw's brief then went into considerable detail about the morbid evidence. "As if movies of the bloody scene upstairs were not enough, the jury was then subjected to eight inch by eleven inch glossy colour photographs...the photographs showed the blood in varied colours, smears and splatters on the ceiling and furniture, and a fluorescent lamp covered with flecks of blood. Then, in a truly astounding display of cumulative prejudice, eight minutes worth of the videotape dealing with the upstairs were (sic) played for a second time to the jury...

"More graphic descriptions of the gruesome details of Al Podgis's killing were presented by the prosecution pathologist who contradicted Scott Franz's version of the shooting of Al Podgis. Even for seasoned criminal trial attorneys, the rendition was singularly gory...the pathologist vividly described Al Podgis's autopsy and bullet wounds, including references to the fly larvae or ants and maggots embedded in Al Podgis's flesh; the erosion of the armpit; a demonstration of the missing part of Podgis's head; the gaping lacerations; the brain extruded, the shattered jawbone..."

With an ironic flourish, Shaw then pointed out that according to the testimony of Dominick Di Maio, "the prosecution's insistence on trying to prove that Franz killed his stepfather in a particularly gruesome and presumably purposeful way was not only entirely irrelevant, but quite possibly utterly wrong as well."

On December 21, the Supreme Court of New Jersey refused to hear Shaw's appeal.

By the New Year, the Curtis family was experiencing a welter of emotions: rage and depression, the agony of defeat inspiring a ferocious resolve to continue their campaign. There had been some triumphs. Letters of support continued to arrive, the defence fund had grown to nearly $10,000, and Lorraine Peever had just mailed out the fourth newsletter. The previous November, Southam News reporter Dave Todd had accepted an invitation from Peever to address a public meeting in Brantford, Ontario sponsored by the local Bruce Curtis Defence Committee. Todd told about seventy-five people that Curtis's trial had included perjured testimony and irrelevant evidence. While visiting in Vancouver a few weeks later, Jennifer Wade had appeared on a popular TV talk show hosted by an intractable broadcaster named Jack Webster. ("Convince me, Jennifer Wade," Webster had growled, "that people who watch Webster should send money and that this really is a raw deal for Curtis and not nationalistic maudlin sentiment trying to help a guy who deserves to do twenty years in the bucket.") Wade was apparently convincing; the show generated considerable interest and the Vancouver defence committee reported more than sixty donations from British Columbia and the state of Washington in the weeks that followed.

But for all the encouragement, the Curtises were more frequently disillusioned. In December, while going through some of their son's personal effects, the Curtises discovered what they would come to describe as the "astounding letter" that Colleen Smith had written to Bruce. A neighbour who read it exclaimed, "Why, she's offering him her body!" That discovery, along with an exchange of correspondence with King's-Edgehill that the Curtises regarded as "remarkably unsupportive," further lowered their regard for the private school.

Neither had a change in Canada's government produced the action Jim and Alice had expected. In September, after a volatile election campaign, the Progressive Conservative Party of Brian Mulroney had won a landslide victory over the Liberal party. The new justice minister was John Crosbie, a Maritimer from the province of Newfoundland. The external affairs posting went to former prime minister Joe Clark. There was every reason to expect that the new administration, many of whom had responded sympathetically, while in opposition, to the Curtises' overtures, would take action. But by January 1985, after a frustrating four months of exchanges with the new government, Jim Curtis angrily concluded: "They're keen as hell when they're out of power, and forget everything when they get in."

In letters to politicians and the media and in conversations with supporters, the Curtis family drew attention to the recent misfortunes of two other Canadian citizens abroad: junior hockey league player Allan Chatlain, who had been arrested on assault charges in Prague, Czechoslovakia, and journalist Jonathan Mann, arrested in India after violating a travel ban to an off-limits area. In both cases, the family claimed, officials had intervened in the affairs of a foreign government on behalf of Canadian citizens. Why, they asked, couldn't the same be done for their son? That emotionally charged question became an apocryphal battle cry amongst family members and supporters. (In fact, Canadian consular officials merely provided routine services for Chatlain and Mann, and in both cases the men were released following court appearances without the benefit of diplomatic interference.)

The family also cited the 1981 case of Sidney Jaffe, a Toronto land developer who was abducted by Florida bounty hunters to stand trial in that state for breaking land-sale laws. Jaffe was convicted and sentenced to thirty-five years in prison. The Canadian government protested that Jaffe's abduction violated Canadian sovereignty and the U.S.–Canada extradition treaty, and was a breach of international law. After a gradually escalating campaign of diplomatic communications, high-level discussions — resulting in a memorandum from U.S. Secretary of State George Schulz on Jaffe's behalf — and, finally, an extraordinary habeas corpus petition in which Canada demanded that Florida free Jaffe from his "illegal custody," he was released in October 1983.

One of the many people to receive letters from the Curtises was Arthur Andrew, the retired diplomat who had been the guest speaker at Bruce Curtis's graduating ceremonies at King's-Edgehill in 1982. The widely respected Andrew, an alumnus of the school who was teaching at King's College in Halifax, still maintained strong connections within the department of external affairs. He wrote a letter, dated January 21, to the minister, Joe Clark.

> While I do not accept the analogy Mrs Curtis makes between her son's case and those of the journalist in India or the hockey player in Czechoslovakia, I do think the Bruce Curtis affair has one point in common with them; it is arousing a good deal of public interest and, in this case, having a very unfavourable effect on the reputation of the U.S. justice system in the eyes of Canadians. Coming on top of the Jaffe case in Florida, the way in which Bruce Curtis was tried, and sentence he was given by the New Jersey courts, is bound to raise

serious questions about American justice as it applies
to Canadians...

If justice ought not only be done but be seen to be
done then, at least in the eyes of a growing number of
Canadians who are aware of the Curtis case, this has
not applied to yet another Canadian appearing before
yet another American court. This perception of U.S.
justice should be a matter of some concern to the U.S.
government.

The Executive cannot, of course, interfere with the
Judiciary under the U.S. constitution but it could and
in its own interests should at least take an interest in
the ill-effects this case is having on the bilateral relationship. It is possible that there is an explanation of
the actions of the New Jersey court that have not been
made public in Canada... On the other hand, after
looking into the matter, the State Department might
agree that the Curtis trial was not in the best traditions
of the U.S. judicial system and consider it to be in the
national interests of the United States to take the
necessary legal measures, itself, to seek a new trial in
a different jurisdiction.

If you agree that the situation is as I have attempted
to describe it, you might think it useful to draw it to the
attention of the appropriate American authorities as a
matter likely to affect good relations between the two
countries and trust that they will either rebut or
remedy the complaint."

Sincerely,
Arthur Andrew

"I think things went their usual course," Andrew remarked,
observing that Canadian consular officials did what was required of them, "but the family was pretty upset by that
response. People are reluctant to accept the fact that the laws of
a foreign country apply to Canadians travelling in that country. It's especially difficult in this case because the country con-

cerned claims to have a pretty high calibre judicial system. My emotional feeling is that one fact alone probably should have brought about an acquittal: when the gun expert said in court that the gun was safe and bang, it goes off.

"No one says due process hasn't been observed in this case, but due process can produce a miscarriage of justice."

On Sunday, January 20, 1985, the eve of Bruce Curtis's twenty-first birthday, defence committees in five Canadian cities organized vigils to increase public awareness of the case. In Halifax, as a light snow fell, Alice and Carol Curtis joined Alexa McDonough and about fifty other supporters in a march from the U.S. Consulate to a downtown parade grounds, carrying candles. Two marchers held a banner that read: WAITING FOR JUSTICE - REMEMBER BRUCE CURTIS. In Montreal, Jim Curtis addressed a candlelit vigil in a church. Lorraine Peever joined a small group of people protesting outside the U.S. Embassy in Ottawa as the temperature sank to -14°F. At the American Consulate in Toronto, Anne Curtis-Woodside and her husband, Blake, met several dozen supporters from the Paris-Brantford area who had arrived in a rented bus. The bus was used to conduct media interviews and as a warming-up station. Reports came from across the country describing candles being lit in front of homes and yellow ribbons being tied to trees, poles and perches — a symbol that, four years earlier, had been used in the United States to indicate support for American hostages held in Iran.

News of the vigils was carried in Canadian newspapers and on radio and television. The story was also reported in the New Jersey media. Many Americans began writing to the family. One letter, from West Berlin, in central New Jersey, read: "We are accustomed to violence, rape, murder and we constantly lock our doors night and day, not as do Nova Scotians. I can understand your son's panic." A couple wrote: "The purpose of this letter is to offer our help. We live in Monmouth Beach, N.J., only about an hour from your son. If you so choose, anytime you or your family make a trip this way, feel free to use our home, anytime, as a base."

Jean Benham, a retired schoolteacher in her seventies, living in Spring Lake Heights on the Jersey shore, was asked about the case by her daughter, who was then teaching in Quebec and had read Dave Todd's first article. When Benham said she had read about the "psychopathic Canadian killer," her daughter suggested she find out whether he was really a psychopath. Soon Benham became a regular visitor to Bordentown, discussing teaching methods with Curtis and sending him articles on education and her back issues of *The Smithsonian*.

"The relationship I have established with him is like that of a surrogate parent; my first reaction was, 'my goodness, he's so pale and thin,' " explains Benham, who often calls Alice Curtis to report on her son's welfare. "When I visit, I'm sure I'm the only one who brings fruit instead of bags of potato chips and pizza. I bring grapes and big, black Byng cherries, and in the winter I bring oranges and grapefruit by the crate.

"I never once questioned him about the event in Loch Arbour. He has referred to Asbury Park but never to the accident or Scott. I think he's going ahead with his life instead of going over the past."

But despite the publicity and the growing protests of Curtis sympathizers in Canada and the United States, Jim and Alice Curtis regarded with dismay what they felt was the continuing intransigence of the Canadian government. Responding to a question about the case in the House of Commons on February 6, External Affairs Minister Joe Clark said: "It is the view of this government that those court proceedings fully followed American law. It would be as inappropriate for us to interfere in the judicial proceedings of the United States as it would be for us to accept interference in judicial proceedings by the United States in Canada."

Among the many observers who disputed Clark's position was a Newfoundland lawyer named Donald Mercer. A former president of the Federation of Law Societies of Canada and an executive member of the Canadian Bar Association, Mercer's interest in the case began in the summer of 1982, when he first heard about the arrest of the two boys. His daughter, Anne, had been a student at King's-Edgehill and one of Franz's closest friends. "He was a shy boy, and a great admirer of Anne," Mercer says, recalling the occasions he met Franz on the campus. "He wanted to over-impress her with his position in an effort to win her special friendship. Now I feel he lived in this false world to escape from his background."

Mercer's first concern had been for Franz, admittedly combined with an enormous sense of relief that his daughter had not accepted the boy's invitations to visit. Mercer remembers writing to Franz in prison offering his assistance if there was anything he could do. But as he learned more about the trial, he became disturbed by Curtis's predicament. He knew that it was a recognized principle of law in both Canada and the United States that prejudicial evidence, unless it was directly relevant to the charges, should not be admitted. "It states in P.K. McWilliams's *Canadian Criminal Evidence* that photographs of a victim of a crime may well cause in the jury, and in judges too, feelings of indignation, abhorrence and shock, and serve to inflame them against the accused," Mercer explains. "This in itself is not grounds for rejecting their admission, but in this case the photographs and video were relevant only to the death of Al Podgis, and should not have been admitted. That is a rule under both American as well as Canadian jurisprudence.

"The difficulty you're confronted with," Mercer continues, "is that you have to believe the prosecutor had a preconceived notion that although the conspiracy charge was dropped, there was a conspiracy between these two boys to kill the parents. I think there were references to Leopold and Loeb, the teenagers who killed for the joy of it, for the thrill. So he had this diary that may seem to the average person to be very intense, philosophical, unusual, and he convinced himself that he [Curtis] could be the type of near-genius who would be thrilled by these incidents. But there was no evidence introduced that I am aware of that there was ever any feeling of having to bring about the death of Mrs Podgis. All the evidence suggests the contrary."

Mercer had written to John Crosbie, an acquaintance and fellow Newfoundlander, before the Progressive Conservative party took power. He recommended that recognized leaders in Canadian criminal law review the case to determine whether there had been a miscarriage of justice, a suggestion that was apparently never acted upon.

"I have discussed this case with people in prosecution departments in Canada, and I believe he [Curtis] wasn't dealt with justly. I am personally revolted by it."

On Saturday, March 16, five weeks after Clark's statement in the House of Commons, *The Toronto Star* published a feature article, running sixty column inches, under the headline: "The anguish shadowing a family." Reporter Ellie Tesher's account was mainly a well-researched summary of the case to date, but there was one intriguing element buried midway through the piece. Although the jurors in the Curtis case have, for the most part, followed the well-established tradition of not commenting on their case afterwards, Tesher contacted juror Wayne Schmidt, a father of two who lives in Colts Neck, New Jersey, who told her: " 'There was a movement among the jurors to go for first degree murder because we were charged to take the verdict to the most severe degree . . . '

"Interested in the Canadian support for Curtis, Schmidt asked several times why the defence did not bring out Bruce's character as described by Canadian media reports, and why Bruce never took the stand to testify on his own behalf.

"The only evidence that was presented was 'overwhelming' in pointing to guilt, he said. 'I searched my own soul many times . . . ' "

January 21, 1985

Dear Bruce,

A 21st birthday is a time for reflection on the past, projection to the future and the formulation of a tentative philosophy of life. Your life, for the past 2 1/2 years has been so chock full of the extremes of emotion of hope and despair, that your reflections must be, to say the least, extraordinary.

How do you feel, knowing that you are at the centre of an international storm? I'm sure, among other things, that you must feel very grateful to know that so many people are working so hard on your behalf and on behalf of justice. For those, like yourself, who admire Socrates, it is a comfort to know that there are people who still care about the ideals that were so important to him and who are willing to work toward attaining them. Knowing that your situation has, in many ways, been the catalyst that started such activity must surely make you feel very humble. Knowing that it is your countrymen who have instigated the activity must make you proud to be a Canadian.

I hope that one day you will be able to express gratitude to your wonderful parents. Without their unfailing love and support, your life, at this time, might have been vastly different. Without their support I fear that your spirit would have been utterly destroyed. It has been largely through their efforts that your spirit has been able to survive this continuing horror and look, with a measure of hope, to the future. It has been not only their efforts of the past 2 1/2 years that have been instrumental to this process but their untiring concern and boundless love that they have given to you all your life.

The stability and security of your early life has acted as a kind of rudder that has steadied you through these past, tumultuous times. When you reflect upon your past you will see, perhaps, from a different perspective, the value of a stable, secure and loving home where you were able to indulge in the pleasures of an orderly and uncomplicated lifestyle. Your parents taught you, quite wisely, not to place undue value on material possessions for these things decay and erode, whereas treasures of the mind and spirit do not. You were encouraged, therefore, to appreciate such things as the logic of Pythagoras and Socrates, the music of Beethoven and Bach and the beauty and order of the natural world that surrounded you and of which you felt a part, on the North Mountain. Through the study of these things one eventually comes to a recognition of certain steadfast values that serve one well throughout life, such things as integrity of character and a capacity for human understanding.

One thing that pleased me greatly upon hearing your interview with CBC Inquiry were your statements:

"Scott was my friend, I thought I should support him."

and "I felt very responsible.... I wanted to go to her [Rosemary Podgis's] family and tell them what had happened so that they would know."

These statements told me that even in the midst of your obvious shock and state of mental chaos, that somewhere in the back of your mind you knew that there were certain standards of honour and integrity that you should attempt to uphold. I was very proud of you when I heard that interview. I hope that whatever your future circumstances might be that you will never compromise your integrity.

The stability and sense of order that was a gift of your childhood has been a tremendous help to you throughout your long ordeal in N.J. Even in the midst of chaos, you had the advantage of knowing that such things as order and stability do exist. Can you imagine how chaotic this world must seem to those who have never known such things? Many of your fellow inmates have not. Therefore, they are worthy of compassion. When you were in Monmouth County Jail, enduring all of its horrendous conditions, you once told me that your life consisted of bouncing from moment to moment, never knowing what might happen next. Some people live their entire lives like that. They know no other way. You are privileged. Not only have you known another way but you have been given the opportunity for insight.

As for your parents, they have always given you unconditional love. Many parents would have turned their backs on a son who landed in the mess you did, in order to preserve their own selfish vanity. It would have been easy for them to have come back to Canada and invented some sort of story to explain your disappearance but they didn't. Why not? First of all, they are people of much integrity. They could never fabricate and pretend to live with a lie. Also, they felt that the only way to fight this horrible injustice was to bring the true story to light and to the attention of the public because, in a democracy, this is the way that justice is safeguarded. By doing this, however, they risked public scorn, ridicule and the loss of the social respect that they have always known. They also risked an increase of stress with its inevitable physical repercussions. By defending you through a trial and 2 appeals they have made great financial sacrifice. Why have they done all this? Because they love truth and justice as much as they love you.

When you were born and came into our family we had hope that you would fill our lives with happiness and bring us much joy. You have never disappointed us. Now, on your 21st birthday, you must look to the future while reflecting on the past. Count your blessings. Set positive goals. Look for the good that is mixed with the bad. This dark cloud that is passing over your life must have a silver lining. I have watched the way you have conducted yourself in prison. I have been impressed by your statements on TV. You have given me reason to hope that from this devastation a beautiful phoenix will rise.

Much love,
Aunt Lorraine

GRANDMA SENDS THIS POEM

My life is but a weaving between my God and me
I do not choose the colours He worketh steadily.
Oftimes He weaveth sorrow and I, in foolish pride
Forget He sees the upper and the underside.
Not til the loom is silent and shuttles cease to fly
Will God unroll the canvas and explain the reason why.
The dark threads are as needful in the skillful weaver's hand
As the threads of gold and silver in the pattern He has planned.

For months, Nova Scotia politicians and the RCMP had been the targets of letters of protest from Bruce Curtis's family and supporters over the RCMP's co-operation with New Jersey investigators and its own partial investigation into the poisoning allegations. In January 1985, Jennifer Wade wrote an angry letter to provincial Attorney General Ron Giffin:

> "I am told the RCMP in Nova Scotia passed on unsubstantiated allegations to the Loch Arbour, New Jersey police. No investigation was made here, and ironically the boy's parents have been denied access to the file — even to this date. It is incredible what stories police have been circulating on information which supposedly would have come from your office and from other official sources, and none of this

information has yet been substantiated by any investigation... There is a story circulating about two foreign students at King's-Edgehill having been 'poisoned.' I recently saw a medical report on these two boys and found they were admitted to Hants Co. Community Hospital at 10 p.m. at night, given gravol and dismissed in 20 minutes.* The Curtis boy and Scott Franz both left the school at noon that day: there are people to vouch for this. Bruce Curtis was home by mid afternoon. Then there's a story about a teacher having been 'poisoned' by Franz. A recent letter which has just come to light calls into question the maturity of this teacher and therefore the veracity of her story. Certainly she had more than a passing interest in these two boys. It is such questionable events that have deliberately been used to discourage public support for the boy's case. I understand Bruce Curtis was puzzled, shocked, and saddened when his parents confronted him in October with some of these stories.... Is it not an obligation of your office to clear up some of these lies and innuendoes and stories and reveal the truth as your office knows it and thus somehow try to lessen the sorrow for this family already suffering because of the miserable way this has all been handled...?"

The RCMP in Halifax finally assigned Sergeant Eric Calder to renew the investigation. At 10:30 A.M. on Wednesday, March 20, he sat across from Curtis in a room at the Youth Correctional Institution at Bordentown. Also present was Mary Kennedy, a lawyer from Mike Shaw's office. After presenting Curtis with his card and reading him his rights, Calder discussed a number of incidents that were said to have occurred at King's-Edgehill.

*According to the medical report, Antonio Maher was in the out-patient department of the hospital for 55 minutes, from 2225 hours to 2320 hours. Steven Ho was there for 48 minutes, from 2227 hours to 2315 hours.

Q: The incident relating to you and Scott Franz allegedly going to New Minas, N.S. at the Dairy Queen with Colleen Smith, and Colleen Smith receiving a bad milkshake from Scott Franz. Do you recall that?

A: No, because I'd been out with her numerous times and one particular incident would not stand out.

Q: The incident I referred to concerning Colleen Smith locating her pocket calculator in Scott Franz's possession one day during Math class. Do you recall that?

A: Yes. I recall that she could not find her calculator and one day she noticed the calculator in Scott's possession had the same serial number as the one she had previously had. Miss Smith asked him about it and he passed it off as an error or mistake or a mix-up on both of their parts. It might have embarrassed him because it questioned his reliability or honesty. The whole incident was conducted in a non-offensive manner. Scott never mentioned the incident to me.

Q: The incident we discussed concerning Rea deBoer and his wife, Heidi deBoer catching two students who she described as Scott Franz and possibly yourself after normal hours one evening in the Biology lab. Were you one of those or were you with Franz on that occasion?

A: No.

Q: Do you have any knowledge of Scott Franz stealing an insecticide known as Green Cross containing Nicotine Sulfate, or any Chloroform from the Chemistry lab?

A: I do not know Scott obtaining in any manner an insecticide known as Green Cross, however I am aware of Scott obtaining from the Biology lab Chloroform the latter part of grade eleven. I was in possession of the container which contained the

Chloroform. The reason for me having it was that I used to hold for Scott some of his drugs since he was known to use drugs. He was afraid that he might get caught with them and since it was known that I did not use drugs, people would not look to me as having drugs in my possession.

Q: How did you know that Franz took the Chloroform from the lab?

A: He told me.

Q: Are you aware of the Chloroform being placed in another bottle? If so, describe what you know.

A: I did not specifically witness Scott transferring the Chloroform from one container to another. However, I do believe that Scott had another container containing Chloroform. This container was offered to Scott's friends as a means of getting high. I never took a whiff from the container.

Q: Do you recall the incident whereby you and Scott Franz are alleged to have been in Rory Kempster's and your room late one night while Rory apparently slept? Rory awoke and got angry at you and Scott. If so, give details including what was in the spray bottle that we discussed.

A: Yes, I remember the incident about 2 o'clock in the morning. It was part of a school prank in which Rory would be taken and tied to a tree in the quad. A number of students were involved in the carrying out of the prank. The purpose for Scott's presence that night was to test Rory's sleeping pattern. Scott had with him a spray bottle containing either Johnny Walker or Bacardi rum mixed with Coca-Cola. The prank was never carried out. Rory's interpretation of the incident was influenced by his recent viewing of The Exorcist and my knowledge of the movie and practices of black magic. Rory thought that it contained elements of black magic when in fact it was in preparation for this prank.

Q: The main incident here that we discussed involving Antonio Maher and Steven Ho being poisoned on 19 June 1982 by drinking cream soda pop. Did you put anything in a bottle of pop in Antonio Maher's room?

A: No.

Q: Do you know who did?

A: No.

Q: Were you and Scott Franz in Maher and Franz's room on Saturday, 19 June '82?

A: Yes.

Q: Did you leave Franz in that room alone at any time that day?

A: Yes.

Q: Will you submit to a polygraph examination at some future time concerning questions surrounding the poisoning of Maher and Ho?

A: No. I do not believe polygraph machines are a valid indication of truth; therefore I would not submit myself to a polygraph test for any type of question no matter what the subject is.

Q: Is there anything further you wish to add to this statement?

A: Yes. Scott would not tell me anything which would reflect badly on his character other than obtaining drugs. He attempted to present an image of wealth and worldliness. Any deviousness on his part would be kept to himself since it would detract from his image.

Q: When you came to New Jersey from Nova Scotia, did you bring any prescription drugs with you with your name on the bottle label?

A: Yes. "Alupent," which was a prescription drug.

Q: I just told you that the New Jersey police found such a bottle with your name on it and the bottle contained a white powder later analyzed and found to be arsenic. Was that arsenic yours?

A: No.
Q: Do you know how the arsenic got there?
A: No.
Q: Do you know of Scott Franz ever having any arsenic?
A: No.
Q: Is there anything further you wish to add?
A: Yes. I brought a bottle of Alupent to New Jersey. I do not know if this is the same bottle found by New Jersey officials, so it is not correct for me to agree that it was "such a bottle" in the above question and answer.

In an effort to clear up the lingering question of the trace of arsenic found in the bottle, Curtis's sister Anne, in her capacity as a physician, requested information from Boehringer Ingelheim (Canada) Ltd., manufacturers of Alupent®. The company's manager of Regulatory Affairs and Quality Assurance confirmed in a letter that: "We do not add Arsenic to any of our formulations, however, since even water contains traces of Arsenic and is widely used as a solvent, almost any product may contain a trace amount of Arsenic."

The letter added: "If an ingredient was released with a 3 ppm [parts per million] content (which is doubtful since most companies have internal Acceptable Quality Limits which are more stringent than compendial limits) and was diluted in a preparation the concentration of Arsenic, if it was at all present, would be in the parts per billion to parts per trillion range."

The quantity of powder in Curtis's pill bottle was so small that the first lab test, submitted on July 28, 1982, was returned marked "Insufficient quantity for analysis." It was only when the powder traces were retested for nicotine sulfate eight months later — one week before Curtis's trial began — a trace of arsenic was detected.

After the New Jersey Supreme Court's refusal to hear Curtis's appeal, Mike Shaw had to make a strategy decision. The case could be taken to the U.S. Supreme Court, the highest court in the land, but the majority of appeals there were denied and those that succeeded turned on general constitutional principles likely to affect the entire American judicial landscape. Instead, after consulting with Jim and Alice Curtis, Shaw chose an alternative route: he filed a petition for a writ of habeas corpus to the federal district court for New Jersey.

Habeas corpus, Latin for "you must have the body," was sometimes called the Great Writ of Liberty. It was used to test whether a prisoner had been accorded due process under the law. Thus, Shaw intended to appeal Curtis's criminal conviction in New Jersey to the federal court on the grounds that Curtis's 14th amendment rights had been violated, that the state had unlawfully deprived him of his liberty. Petitions were assigned to a federal judge, who in turn assigned the case to a magistrate whose job it was to submit a recommendation to the judge on whether the petition should be granted or denied. Although a magistrate's conclusion was not binding, it reflected a judicial official's professional appraisal of the case's merits.

"At some level," explains Shaw, "any criminal case can be so devoid of evidentiary merit that an argument can be made that it lacks due process, that it lacks fundamental fairness. There's nothing new in it (the petition for habeas corpus). It's the same fundamental principle that we raised before, that in Bruce Curtis's trial there should have been none of the awfully gory proof of what happened upstairs when Scott Franz shot and killed his stepfather. That's the shoehorn we're trying to use to convince the federal court that they should see this as a constitutional [14th amendment] situation.

"Our first appeal (to the New Jersey Supreme Court) was a particularly distressing and surprising loss. Now we have even less of a chance because so many petitions of habeas corpus are filed. And to get a magistrate, and then a judge, to pay attention is even harder. Their natural inclination is to say, 'gosh, this has been heard all the way through the state system, it's been passed upon by two appellate courts in a very sophisticated state. Should I really spend too much time worrying about it?' "

The petition was filed on April 10, 1985, in the federal district court, Trenton, New Jersey. Five weeks later Shaw wrote a letter to the magistrate assigned to the case:

May 17, 1985

Honourable John W. Devine
United States Magistrate
United States Courthouse
Federal Building
Trenton, N.J.

Dear Magistrate Devine:

I am writing to urge that Your Honor permit us oral argument on our habeas corpus petition in this case. The denial of a fair trial to Bruce Curtis — now in his third year of imprisonment — is the most extreme that I have ever encountered in over twenty years of prosecuting and defending criminal cases.

We did not represent Bruce Curtis at his trial or in his appeal to the Appellate Division, and although the obvious and overwhelming point which we raise was sketched by Curtis' then counsel amidst a series of other points, the Appellate Division did not even address the issue in its opinion. Although our petition to the New Jersey Supreme Court made the same points we have made in our habeas corpus petition in this court, we were not afforded oral argument, and no opinion was written.

I beg the court to grant us the opportunity for oral argument. We believe we can readily satisfy Your Honor that the trial court committed an obvious, hugely prejudicial error in receiving detailed evidence of an utterly irrelevant killing as to which it is conceded that Bruce Curtis has no involvement whatsoever, and that this almost unbelievably gory evidence, repeated again and again through photographs, movies and lay and expert testimony, so dominated Bruce Curtis' trial as to wholly deny him due process.

Respectfully yours,
Edward M. Shaw

Although he believed the habeas corpus to be the best move, Shaw was aware of other, less conventional possibilities. One was filing an application for clemency to the governor of New Jersey. Another involved arranging for Curtis to serve his sentence in a Canadian prison, closer to friends and family. But when he looked into that alternative, Shaw discovered that although a Canada–U.S. prisoner transfer treaty had been signed in 1978, each state was required to ratify it individually. New Jersey was one of about half the states that had not done so.

A prisoner transfer was regarded as a last desperate measure by the Curtises and Shaw because it would not alter the terms of Curtis's sentence. The Curtises told the attorney that they had come too far to accept so little.

In the spring of 1985, the efforts of Jim and Alice Curtis, Lorraine Peever, Jennifer Wade and others to bring the case to the Canadian public had succeeded beyond their wildest dreams. Over Christmas, Wade had been in touch with Jan Tyrwhitt, a staff writer for the Canadian edition of *Reader's Digest*. Although *Reader's Digest*, noted for its simply written, eternally optimistic articles aimed at what one senior editor referred to as "Mr and Mrs Front Porch," seemed an unlikely publication to carry the story of a murder trial that had no happy ending, Wade was only interested in its five-million Canadian readers. Tyrwhitt sent her editors a copy of Dave Todd's article and was told "they wanted nothing to do with this nasty, violent stuff." Yet they finally agreed that Tyrwhitt could look into the case since she was going to be in Halifax researching another assignment.

Tyrwhitt met with Wade and was taken to Mount Hanley to talk to Jim and Alice. After visiting Bruce in Bordentown, Tyrwhitt convinced her still-skeptical editors to grant approval. Although Tyrwhitt wasn't entirely satisfied with all aspects of the story herself, she decided that the irregularities of the plea bargain and trial were the real issue, and that it justified doing the story. At the same time, Joan Melanson and Roxanna Spicer of CBC Halifax's *Inquiry* had been assigned to produce a documentary on the case for *The Journal*, the CBC's week-night current affairs program that followed the network's flagship news show, *The National*. There were also several film production houses interested in acquiring the rights to the story, and a playwright and drama professor in Nova Scotia, Jack Sheriff, was writing a play.

On a more modest scale, the proceeds from bake sales, raffles and flea markets were being donated to the Curtis fund in Middleton. Buttons had been produced bearing a photo of Curtis and the phrase, "WAITING FOR JUSTICE." Dalhousie University's colours — yellow and black — were used to symbolize Curtis's lost educational opportunities. (Later a supporter donated eight hundred yellow-and-black bumper stickers that read: "HELP BRUCE CURTIS.") Letters of support protesting a tragic miscarriage of justice, mainly from Canadians from as far away as Mexico, Japan and Australia, were being sent to Bruce, his family, and both the Canadian and New Jersey governments. The volume of correspondence was so great that Peever's newsletter, by then half-a-dozen pages of single-spaced type and photocopied articles and observations that reached an estimated one thousand supporters, had incorporated a section called: "What you might do." In the June 1985 newsletter, readers were urged to:

SPEAK — about the case to groups and individuals or arrange for a speaker by contacting one of the Bruce Curtis Defence Committees.

WATCH — for an article in Reader's Digest Magazine (Sept. or Oct. 1985) and draw the attention of others to it.

WEAR — A Bruce Curtis - WAITING FOR JUSTICE - button or distribute a pamphlet (both available from Bruce Curtis Defence Committees).

WRITE — To members of Parliament and urge for protest on the grounds a minimum standard of justice has not been met.

WRITE — To friends and relatives overseas, sending them a newspaper article and a brief outline of the case. Ask for their support by way of writing to the Governor of N.J. if a petition for clemency becomes necessary.

WRITE — To the editor of your local newspaper, expressing your view of this case.

COMMUNICATE — your ideas to the Committees.

The June newsletter also recommended that supporters read British journalist Ludovic Kennedy's recently published book, *The Airman and the Carpenter: The Lindbergh Case and the Framing of Richard Hauptmann*. Kennedy maintained that Bruno Richard Hauptmann, accused, convicted and eventually executed for the kidnapping and murder of aviator Charles Lindbergh's infant son in 1932, was a victim of an extraordinary conspiracy engineered by the New Jersey prosecutors and police officials. Hauptmann's wife, Anna, was still alive and struggling to clear her husband's name after fifty-three years. As if to confirm the family's worst fears about the state, they learned that the Chief Justice of the New Jersey Supreme Court, Robert Wilentz, was the son of David Wilentz, Attorney General at the time of the Hauptmann investigation and trial. After writing to Kennedy in England, the Curtises received a letter from him dated July 8: "Your son's story is appalling," Kennedy wrote, "but appalling miscarriages of justice, whether in New Jersey or elsewhere have long ceased to surprise me. They are one of the casualties of the adversarial justice system as practised in Anglo Saxon countries. The inquisitorial system as practised in France, Germany, Italy and elsewhere has many more safeguards. I very much hope your son's appeal is successful."

At ten P.M. on June 6, CBC's *The Journal* aired "Tie A Yellow Ribbon," the documentary that the Curtises expected would present the tale of their son's injustice to a million-and-a-half Canadians. Although most of the details were anticipated by the Curtises, they listened in horror as Joan Melanson told the national viewing audience: "But just when the family needed support the most, there was another setback. The Nova Scotia government refused to help Bruce. Why? A cabinet minister, Gerald Sheehy, said charges might be laid against Bruce Curtis because of incidents at King's-Edgehill School, before his fateful trip to New Jersey. There were rumours that Bruce and Scott Franz put something in the drinks of three people...to make them very sick. At the time of the incidents, police did not investigate. But the rumours persisted and reached the government.... After months of pressure there was an investigation. The police report said there was not enough evidence to lay criminal charges. But the Attorney General, Ron Giffin, refuses to clear Bruce's name. He won't say why. The Curtises have been refused a copy of the report which could help them; the rumours have already hurt them."

Although the tone of the program was predominantly sympathetic, all the Curtises could think about was the news, previously unknown to them, that their son's name was not going to be cleared. "These were rumours," Alice protested. "Bruce is caught in a Catch-22 of not being guilty because it can't be proved he did it and not being innocent because it can't be proved he didn't do it. With that kind of logic everyone who was in the boys' residence that Graduation weekend is a suspect. I stayed and collected Bruce's stuff out of his room. Am I a suspect? Bruce got roped into everything that happened. If Scott was involved, Bruce must be involved."

May 27, 1985

Dear Mom and Dad:

This paper was made for me by the inmate who worked in the print shop. He, of course, left but the person who replaced him was a former teacher's aide and I get along with him. Connections like that are very important since everything is controlled by someone and all things are treated as personal property to be doled out to friends. This gives some meaning to the trivial positions that are held by most of us. The attitudes and jealous guarding of domains resembles, somewhat, the court of Louis XIV, where nobility vied for the chance to put on the king's stockings, grovelling before an absolute power. Sycophany running rampant.

Among the concepts and perceptions of <u>Shaking it Rough</u>*, this was probably the truest — how everything is warped and directed toward pleasing an insatiable, invisible authority which exercises immense control over your life. Words are not spoken, deeds not acted out, morality and dignity suppressed for an ultimate reward of freedom. We are as children told when to cross the street, joined together by rope so in adventures we do not stray, guarded at every turn, watched for bad behavior, reduced to creatures that cannot function or feel comfortable without our world strictly outlined for us in concrete terms. Other perceptions [in <u>Shaking it Rough</u>], though the author distorts and exaggerates, I doubt the desire to express joy or even happiness, except at a visit, would be suppressed for fear of offending your fellow inmate. Moments of joy

---

* Curtis was reading Andreas Schroeder's *Shaking It Rough*, an account of life inside a prison.

are eagerly sought here, and fully expressed, sometimes to the point of hysteria. Laughter is heard, smiles cross faces, joy is expressed in form and motion....

A place like this is almost impossible to comprehend, totally, unless personal experience is used for it is an unique distillation of attitudes which, outside of prisons, are found only in rare and isolated instances. One of the best portrayals of some of the warping which occurs here I found in Thomas Mann's The Magic Mountain. It is about a TB sanitorium high in the Swiss Alps, just before WW1. Like here, the community was very isolated and insular, all contact was with those already present, little variation of thought and space. Time periods were considered in chunks of six months and years. People considered sick were shunned by society and were forced to take refuge high in the mountains, away from the amazing change of the world down below. He describes, perfectly, the perception of time that eventually grips one, the attitude of not caring and how the outside world begins to assume a mythological tinge. Of course, many things were different but the differences are mainly external which, to the unconsciousness, matter little.

Shaking it Rough was again thoughtful in its touching upon the need to reduce desires, needs, external decoration to nothing but the mind and body, throw away the trappings and finery of society. Few ever achieve such a state of asceticism, certainly not among this bunch who still cling to the most primitive and crude forms of gratification. For these many, the experience of imprisonment does nothing to transform their personality or educate them in what is really needed for a harmonious life. They emerge the same and take their place beside their fellowman an identical creature of non-perception. Some, such as Dostoevsky, were able to find from their prison experiences, profound hope and gladness in the hearts of their fellow inmates. Such a stance is delusion, denial in the participation of ugliness.

For those who would look, the blueprints of society can be read but to say that they describe and build paradise is sad and of little use. Advancement and progression can be made but only by accepting the real nature of things and then shrugging them off as constricting to movement forward. Others would hide in the squalid huts of yesterday. I cannot. I like to walk.

Love, Bruce

By the fall of 1985, when Jim and Alice Curtis had expected to be feeling encouraged by at least a suggestion of victory in a foreseeable future, instead they felt only disillusioned and bitterly discouraged. Despite the vigorous support of a nationwide Justice for Bruce Curtis movement and the almost consistently favourable media coverage, their son still languished in prison. Sometimes Jim and Alice felt as though he was no closer to freedom than he had been three years earlier. The power of so many voices and letters — including those of influential community leaders, politicians and clergymen — had failed to sway officials in the federal department of external affairs. In New York, Mike Shaw had requested that the habeas corpus petition be expedited, but the magistrate assigned to the case had flatly refused. And even if the petition were finally granted, Shaw warned the Curtises that the state would probably take the case to the United States Court of Appeals for the Third Circuit, which had jurisdiction over New Jersey and was the next tier in the federal court system. The process of litigation could take years.

The Curtises' health had suffered as well. Friends noticed that Alice had aged terribly. Jim had suffered a mild stroke that resulted in a partial loss of vision in one eye. They had spent

$100,000–all their life savings including insurance policies. Yet there was never a question of accepting defeat. "It was a family effort," Alice explains. "And we kept advancing from one level to another. First there was Dave Todd's article. Then Mrs Wade, who was so experienced, became involved. Then the next article to the next article to this or that TV program. Always bigger every time. If we had ever come to a dead halt, maybe we would have thrown up our hands, but there were always minute advances."

Jim Curtis adds: "And we're gonna get those rotten bastards, no matter how we do it."

"If we ever felt like giving up," continues Alice, "there was always Lorraine pushing it."

It was Lorraine Peever who seemed indefatigable. If her long-suffering brother and his wife were the spiritual figureheads of the movement, Peever was the main power source. When she wasn't conferring with local supporters, sifting through letters, collecting articles about the case and related issues (just about any miscarriage of justice or, conversely, evidence that a hardened criminal had been acquitted or paroled early was of interest to her), or preparing the newsletter, she was assisting reporters with their stories, putting them in touch with the appropriate contacts and sending out packages of research, all of it carefully annotated, relevant passages highlighted. It was fair to describe Peever's commitment to her nephew's case as an obsession. If asked, she would admit it herself. "It's a continuing nightmare that doesn't end," she has said repeatedly. "It's like there is no time element."

Peever had spent a great deal of time with Jan Tyrwhitt, the writer for *Reader's Digest*. She had liked the woman's intelligence and particularly her sensitivity. The article represented the most in-depth study of the case to date — considerably more so than the trial itself, Peever noted ruefully — and that made her even more anxious than she usually was before an article or TV show on Bruce was run. Peever was like a completely guileless public relations officer: she understood that nothing less than total honesty was essential when dealing with the

media, because good reporters find it all out anyway and then
you're given the appearance of having concealed something,
compounding the damage. But she was also utterly convinced
of her nephew's goodness and innocence. She gently warned
reporters that there were some "curves" to be encountered, referring to the homoerotic passage in the diary and the poisoning
allegations. These, however, were counterbalanced by Bruce's
gentle nature and his intellect, and by Peever's absolute conviction that whatever else had happened, the shooting of Rosemary
Podgis had been an accident, the cover-up a panic reaction, and
the trial a dreadful corruption of justice.

The November issue of *Reader's Digest* contained Tyrwhitt's
20,000-word article, entitled "Web of Violence." It was a departure for *Reader's Digest*, and as much a relief for Tyrwhitt as for
Peever when it was finally published. In June there had been a
change of senior editors at the magazine's head office in Montreal. The Curtis article, scheduled for September, was killed by
a new editor who decided that since Tyrwhitt couldn't prove the
boy was innocent, the story lacked the magazine's patented
uplifting ending. There was no resolution, Tyrwhitt was told.
She defended the article on the grounds that the boy was the
victim of an unfair trial, and that the benefit of doubt was clearly
on his side. At the end of what Tyrwhitt now refers to as "the
worst week of my career," the story had again been approved.

It was a scrupulously objective account that earned two National Magazine Award nominations that year. Tyrwhitt would
later lament that even at three times the length of most *Reader's
Digest* articles, there was insufficient space to really explore the
complexities of the case, although she was not convinced that
her conclusion would have been any different. "What really
happened at 401 Euclid Avenue during that terrible
weekend...?" she wrote. "Only Curtis knows."

Peever thought the article was splendid, and was very happy
that Tyrwhitt had focused primarily on the trial. Peever had
always been struck by one irony. During the "awful winter" of
1982-83, when she had exchanged weighty discourses with
Bruce by mail to help him with the philosophy course he was

taking from Queen's University, he had been studying Plato's *Apology*, in which Socrates proclaimed the rights and necessity of free thought at his trial, was condemned by an angry mob and drank hemlock as his sentence. "I found it immensely ironic that Bruce had his head filled with thoughts of the ideals of justice when he entered the courtroom of Judge Arnone," Peever wrote in a letter to a journalist. "Rarely does one have the opportunity to make such a comparison between these ideals and man's inadequate attempts to meet these ideals. The American democracy is supposedly founded on the principles of the Greek democracy. To an inexperienced observer such as I, it seemed there was very little attempt to meet the ideal of Socrates in the Monmouth County court. I often wonder what the effect of all of the above will be on Bruce, who is so sensitive...."

The way her nephew was attempting to rebuild his life in prison, judging by letters, visits and his comportment during televised interviews, impressed Peever. She was reminded of a hymn she used to sing in the old country church she attended as a child: "Will your anchor hold in the storms of life...?" Peever concluded the letter: "We are quite hopeful that Bruce's anchor will hold from now on."

It was towards the end of October 1985, shortly after Thanksgiving Day in Canada, that Gerald Morris, a University of Toronto law professor, talked with Lorraine Peever in Toronto. Morris had grown up in southeastern Ontario and graduated from the University of Toronto's law school in the mid-1950s — the first Morris boy in generations not to go into the family's funeral business. After obtaining a graduate degree in international law at New York University, he began working for the Department of External Affairs in Ottawa. In 1960 he was posted for two years to New Delhi, India, followed by four years at the Canadian consulate in New York. In the spring of 1966, Morris was offered a senior position with the legal division of External Affairs. Instead, he accepted an offer to teach international law at the University of Toronto, his Alma Mater. Many years later, he still maintained close ties with officials in External Affairs — both his peers and, increasingly, former students — and operated a one-man, part-time law practice.

Peever had initially contacted Morris on the advice of a mutual friend who believed Morris might be able to help her nephew. After listening to the woman's story, Morris knew instinctively that he wanted to get involved in the case. For one thing, it offered a prospect of success, it was a "potential winner." It was also a case that seemed to cry out for Morris's knowledge and skills as both a practising international law specialist and a former career diplomat who enjoyed access to a powerful old boys' network. The other element that attracted Morris to the case was less pragmatic: Bruce Curtis's plight aroused strong sympathies. "Even before evaluating whether or not the boy might be criminally responsible," Morris would later say, "it was impossible not to be saddened by this young guy who in some way got involved in rather horrendous circumstances that blighted a promising life."

Morris told Peever that he would need several weeks to study the trial and appeal transcripts and other documents. He also explained that because of his commitments to the university, an ailing mother and some eye problems that required him to limit his reading, it would be advisable to involve another lawyer. He recommended Jennie Hatfield Lyon, a young woman with a passionate interest in human rights, for whom Morris had great respect. Hatfield Lyon, a native of Cape Cod, Massachusetts, had majored in international relations at Brandeis University — where she met her future husband, a Canadian named Daniel Lyon and taken an M.A. in international law at Columbia University in New York. Later they both studied law at the University of Toronto, where she specialized in international law. The field was small in Canada, so Morris and Hatfield Lyon would frequently meet at conferences and around the law school campus. In 1982, Hatfield Lyon and Morris submitted a brief setting out the international legal issues raised in the kidnapping of Toronto land developer Sidney Jaffe, who was fighting his legal battle with authorities in Florida while incarcerated in a state prison. They discovered that they made an effective team, and collaborated on other cases.

They were a study in contrasts. At fifty-four, Morris was a tall, distinguished-looking man with broad shoulders, silver hair and an engaging courtly manner. Hatfield Lyon, a former Miss Cape Cod with wavy chestnut hair and a quick, radiant smile, was a quarter-century his junior and no more than two-thirds his height. Where Morris could glide with a veteran's seasoned assurance through the hallways at External Affairs, Hatfield Lyon exploited four personal characteristics: a keen legal mind, charm, audacity and an almost total absence of artifice. Morris, who had worked in media relations while at the Canadian consulate in New York because "someone thought I had a gift for the blarney, I guess," tended to good-naturedly amble around an issue, punctuating a conversation with tangential bits of history and folklore. Hatfield Lyon, although she enjoyed small talk as much as the next person, had the ability to zero in on a subject like a zoom lens pulling a distant object into focus.

Morris and Hatfield Lyon were disturbed by several aspects of the trial. They finally agreed that if nothing else, the sentence was absurdly severe. After making some preliminary inquiries, they learned that the Curtis case was being handled mainly from within the consular bureau of External Affairs, whose principal role it was to aid distressed Canadians abroad. Morris had also learned that consular officials in Ottawa were skeptical of the Curtis family's claims because they were relying on reports from the consulate in New York, which in turn would have received what Morris described as "a rather rose-coloured version of what happened" from the viewpoint of officials in New Jersey. Canada's "official observer" at Curtis's appeal to the intermediate appellate court had been largely symbolic. If the legal division of External Affairs did not seem to be involved at all, Morris suspected that was because no one had ever presented anyone there with a cogent argument for why they should be. Among foreign nations, Britain and the United States were considered to have judicial systems equal to that of Canada, and the troubleshooting role of External Affairs was minimized. Since the Curtis case had made its way in an orderly fashion through the court system in New Jersey and was presently in the able hands of a

New York attorney who had it before a federal court, it was difficult for anyone in the department to see what it was the Curtis family wanted them to do. When Joe Clark had told parliament that this was not a case that justified intervention he was, in a sense, right. Neither Morris nor Hatfield Lyon believed that the Canadian government could ask the Americans to give Curtis a new trial or challenge the court proceedings that had already taken place. Morris was convinced that the reluctance of External Affairs to act on the Curtis case did not indicate its unwillingness to confront the Americans so much as its inability to translate the slogans of a well-intentioned but shrill grass-roots movement into a blueprint for diplomatic action.

Both Morris and Hatfield Lyon agreed that their first objective might, in certain respects, be the most difficult. After two years, the Curtis family and their supporters had finally succeeded in bringing their son's misfortune into a national forum. The dynamics were almost a reprise of the 1960s protest movements, with External Affairs cast as a beleaguered university administration beset by a small but vocal core group of activists. When officials refused to take prompt action — whether for reasons of indecision, misunderstanding or an acceptance of the status quo — that rejection attracted more sympathizers to the protest. As public pressure mounted and the rhetoric grew angrier, the public servants, predictably, dug in their heels and adopted a seige mentality. By the end of 1985, the two sides had polarized. Letters to both the Canadian and New Jersey governments, for example, had once been supervised by defence committees. Now they were pouring in by the hundreds, and it was often impossible to trace their origins. Several that Morris had seen ordered Joe Clark to "do something!" At a certain point the sheer vehemence of the protest began to undermine the effectiveness of the message.

So Morris and Hatfield Lyon began to engineer a delicate de-escalation of the grass-roots campaign. They carefully explained to Peever and Jim and Alice Curtis that the case was at a stage where it had gained notoriety, and they both felt that officials in Ottawa had privately acknowledged that it was an important issue that warranted attention. "The Curtises realized they were at a point where they were spinning their wheels," Morris says. "They were frustrated that they weren't achieving any real progress with officials in Ottawa or New Jersey. I knew they weren't going to succeed unless they became a little more low-key, toned the rhetoric down. I guess I'd had enough of a diplomatic background to know that in some situations striking advances can be made by just the most subtle chatting, by being very understanding of the limitations of officials in External. We needed to gradually get them to a point where they were discussing the case using our terms without ever feeling there had been a marked shift in their viewpoint."

Both Morris and Hatfield Lyon had long phone conversations with contacts in External Affairs and flew to Ottawa on several occasions. On Friday, January 17, 1986, for example, three days before the second vigil on the eve of Curtis's twenty-second birthday, Hatfield Lyon discussed the case with Brian Dickson, director of the department's legal advisory division and son and namesake of the Chief Justice of Canada. According to Hatfield Lyon's notes on the meeting, Dickson questioned whether comparisons could be made to the Jaffe case, where Canada actively intervened in the U.S. domestic courts, because in that instance the kidnapping of a Canadian citizen on a Toronto street by Florida bounty-hunters clearly violated an international extradition treaty and Canada's sovereignty. Hatfield Lyon did not dispute that, but alternatively suggested that a case could be made that Curtis's human rights were being violated, that his incarceration was unjust, thereby justifying an official Canadian interest or involvement in the case. Morris and Hatfield Lyon considered it a small victory that they had initiated dialogue on the subject with senior officials. "It's important," Hatfield Lyon explains, "that they [External Affairs] knew people were interested and watching what they were going to do with this case."

When Jennie Hatfield Lyon decided to visit her family in Cape Cod early in 1986, she made arrangements through Mike Shaw's office to visit Bruce Curtis. Despite their efforts, Hatfield Lyon would have to see Curtis as a regular visitor: prison officials, for unknown reasons, had been unwilling to grant her status as a lawyer. Hatfield Lyon had also spoken briefly on the telephone to Dennis Fahey, the private investigator hired by Michael Schottland in 1982, who had been in touch with Lorraine Peever. He wanted to discuss his belief that the trial had been a mockery and the boy was suffering irreparable damage in prison.

At 12:40 P.M. on Saturday, January 25, Hatfield Lyon sat in the cavernous gymnasium that served as a visitor's hall for the Bordentown Youth Correctional Institution, hoping she would recognize the boy whose welfare she had come to care deeply about but with whom she had never met. She was disappointed that the guards had not permitted her to bring in the birthday card or copies of *Popular Science* and *Science '86* that she had intended to give him as a gift. She did recognize him instantly, and they began by chatting, somewhat awkwardly, about his circumstances. Hatfield Lyon explained her belief that human rights concerns within the context of international law might prove to be an effective wedge to pry open the lid on his case. One approach might be an application for clemency to the governor of the state.

Hatfield Lyon's first impressions filled her with sadness. She was the oldest of six surviving children in her family — her older sister died in a traffic accident in 1980 — and she had four sisters and a brother Curtis's age. Curtis even reminded her of her brother, with whom her family had had difficulty communicating for years. He had always seemed at a loss for words, and when he did speak he'd mumble a few words. Hatfield Lyon remembered overhearing him sitting in a room with a few male friends and realizing that they rarely talked. She had thought for a while that this was simply an unfathomable trait of the male species until her brother had gotten married and suddenly opened up and become articulate. Hatfield Lyon felt she had learned a valuable lesson about the kinds of stages through which adolescent boys may pass.

She also remembered a particularly significant incident: once, when he was twelve, her brother and a friend, the son of a judge, had decided they would build a Molotov Cocktail. After lighting it they panicked and threw it wildly towards the street. A car, belonging to the judge, was passing by and was very nearly blown up. What would have happened, Hatfield Lyon speculated, if that stupid and reckless act that today made a funny anecdote had been frozen in time and scrutinized by law enforcement officials, lawyers, judges, psychologists, reporters, curious strangers? It would surely have been deemed the product of warped and dangerous minds.

Curtis told her about the difficulties of maintaining a vegetarian diet in prison. One of Hatfield Lyon's sisters was a vegetarian, she told him, so she understood. He discussed with obvious enthusiasm a computer course he was taking, and said he had an interest in the application of international law to outer space. They talked about art — he favoured modernism, Hatfield Lyon liked the Romantic period — and music. When Curtis said that he did not like classical music, Hatfield Lyon told him that many of her friends who were obsessed with computers found classical music to be highly mathematical. That aroused the boy's interest. Gradually, Hatfield Lyon steered the conversation toward more sensitive subjects. "How do you deal with emotional and ethical matters, Bruce?" she asked. "It must be terribly difficult to deal with having killed someone. Is there anyone here to talk to?"

Curtis admitted there was not. Although he was clearly uncomfortable, Hatfield Lyon knew instinctively that he could be probed more easily by a woman than by a man. He had two sisters, after all, and he was closest to Anne, whose personality most resembled Hatfield Lyon's.

"Is there a psychologist here you can talk to?" she asked.

"Yes," Curtis replied, adding, "but they don't give a damn and they're not very good."

"Do you have any friends you can talk to?"

Curtis shook his head. "There's a couple of people I play chess with, but nobody you would talk to about personal things."

"Could you talk to your parents?"

"Not to my parents," Curtis told her quietly, "but maybe to my older sister."

Hatfield Lyon continued to talk about the issues of guilt and moral responsibility. She told him about her nephew who had been born with a defective kidney. The child was supposed to receive one of Hatfield Lyon's kidneys, which were a perfect match, but at the time when his kidney failed, Hatfield Lyon was at Columbia completing her M.A., and so her mother was afraid that her eldest daughter would end up losing her degree and chose not to notify her. Instead, her father donated a kidney that matched but was infected with hepatitis. After months of combatting the inevitable rejection syndrome following a transplant, the child appreared to have recovered when, one day, Hatfield Lyon took her nephew to the beach. A cup of medication was accidentally kicked over and Hatfield Lyon was uncertain whether she had given him a full dose. A few days later, the child's body rejected the transplant and he died. Although the doctors had assured her it had not been her fault — the medication had not been successful — Hatfield Lyon was tortured by guilt for years afterwards.

When Curtis admitted that he was haunted by his responsibility for the death of Mrs Podgis but that he used private means to resolve it, Hatfield Lyon warned him that guilt can eat away at the soul. When she inquired whether he had considered writing down these hard-to-express feelings, she laughed at his quick, ironic response: "Given my experience with the last diary, I don't think so."

When Hatfield Lyon left the prison she felt a remarkable physical and mental exhaustion. The visit had been cathartic. It had strengthened her convictions about the case. "It became almost inconceivable for me to imagine that he'd purposely done what he was convicted of doing," Hatfield Lyon would say later. "It was even inconceivable to me that he'd initiated or played much of a conscious part in the cleaning up. I could see it if he was in a traumatic state of mind, something approaching what psychologists call 'automatism.' "

Hatfield Lyon met with Dennis Fahey late in the afternoon at a restaurant that she only knew was "somewhere near the Garden State Parkway." There had been a brief film clip of the detective on the CBC *Inquiry* program two years earlier, and Hatfield Lyon noticed that he appeared older now. Fahey told her about his background, the fact that his father and grandfather had been stereotypes of the classic Irish-American "honest cop," and that he had run into problems with bureaucratic police departments because he, too, "was a maverick." As he spoke, Hatfield Lyon studied the man. He had short, severely styled dark hair and a thick, identifiably "New Jersey" accent. She thought he looked like . . . well, he seemed to be a sincere, forthright man, "a fighter for what was right."

Then Fahey told her he was upset that Mike Shaw had never contacted him. He said he had taken notes during a conversation with Barbara Czacherski that proved the Monmouth County Prosecutor's Office had subjected Scott Franz to a gruelling two days of interviewing without his lawyer present immediately prior to his plea agreement. He also said Franz had been fed only chips and Coca-Cola. Fahey felt that a case could have been made that investigators from the prosecutor's office had violated Franz's *Miranda* rights when they interrogated him in Texas after his arrest. Furthermore, Fahey concluded, he had taken notes during a phone conversation he had had with Dr Halbert Fillinger, the medical examiner, around Christmas of 1982. Fillinger had told him at that time that he had no independent recollection of the details of the Podgis autopsies other than the reports he prepared at the time. If Fillinger couldn't remember those details, Fahey asked Hatfield Lyon, how, then, could he testify on the witness stand that Al Podgis had died from a contact wound when his autopsy report made no mention of it?

Hatfield Lyon, who felt a little fatigued after her afternoon with Curtis, was having trouble following some of the intricacies of Fahey's logic, but she thought the essence of his arguments seemed sound. Hatfield Lyon was surprised to discover the degree to which Fahey was emotionally wrapped up in the case, and the depth of his outrage. Then he shocked her. Fahey asked how much she knew about prisons. He asked her whether she had ever considered how the tougher elements within the prison population in Bordentown would be likely to regard Curtis, a slightly-built, withdrawn youth, an aesthete. Hatfield Lyon didn't answer. Fahey said: "He would be like a delicate morsel."

Fahey told her that he had been to see Curtis the previous week and was of the opinion that the boy was probably being brutalized and almost certainly had contemplated suicide. Hatfield Lyon asked the detective whether he would consider coming to Ottawa in order to relate his feelings to officials in the Department of External Affairs. She assured him that the meeting would be confidential. Fahey said that he would consider it.

Later that evening, visiting with her family in Cape Cod, Hatfield Lyon couldn't get her mind off Curtis. "There was an incredible pain in his eyes, like a wounded animal. He tried to mask it but it was obvious to me. I believed it was solely because of problems trying to deal with guilt and moral issues. He seemed very matter-of-fact about other problems in the prison. He mentioned that the new superintendent had banned plants, which symbolized for him something natural and alive in that place. He said he didn't watch TV because sports was usually on. I did see an impassivity, as though he didn't have much ego left, but he never mentioned having to avoid social situations."

Although Hatfield Lyon's visits home were usually a welcome, relaxing respite, she "didn't sleep all weekend."

February 25, 1986

Dear Aunt Lorraine:

My window, of the lights outside, make diamonds. I long to possess them, smother their brilliance and make complete the night. The harsh light which normally casts wide shadows into my room is out, whether through design or fault I am not sure and so at least somewhat I regain a sense of what darkness can be. To delight further and increase the connections with memory snow has fallen lately and stays, somewhat diminished, for a period of time. The pavement is like flakes of obsidian. The snow is like snow for so many figures of speech employ snow that it seems an elemental aspect of description. Now, again things have changed. Snow fell heavily last night and everything has a light white covering to it that obscures the differences, the shades of opposition I wished to see. And my room seems so full of light, pale whitish light as if before my eyes was a veil, thin and finely woven. I cannot look out, cannot survey the brilliance of the land under its pale empty sky. Too long the corridors held dimmers, too long the eye rested on sombre shades of earth, too long like a monk in his cowl, I have seen shadows from a shadowed land and become familiar with its vagueness. Colours are repeated, samness prevails. The lockers are robin's eggs, the bookshelves fallen broken trees, the desks clumps of dirty snow and my wall the shade of a chocolate milkshake splattered and made pale by a sun. In the school area an aide and I made a bulletin board out of strips of seven bright colours woven together in a checked pattern. To those coming in it seems gaudy, too full of colour. To us it attracts with a fascination of oddity, a treasure trove of stimulating combinations that do not occur cannot occur in this dull world. That is why the flowers in the calendar you sent are so special, the range of colour is vast, the memories evoked vivid with fields of flowers, forests rich in grades of green. How odd in winter to think of flowers, of ways through woods dotted with tiny points of colour, of somber darkish stands of trees between green fields. Most certainly one gets used to anything but the process is so painful as parts die, sensibilities wither away to trouble no more the mind. I dare not start another page so,

Love, Bruce

When Mike Shaw's junior partner, Daniel Casagrande, left the firm early in the summer of 1986, his replacement on the Curtis case was a bright young Fordham Law School graduate named Joanne Legano. Until quite recently, Shaw and Casagrande had been regarding Curtis as a "paper case," a habeas corpus petition based strictly on the facts recorded during the original trial. Technically, no input was needed from the appellant so neither attorney had visited Curtis, although a representative from the firm had been present when an RCMP officer had conducted an interview the previous March. But the Curtises, after consulting with Gerald Morris and Jennie Hatfield Lyon, indicated to Shaw their interest in pursuing a form of clemency known as a "commutation of sentence." Since there was nothing to prevent an attorney from filing a petition for clemency at the state level while a habeas corpus was before the federal courts, Shaw agreed.

Often described as "an act of official mercy," executive clemency includes the power to pardon offenders as well as to reduce sentences or fines. In New Jersey, unlike more than half the fifty states, clemency was a confidential process. In the four-and-a-half years since Tom Kean had been elected governor, he had granted twenty-seven pardons and modified thirty-seven sentences. The sentence commutations most often involved crimes such as assault, robbery and weapons violations. Six had involved seriously ill inmates. In July 1986, Governor Kean told *The Philadelphia Inquirer*: "The main guide I have in all these things — the one overriding guide — is public safety.... On the other hand, if there has been a punishment and it looks overly harsh and you combine that with somebody's record, which let's say has been spotless before that — no history of violent crime, no history of drug abuse — yes I'd very much take that into consideration."

Legano, whose job it was to prepare the petition, felt strongly that in order to make a plea for clemency it was necessary for her to meet the client in order to construct the best, most convincing brief. That made professional sense, but it also reflected Legano's personality. She was a native New Yorker, one of three daughters raised by parents who taught their children to develop a social conscience. Legano was torn between a career in social work or law, but eventually decided she could be more effective and have the power to effect social change on a broader scale as an attorney.

The Curtis petition was going to include letters of support from the boy's family, members of the Bruce Curtis Defence Committees from across Canada and lawyers in the U.S. as well as Canada. Dr Harry Brunt's 1982 psychological report would be sent, as well as a recent assessment by Dr Robert Sadoff, an eminent psychiatrist often called upon by criminal attorneys. Although all the materials in the clemency petition were confidential, Legano describes Dr Sadoff's report as containing "no surprises. It's a very good prognosis that says Bruce's release certainly would cause no detriment to society." There were also no surprises in his institutional records, obtained from Bordentown by court order. Legano says, "there were no serious problems, as I suspected." The petition would also include a letter written by Jan Tyrwhitt on *Reader's Digest* stationery that read:

> In December 1984 and March 1985, I interviewed Bruce Curtis while working on a feature article for the Canadian *Reader's Digest*. Contrary to my expectations, I found him frank, forthcoming and similar in temperament to many other young people I have known. He seemed highly intelligent, with a wide-ranging interest in literature, science, philosophy, outdoor nature and current affairs. As well as the case, we discussed books, art, nutrition and the relationship between astrophysics and particle physics.

> For research purposes, I attempted to assess his values and psychological balance. His eagerness for news of former classmates, concern for the suffering he had caused his family, sense of humour and idealism all struck me as morally sound and typical of a normal 21-year-old. He said that he was interested in acquiring knowledge for its own sake, rather than in winning high marks and medals. He had looked forward to university as a place to learn and exchange ideas, and

regretted that he had lost his chance to enter with friends his own age. He was intensely homesick for ordinary life with his family. All these responses seemed reasonable and natural.

When I asked him if he had been "indifferent" to the death of Mrs Podgis, he was visibly moved and answered, "Of course I didn't want her to die. She was Scott's mother, and she was a very nice person who had been very kind to me." He told me that he felt and still feels great remorse over his stupidity and negligence, and agreed to go to Texas with Franz because he considered it his duty to explain and apologize to Franz's sisters.

I was impressed by his determination to continue his education, and by his account of good relationships with teachers, teaching aides and inmates in the Bordentown classroom. He was capable of working patiently with under-educated inmates, explaining basic reading, writing and arithmetic, and feeling satisfaction when he succeeded in teaching an inmate to write his own name. I also interviewed several of Curtis's former classmates, whose unanimous opinion was that he was incapable of violence, was not homosexual and had never taken drugs. I also consulted a psychiatrist, who told me that on the basis of information I supplied, Curtis showed none of the recognized symptoms of a psychopathic personality. He read Curtis' notebook [diary], and commented that it was not untypical of the privately expressed concerns and fantasies of normal, intelligent teenagers.

Since the *Digest* would not ordinarily report a trial for its own sake, I had decided that I could not write an article if I were certain that Curtis was guilty of aggravated manslaughter. I therefore spent a great deal of time assessing his credibility, not only on the basis of my interviews with him but on that of information about his character, and about events, obtained from many other sources. These included Scott Franz, who seemed to me somewhat unreliable. After long deliberation I concluded that I was justified in describing the case for our readers, and after similar discussion my editors agreed.

My personal assessment of Bruce Curtis is that he is intelligent, sensitive to others and increasingly mature in his judgement and experience. If he were allowed to resume a normal life, I believe that he could contribute to society through his concern for human welfare and his eagerness to equip himself to play some part in extending the boundaries of scientific knowledge.

I therefore respectfully request that you consider Bruce Curtis' application for clemency.

> Yours truly,
> Janice Tyrwhitt

The most touching letter was written by Curtis's grandmother. It read in part:

I hope you can understand, Mr Governor, that when Bruce stepped off that plane in Newark, in July 1982, he walked into a different world. He didn't know anything about guns, family fights or battered wives and children. He'd never been locked out in the rain before and forced to sleep under a porch like a stray dog....

I went to Bruce's trial and I've been back to visit him a few times since. It's a long trip from Ontario, but I think it's good for Bruce to get some hugging. When he puts his arms around me, some of my hurt goes away too. I'll be 80 years old, come September. Each time I make the trip it takes the stuffing out of me. Therefore,

Mr Governor, I hope you will grant Bruce clemency and let him come home.

Yours truly,
(Mrs) Jane [Jennie] Curtis

The petition also contained a report prepared by the National Center on Institutions and Alternatives (NCIA), a private, non-profit organization widely respected for its development of alternatives to traditional prison sentences, often involving elements such as financial restitution or a guarantee to provide community service volunteer work. In June, Legano and an NCIA case developer travelled to New Jersey to interview Curtis. The taxi from Trenton had dropped them at Yardville by mistake. Later Legano was struck by the stark contrast between the low, modern buildings at Yardville and Bordentown's medieval character. She understood then why his family complained so bitterly about what seemed to be preferred treatment for the confessed killer and state witness, Scott Franz.

(It was not yet widely known that on February 26, 1986, Franz had been transferred to Riverfront State Prison at Camden, New Jersey, across the Delaware River from Philadelphia. Although he hadn't been convicted of a disciplinary infraction, he was suspected of what an official in the New Jersey Department of Corrections described as "being too sophisticated for the young men at Yardville." When pressed to explain, the official added "it wasn't anything that we could charge him with, but there were other inmates who, by innuendo and direct accusation, said he did thus-and-so, or convinced them to do thus-and-so. I think manipulative is a good description for it.")

Legano and the NCIA worker obtained a social history from Curtis and asked him for a detailed account of his duties in Bordentown's school and the educational credits he had earned. "We said, 'Okay, Bruce, if released, what would your plans be?'" says Legano. "Because that's a real concern of anybody signing a clemency petition. They need to be reassured that if they turn this person out into society there won't be adverse consequences.

Remember Jack Abbott and Norman Mailer?* So we talked about a very detailed release plan, and again there were really no surprises. He would go to Dalhousie University and study astrophysics. Perhaps do some volunteer work with learning-disabled adults, which is what he's been doing in prison. Go back to his family. Pick up from the same place where he left off."

Throughout the first half of 1986, the Curtis case attracted considerable attention in the northeastern United States. In February, a large feature story in the Bergen (County, New Jersey) *Sunday Record* predicted the passing of prisoner transfer legislation that would enable Curtis to serve his sentence in Canada. (In August, the state senate unanimously approved the bill, although Curtis's family considers a transfer a last resort since it would not reduce his sentence.) Paul Chaiet, responding to the suggestion that he had pushed for the most severe sentence in the Curtis case, was quoted as saying: "I don't get notches in my belt for every year served. Everybody kind of forgets that two people were killed."

The April 1986 issue of *New Jersey Monthly*, a glossy consumer magazine distributed throughout New Jersey and the state of New York, ran an article on the case entitled "Blood Knot." In it, the author referred to a state appellate court panel that three months earlier had harshly criticized both Judge Arnone and the Monmouth County Prosecutor's Office "for letting a manslaughter conviction stand after learning that the two key prosecution witnesses in the case had lied." (The appellate court's written decision also included the following observations: "The need for a new trial in the interests of justice leaps out from the pages of the appellate record. Yet the prosecutor, whose interest should be 'to see that justice is done,' opposes a new trial." The court further said that Judge Arnone "abused his discretion by denying the motion for a new trial." The appellate court judge who wrote the decision was James Coleman Jr., who had also sat on the

*Novelist Norman Mailer helped convicted murderer Jack Henry Abbott acquire a publishing contract while Abbott was still in prison. *In the Belly of the Beast* was published in 1981, the same year Abbott was released. Mailer was seen as Abbott's "unofficial sponsor," and was harshly criticized when Abbott killed an unemployed actor in a knife fight.

panel at Curtis's first appeal.)

Michael Schottland told *New Jersey Monthly*: "I don't think most criminal defendants get a fair trial in Monmouth County. The group of judges they have trying criminal cases here are particularly harsh judges and they have very Spartan attitudes."

In Canada, a CBC radio program called *The Scales of Justice* aired a dramatization of the Curtis trial on June 8 that Gerald Morris felt was influential in modifying the government's attitude towards the case. The program's host, Edward L. Greenspan, was one of Canada's best — and best known — criminal defence lawyers. Throughout each of the program's episodes Greenspan provided clear and erudite analysis of legal issues. In the Curtis episode, "A Mansion By the Sea," Greenspan remarked on the prosecutor's reliance on the details of a murder for which the defendant was not charged. Of Dr Halbert Fillinger's role as the prosecutor's expert medical witness, Greenspan said: "In my view, this autopsy evidence was gravely prejudicial and irrelevant to the charge involving Bruce Curtis. It should never, ever have been admitted." Greenspan referred to "the personal animus against Bruce" caused by the local police chief's public statements comparing Curtis and Franz to Nathan Leopold and Richard Loeb: "This outrageous, but deadly, comparison to Scott Franz and Bruce Curtis did not apply at any point whatsoever. But it had been made and the ominous names echoed outside the courtroom." He pointed out that the publication of the diary evidence presented during a *voir dire* was "strictly forbidden in Canadian legal procedure," and described Curtis's punishment as "the over-sentencing of a panic-stricken child."

In the meantime, Dennis Fahey had agreed to go to Ottawa, and his meeting with officials there and *The Scales of Justice* broadcast came at a time when officials at External Affairs were making a decision on a request from Mike Shaw's office for a letter to accompany Curtis's clemency petition. Morris knew the letter's influence in New Jersey would be directly related to whoever signed it: a consul in New York, a senior official in Ottawa or the minister, Joe Clark, himself. When Joanne Legano delivered the petition to the Canadian consulate in New York on July 3, it included an appeal on Curtis's behalf signed by Clark.

"Several things in May and June convinced them [External Affairs officials] that they were on the right track in making this a very special case," says Morris. "Eddie Greenspan is taken very seriously as a legal scholar. He's a heavyweight who rarely speaks out on a case he's not personally involved in without careful consideration and investigation. He and Dennis Fahey tended to confirm in the minds of people in Ottawa, probably right up to Joe Clark, beyond anything that I could say to them, that there really was something badly wrong with this case."

Morris adds: "In all fairness to External, once the case was presented to them in a way they could relate to, they were quite forthcoming, very positive. I think finally, in their bones, in their guts, they believe that Curtis was a victim of a serious miscarriage of justice no matter what one might say about his behaviour after the central events occurred in that house."

That behaviour had troubled Morris. He admits he discussed the boy's actions with a friend, a psychiatrist in whom he had "an enormous amount of confidence." She told Morris that in her work with victims of shock — among them Vietnam vets towards the end of that war — she had observed periods of days or weeks where they were "living in a nightmare, not really knowing what was reality, highly suggestible." She added that it was certainly *possible* for a teenager from the kind of background Morris had described to have had that kind of reaction to the events in the Podgis house. Morris says thoughtfully: "That's all I have to go on that might provide some explanation for that behaviour."

Morris concedes that the greatest stumbling block he encountered in his efforts to aid Curtis remains the story's central mystery. "Did you know that that was the first thing they said to me when I went to visit people in the Department of Justice? They said, you know, 'Whatever you say about the trial and the suppression of evidence and all of that, his behaviour afterwards was awfully suspicious.'

"That was the impression left with everyone. I don't know that I've ever been given a totally adequate explanation for it. I'm not sure that any of us have, or ever will."

EPILOGUE

When I began work on this book in March 1985, my impressions of Bruce Curtis had been shaped by clippings from Canadian newspapers. He was depicted as a shy, nature-loving scholar from rural Nova Scotia who had been hoodwinked by his schoolmate, Scott Franz, a cocky, fast-talking hustler from New Jersey. After being thrust into terrifying circumstances involving Franz's brutish, gun-toting stepfather, Curtis was persecuted by a corrupt justice system. Even national stereotypes were subtly confirmed: Curtis, a farm boy, embodied the wide-eyed, virtuous Canadian cast opposite Franz, a worldly, aggressive Yank from a heavily urbanized state.

The Curtis story was of interest to me for several reasons. First, he killed someone, and the story of any unnatural death provides a window through which to view an incredible panorama of human emotions. Secondly, if Curtis was wronged, as his family insisted, the story would serve to expose an injustice and perhaps even correct it. And thirdly, Curtis's life had been frozen in time — at July 1982 — and subjected to an intense scrutiny that few of us will ever experience: I suspected a mythology had been established that obstructed an understanding of the tragedy, and I wanted to penetrate it. Finally there was the haunting spectre of the devastated families: the Curtises, the Podgis and Franz children, who still wonder what happened that Independence Day weekend in 1982.

As my research progressed, complexities began to unfold. If an investigation is like a jigsaw puzzle, this one was growing larger as the pieces shrank in size and multiplied in number. Curtis's aunt, Lorraine Peever, warned me that I would encounter "curves," and I did. She was referring, of course, to the diary and allegations of poisoning at King's-Edgehill School, but I was also hearing unsettling accounts of Curtis's attitudes and behaviour from former classmates and teachers. A coincidence of events had occurred over an eleven month period that I, as a journalist, not a family member, could not easily rationalize or accept.

Nor were the "curves" confined to Curtis. I had always seen this story as one that involved Curtis and Franz equally, a tragedy that devastated two families. But Scott Franz was, by the early summer of 1985, refusing all interview requests, including mine. Although I met with Franz's sister, Barbara Czacherski, in New Jersey, and she indicated a willingness to participate, she later declined after consultation with her sisters, Noreen and Rosie. I did not feel they were hiding potentially damaging evidence; their mechanism for coping with this trauma simply did not include sharing it with outsiders. (Eventually, Barbara did co-operate with me in a limited way.)

I had better luck with Al Podgis's children: Terry, Ted, Tim and Tom. When I met with them at their homes in Florida, I found them to be candid and forthcoming, still baffled, after three-and-a-half years, by what had happened. They remembered growing up with a caring, if strict, father, a man who became increasingly moody and troubled following his disappointments in business and his experiences with a delinquent stepson, Mark, and a difficult stepdaughter, Dawn. But they insisted that Al and Rosemary's relationship was founded on a turbulence acknowledged by them both, that Al's "bark was worse than his bite," and that he would never have threatened his youngest stepson with a gun.

My meetings with Curtis deepened the mystery. He seemed a bright, articulate young man whose retiring nature made him somewhat reticent but who was clearly willing to co-operate with me. He tried his best to summon memories that were deeply buried or, in some cases, had faded beyond retrieval. He spoke most fondly and happily about his childhood, his family and his love of rural Nova Scotia. He vigorously resisted discussing only one subject, perhaps understandably — his diary — although we did touch on it.

But Curtis also revealed a streak of arrogance and a contempt for authority that supported many of the reports I had collected from his schoolmates and teachers. Once I asked him about his views on police:

> CURTIS: You see, even back then [the time of the killings] I had the perception that the police were, you know, not for society itself. They were a corrupt organization that tried to manipulate people.
>
> HAYES: Where'd you get that?
>
> CURTIS: From cop shows. And I just don't like any authority at all. I don't like, you know, I'm sort of an anarchist. I don't like anything that has to do with established authority. I'm violently opposed. That's why I don't get along with teachers.... I refuse to accept what they say just because they're a teacher. So I've always been very much against people who think they're in a position of authority and think they're more right than I am because of that.
>
> HAYES: Is that really the reason you didn't give a statement [after being arrested in Texas in 1982]?
>
> CURTIS: Because I don't like police. It was also very rude too because it was so obvious he [Detective Lucia] was running a game. He was rude, you know, he said, "We have ways of making you talk." That's another thing: when people are rude to me I get rude back. So by this time I was getting mad because it was so obvious he thought I was just a scared little kid that would spill his guts out....

When I asked him how Franz's testimony and his own failure to take the stand may have affected the jury, he replied: "To me, it seemed quite obvious that Scott was lying. It seemed to me that any rational person could figure that out with no problem whatsoever. I happen to be a very stubborn person in that sense. I refuse to accept that other people do not think in a rational way, that they use their emotions, and things such as that, to come to conclusions....

"I realize that, but I still won't make allowances for it. I happen to be a very idealistic person. I accept a principle and I follow it, regardless of what consequences or ill effects it has upon me, because I refuse to give in to the system. I refuse to make allowances for reality... That's like Socrates. He refused to give up his principles just for physical health, or even life. And I would do that."

Suddenly my initial assumptions about the story were being challenged from all sides. Earlier theories had to be tested, new information considered. The possibility that Franz had murdered his stepfather in cold blood had become increasingly plausible. The fact that the shy, scholarly *naif* from Nova Scotia had a dark, even perverse side to his character complicated matters considerably. Like Gerald Morris and many others associated with the case, I have never heard an entirely satisfying explanation for the behaviour of the two boys after the shootings: the cleaning up, the dumping of the bodies, the hiding of the guns, the flight. But in Curtis's case, do snobbery, petulance, fantasies about vague, unspecified acts of violence and power, and a supposed glibness in reacting to violent death constitute sufficient reasons for accusing him of murder?

Disturbing though some of this may seem, I always return to the police investigation and trial. There was a bias against Curtis from the beginning, although not, as some have suggested, because he was a Canadian but because he appeared to most of the New Jersey law enforcement officials to be some kind of "weird, brainy kid." The police chief in Allenhurst started the speculation about a Leopold and Loeb-style "thrill killing" because there was so little concrete evidence to provide a better explanation and because of the homoerotic passage in Curtis's diary. When the investigation turned up an alleged poisoning incident involving the two boys in Nova Scotia, it provided further confirmation in the minds of the investigators that Curtis and Franz were sinister, dangerous teenagers.

Just as Franz was a shadowy figure at King's-Edgehill — a great deal of his persona was based on exaggeration and deceit — he remains a shadowy figure today. Even his testimony in the courtroom was cunningly elusive. There remain unsubstantiated suggestions from various sources, however, that raise questions as to whether Franz struck a deal with the state against his will. The factors most often cited include doubts about his family's ability to finance a full-scale defence, his attorney's commitment to the case, and the techniques employed by the Monmouth County Prosecutor's Office to convince the state's only effective potential witness to plea bargain. (Dr Halbert Fillinger's incomplete autopsy reports and expert testimony — the wedge that convinced Franz to accept a plea agreement — must be regarded, kindly, as vague.)

About Curtis's trial, however, there is less doubt. The state's only real evidence suggesting that Curtis had deliberately shot Rosemary Podgis was his behaviour after her death. Everything else — the physical nature of the woman's wound, the lack of motive, the rifle misfiring in court and Curtis's inexperience with firearms, even Franz's self-contradicting testimony — tends to support Michael Schottland's contention that the shooting was a "tragic accident." Common sense, as well as the opinions of countless legal experts who have looked at the case, further supports Schottland's charge that the repetitious barrage of evidence concerning Franz's shooting of his stepfather was improper and gravely prejudicial, and that Curtis's sentence, under the circumstances, was Draconian. Thus Curtis — innocent or guilty — and his family were hostages in what amounts to "the game of law," a game that too often involves amoral factors such as timing, luck, bartering, strategy and ego. To the extent that these factors played a role in the investigation and trial of Bruce Curtis, their cumulative effect resulted in a miscarriage of justice.

The offence was committed in a law-and-order county at a time when a general crackdown on crime was occurring throughout New Jersey. That may explain, in part, the severity of the sentence. The case involved the controversial practice of plea bargaining as well as the concessions and trade-offs that occur routinely in every courtroom. Both lawyers made strategic decisions that were likely crucial in the jury's final decision. For the prosecution, Chaiet stressed repeatedly the sickening details of Al Podgis's death upstairs, a crime for which Curtis was not charged. In his wisdom, Schottland chose not to put his client on the witness stand: his failure to testify may have left serious questions in the minds of the jurors. And, of course, there were many egos on the line — as there are in any criminal investigation and trial — from the police officers, detectives and expert witnesses to the attorneys on both sides.

Perhaps the ultimate illustration of the role the game of law played in the case is the difference of legal opinion over the judge's charge to the jury. Within certain limits, a judge has considerable discretionary powers over the selection of that charge. Schottland argues that Judge Arnone's omission of a fourth alternative — accidental manslaughter — may have robbed Curtis of an acquittal. Chaiet maintains that the alternative does not exist in the New Jersey Criminal Code, and that even if it did the circumstances of the Curtis case would not warrant it.

Clearly, the research gathered by the state in order to decide Curtis's fate was limited. Apologists argue that the system is overloaded with cases; in order to dispense a rough but serviceable kind of justice — bearing in mind Paul Chaiet's insistent reminder that in the case of Curtis and Franz "people kind of forget two people were killed" — the prosecution team is only required to gather enough of "the truth" to convict.

Not that I can claim greater success in gathering the truth, even though my research went considerably further than the state's. The eternal human impulse to simplify complexities, to find easy answers where none exist, is a fool's errand. Neither the legal system, nor the media, nor the most sincere of family members and friends will ever know precisely what happened at 401 Euclid Avenue on the morning of July 5, 1982. No one knows except Bruce Curtis and Scott Franz, and perhaps the truth has eluded even them. The only theory I have not altered since my early exploration of this case is that Curtis and Franz may have been like two chemicals in separate bottles, each inert until combined to form an unstable third element. If this is correct, I doubt that either boy could have been conscious of it.

Curtis wrote to me once to tell me about some books I'd arranged to send to him, among them the first volume of Virginia Woolf's diary. During our discussions in the prison at Bordentown, he had told me that, after reading Woolf, he felt strongly that no one could truly understand anyone else's mind—not even Woolf. At the end of his letter, Curtis observed:

> It was she [Woolf] who gave me the clue of why when you write about me the product will be false, not through any fault of yours, but because of the construction of the world. I had meant to speak more on this matter but the place does not allow that. Perhaps another time.

> Sincerely, Bruce